MAY GOD
HAVE MERCY
ON YOUR SOUL

The Story of
the Rope and the Thunderbolt

Edward Baumann

Bonus Books, Inc., Chicago

97   96   95   94   93   5   4   3   2   1

Library of Congress Catalog Card Number: 92-75931

International Standard Book Number: 0-929387-90-2

Bonus Books, Inc.
160 East Illinois Street
Chicago, Illinois 60611

Printed in the United States of America

To Jack Johnson
The Last Executioner

CONTENTS

v

BOOK III   Illinois Makes the Switch

BOOK IV   The Thunderbolt

PREFACE

At this precise moment, there are 2,589 condemned killers on death row in the United States of America, give or take a few who might have been gassed, fried, hanged, shot, injected or added to the list since these words were put down on paper. Of that number, 38, or just over one and a half percent, are women.

The manner of doling out the death penalty down through the ages has been both fascinating and horrifying. In England it was once customary to chain a condemned prisoner to a wall on the banks of the Thames. When the tide came in, the prisoner was drowned, and no one laid a hand on him. Another method of execution in jolly olde England was to place the prisoner's head on a block and hack it off. The sword was reserved for the nobility, whereas commoners got the axe. It sometimes took the hooded executioner three or four chops, while the blood-soaked victim writhed in agony, to get the job done.

Then the French invented *tenaillement,* in which the unfortunate recipient's skin was stripped from his body with red-hot tongs, and hot lead or boiling oil was poured into the wounds. Burning at the stake was also popular—a punishment generally reserved for Jews, Protestants and other heretics.

The rack was another method of sending a prisoner out of this world. His wrists and ankles were attached to a frame with a roller at each end. As the frame rotated, the joints were stretched and the limbs painfully dislocated.

The Germans improved on this method with a form of punishment called breaking on the wheel. The victim was stretched out on a cart wheel, and as the wheel revolved the executioner smashed his bones with an iron bar. This method proved so effective that other countries soon picked it up.

Less painful, perhaps, was *estrapade,* the dropping of the victim from a great height. Other means of execution ranged from simple drowning to being flayed alive, drawn and quartered, or boiled in oil or water.

One of the more memorable executions in France was that of Robert-Francois Damiens, on March 28, 1757. Damiens never killed anyone, but he had made an unsuccessful attempt on the life of Louis XV.

In condemning him to death, the Parlement of Paris decreed that he "be taken in a cart wearing only a shirt... and, on a scaffold erected for the purpose, that his chest, arms, thighs and calves be burnt with pincers; his right hand, holding the knife with which he committed the said parricide, burnt with sulfur; that burning oil, melted lead, and rosin and wax mixed with sulfur be poured into his wounds; and after that his body be pulled and dismembered by four horses, and the members of his body consumed in fire, and the ashes scattered to the winds...that the house in which he was born be demolished, and no other building be erected on that spot."

Four strong horses were purchased for 432 livres to perform the horrendous task, after the screaming prisoner's right hand was burned in a flaming brazier, while red-hot pincers were applied to his body and boiling oil and lead poured into the wounds. Three times the animals surged ahead, under the whips of the executioner's helpers, and three times the animals succeeded in dislocating Damien's limbs, but were unable to separate them from his body.

The macabre job was finally finished with an axe.

France, of course, improved on the method of execution with the introduction of the guillotine in 1879. The death machine took its name from Dr. Joseph Ignace Guillotin, a physician, who advocated its use in preference to less humane methods. Imagine a condemned person's last thoughts, on hearing the razor-sharp blade whirring down the grooved track. The last person to hear that sound in France was Eugen Weidmann, a convicted murderer, who was guillotined before a large crowd at Versailles at 4:50 a.m. on June 17, 1939.

In our own country, the first documented execution took place in what is now Virginia in 1608 when Captain George Kendall, a governing councilor, was shot as a spy. Another popular means of execution in colonial times was burning at the stake. In some cases the victim would be tied to an upright stake and set afire for several minutes, until he had sustained painful third-degree burns. Then he would be snatched from the blaze and placed in a cell to suffer for a couple of days before being put back on the fire to be finished off.

In Louisiana in 1767 a man was executed by being nailed in a box, which was then sawed in half.

The youngest person ever executed in the United States was fourteen-year-old George Stinney, who was electrocuted in South Carolina in 1944 for the rape-murders of two girls. A subsequent investigation indicated the boy was innocent.

Today, thirty-six states dole out death legally in five different fashions. Electrocutions and lethal injections are equally popular, being the manner of capital punishment in eleven states each.

In Colorado, Illinois, Nevada, New Jersey, New Mexico,

Oklahoma, Pennsylvania, South Dakota, Texas and Wyoming they give their killers the needle. In Alabama, Connecticut, Florida, Georgia, Indiana, Kentucky, Nebraska, Ohio, South Carolina, Tennessee and Virginia they give them the juice.

The electric chair is affectionately known as "Old Sparky" in Florida, "Yellow Mama" in Alabama, and "Gruesome Gertie" in Louisiana.

Arizona, California and Maryland employ the gas chamber, sometimes known as "the green room." In New Hampshire, it's the gallows.

In Delaware, prisoners sentenced to death prior to June of 1986 can choose between lethal injection and the gallows, while those sentenced after that date will get the needle, whether they want it or not. Mississippi gasses prisoners sentenced to death prior to July 1, 1984, and uses lethal injections on those sentenced after that date. In Idaho it's up to the director of the Department of Corrections, who can stand the condemned prisoner before the firing squad if he deems a lethal injection to be impractical. Louisiana electrocutes prisoners sentenced to death before January 1, 1991, and uses lethal injections for those condemned after that date.

Seven states give their condemned prisoners a choice. In Arkansas, Missouri and North Carolina they can choose between the gas chamber or the needle. Montana and Washington let their death row inmates opt between the needle and the noose. And in Oregon and Utah, they can go to glory by lethal injection or the firing squad.

States without the death penalty are Alaska, Hawaii, Iowa, Kansas, Maine, Massachusetts, Michigan, Minnesota, New York, North Dakota, Rhode Island, Vermont, West Virginia and Wisconsin—although some state senator or representative is always calling for it whenever there is a particularly heinous homicide.

The only legal execution ever to take place in

Wisconsin occurred on August 21, 1851, when John McCafferty was hanged in Kenosha for throwing his wife, Bridget, down the well. McCafferty died such a horrible, lingering death on the gallows that an aroused public opinion forced the repeal of the death penalty, and Wisconsin hasn't had one since.

In neighboring Illinois, the way of death has advanced from the gallows, to the electric chair, to the needle as the world becomes more and more civilized.

The focus of this book is on one county alone, Cook, which accounted for the execution of 171 convicted killers by the People of Illinois since the first settlers chased the Indians out of Chicago in 1833.

You will walk up the steps to the gallows with each of these forlorn, or frightened, or sometimes defiant and brave individuals. You will walk down the corridor with them as they cover those seventeen steps that the cons like to call "the last mile."

This book is neither for, nor against, capital punishment. There are indeed some killers whose homicidal acts are so foul and repugnant that they certainly do not deserve to remain on this earth. As Florida Justice James C. Adkins, Jr., put it, "Some people just ought to be eliminated. We kill rattlesnakes. We don't keep them as pets."

On the other hand, there are killers who made one dreadful mistake in a moment of passion, and, perhaps, should be given a chance to repent for their misdeeds.

The Bible says "an eye for an eye" and "thou shalt not kill." Which will it be?

There is also this to consider: A University of Florida sociology professor, Michael Radelet, documented 343 cases of people convicted of murder between 1900 and 1985 in this great land of ours who were actually innocent. Of that number, twenty-five were put to death before it was discovered that they were not guilty of the crime for which they had been executed. Yes, the courts convicted and the government executed 25 innocent people in the United States this century alone. And that is only the number we know of for sure. Unfortunately for them, capital punishment is irrevocable.

One of those wrongly executed was a woman, Barbara Graham, whose last words as she went to the gas chamber were, "Good people are always so sure they are right."

Since 1970, forty-six Death Row inmates in the United States were released after they were proved innocent.

In Sidney, Australia, a condemned man was granted a reprieve in 1803 for yet another reason. The executioners gave up on attempting to hang Joseph Samuels after three unsuccessful attempts in which the rope broke twice. What an ordeal that must have been for Samuels' neck!

In the United States, perhaps no man met his maker more resolutely than handsome Harry Pierpont, one of the original members of the John Dillinger gang of the 1930s. When the warden of the Ohio State Penitentiary in Columbus asked Pierpont whether he had any last words, after he was strapped into the electric chair, Pierpont was said to have replied, "Turn it on."

Edward Baumann
Kenosha, Wisconsin
1993

ACKNOWLEDGEMENTS

The author wishes to thank former *Chicago Daily News* cohorts Harlan Draeger, Bob Herguth and Jack Lavin; Ralph Otwell, Art Petacque and Walter Spirko, of the *Sun-Times;* Augustine Jewell, Joe Pete, Kenan Heise, Joe Mastruzzo, Vern Whaley and the late Basil "Gus" Talbott of the old *American;* and *Chicago Tribune* colleagues Don Agrella, Brian Downes, Tom Hollatz, Linda Hubbs, Mary Huschen, Barbara Newcombe, John O'Brien, Mary Wilson and Walter Wojtowicz for their enthusiastic assistance in researching this book. It could not have been done without them. And a special thanks to Chuck Hallberg of Delavan, Wisconsin, who suggested the title.

BOOK I

A BIZARRE PRESS CONFERENCE

1

COUNTDOWN TO DESTINY

As the scrawny black hands of the round-faced clock ticked off the remaining seconds of the waning minutes of the final hour of the last day he would ever know, Vincent Ciucci, a 35-year-old grocer from the Little Italy neighborhood on Chicago's teeming West Side, puffed insatiably on a smelly cigar and postured self consciously for the press. The highly unusual drama unfolded shortly before the stroke of midnight on Thursday, March 22, 1962, in a dimly lit 10-foot square cell in the basement of the hoary old Cook County Jail.

Vince was about to ride a thunderbolt.

The macho Ciucci had been convicted of killing his wife and children, after she found out he had a pregnant girlfriend on the side.

Firefighters found the bodies of his wife, Anna, 28, along with those of 9-year-old Vincent, 8-year-old Virginia and 4-year-old Angeline, in the charred ruins of the family grocery on West Harrison Street on the night of December 5, 1953. An autopsy uncovered a rifle bullet in each of their heads.

A jury found Ciucci guilty of murder, and on January

11, 1955, he was sentenced to die in the electric chair. Cook County carried out its own dirty work in those days. No sending its killers downstate to be dispatched by anonymous strangers.

For seven years, two months and 12 days Ciucci avoided the death penalty while his lawyers filed an unending series of motions for hocus-pocus and mumbo-jumbo. Twelve times the grotesque chair was dusted off for Ciucci, and 12 times he won eleventh-hour reprieves. And now the appeal process had run its course. Thirteen would not become Vince's lucky number.

Thirty-five witnesses—mostly police, press, influential politicians and relatives of the victims—were gathered outside the execution chamber just 17 steps down the hall from Ciucci's death cell. All had been thoroughly searched, right down to the heels of their shoes, to make sure none carried a hidden camera. They had been relieved of everything in their pockets, and allowed to bring in only pencils and paper that had been provided for them.

On the night of Ciucci's appointment with death the basement room was oppressively hot, thanks to a network of live steam ducts running directly above the five rows of wooden benches, as the witnesses waited for the midnight hour. Like the star of the show, the audience was all male.

Some, who had been through it before, chatted in hushed tones with their benchmates. Others surveyed the pipe-crossed ceiling, and occasionally glanced, bored, at their watches, trying to project what time they would get out of there. Several, who were virgins at the legal killing of another human, fidgeted uneasily on the hard, backless picnic benches, offering feeble wisecracks while inwardly worrying whether they would puke or faint.

At 11 o'clock Sheriff Frank Sain, who was half in his cups, slipped into the room from a rear door. The long-time Democratic party hack and one-time warden, who was put into office by the Daley machine because he was considered harmless, beckoned to several newspaper reporters whom he knew.

As they joined him in the hallway the affable Sain declared, "'C'mon, boys. They tell me I can't do this, but I'm the sheriff and I run this place, so if you boys want to hear the condemned man's last words, I say it's Okay." He then motioned the reporters into line behind Assistant Warden Frank Trankina, who was shaking his head in disbelief.

The select group included Ron Koziol and Aldo Beckman of the *Chicago Tribune,* Don Sullivan of the *American,* Ray Brennan and Art Petacque of the *Sun-Times,* and Jack Lavin and the author, representing the *Chicago Daily News.* Brennan, who reeked of Chivas Regal, was listing slightly to port.

"Ray's drunk as a fukkin' skunk," Lavin snickered, jabbing Koziol in the ribs. "Are you telling me? I got half a jag on sitting next to him," Koziol stage-whispered.

The 54-year-old Brennan, one of the best crime reporters ever produced by the lusty old rough-and-tumble school of Windy City journalism, was indeed sauced to the gills. He had been on the Ciucci story for nine years, from the discovery of the bodies to the arrest, the trials, and the appeals. He had gotten to know the prisoner as well as anyone over the years, and had stopped somewhere for a few jolts to fog his mind before coming down to see him off.

The beefy, red-faced Trankina banged with his fist on the heavy steel door at the end of the short hallway. A slot opened, and a guard peered out inquisitively.

"Open up," Trankina commanded.

The group entered a large, windowless corridor that contained three "death cells" side by side against one wall. The cells on either end had been temporarily vacated, so their occupants would not have to watch the condemned man being led to the chair like in the movies. Ciucci, who had been sitting bleary-eyed on his cot in the middle cell, puffing on his cigar, got up apprehensively to study his guests.

"These boys are from the press, Vincent. They've come to see if you have anything you want to tell them before, um, before, ah, if you have anything to say," Sain fumbled tactlessly.

"Hi, Ray," Ciucci said, reaching through the bars to shake Brennan's hand. Several others in the group also self-consciously shook hands with the soon-to-be-dead prisoner, as though social intercourse demanded it. Ciucci thanked Brennan and one or two of the others for stories they had written about him, and chided others for what he claimed were "distorted" reports.

He had turned down the traditional "last meal." He knew that the massive electrical jolt delivered by the chair would cause the bladder to burst and the bowels to cut loose, and he did not want to mess his pants in front of a crowd.

In violation of his own rules against liquor in the jail, Warden Jack Johnson had slipped Ciucci several straight shots to calm his nerves, although he had not yet reached Brennan's plateau.

Blowing cigar smoke into the air, the handsome Ciucci cockily declared, "I don't fear that chair. They could open that fukkin' door right now. My conscience is clear."

As the minutes ticked away, he leaned against the bars of his cell and recited a remarkable story. He had, indeed, murdered his wife as charged, he said, but he would deny to the very end that he had harmed his three children. He then offered a new version of what happened on the night his family was slain — a far different story than that of total denial he had told in court.

"I was in the bathroom when I heard strange sounds, like a cap pistol going off. I rushed out, and noticed my wife leaving the children's room with a rifle in her hand. I snatched the rifle from her, spun her around and knocked her across our bed. Then I went into the children's room.

I picked up my son Vincent's head, and his face was completely covered with blood. I looked at my little daughters. It was the same thing.

"I then picked up the rifle and went back into our bedroom, where my wife was lying. She was mumbling something, and I emptied the gun into her."

Ciucci rambled on. "I don't want no last meal. The thing I want more than anything else in this world is the opportunity to take truth serum, a lie box, or anything to substantiate my story."

As the clock ticked out 11:15 p.m., Ciucci turned the conversation to his former mistress, Carol Amora, who bore him a child. "My wife talked with Carol and told her, 'You may get my husband, but you never will get my children,' " he said.

"Do you still love Carol, Vince?"

"Carol to me is another female—just like the rest of them on the outside world," he scoffed.

The hands of the clock slipped down to 11:20.

"How do you feel about going to the chair 40 minutes from now, Vince?"

Taking a long drag on the cigar he smiled. "I myself know what transpired that night...and I have made peace."

At 11:22 a doctor and a nurse entered the cell to give Ciucci a cursory physical examination. Under Illinois law, one had to be in good health to be put to death. Ciucci rambled on as they put a stethoscope to his chest and made him stick out his tongue and say "aaah." "Why would it be necessary for me to do away with my children?" he asked.

At 11:28 p.m., after the medical contingent departed, a jailer entered the cell, unscrewed an overhead light bulb, and plugged in an electric razor. Ciucci obediently pulled off his T-shirt, sat down, and continued to chatter above the buzzing while the dark, curly hairs of his head tumbled into his lap.

"Let me ask you something," he said to no one in

particular. "Do you think it's fair to deny a dying man his last request? Truthfully, I believe society is not caring about a human being's life."

The barber's job took two minutes. By 11:30, with only a 5 o'clock shadow delineating where his locks had been, Ciucci looked smaller as he continued to ramble.

"What more can a man say? I'm willing to take any steps to prove that I did not touch my son or my daughters."

At 11:31 he was instructed to strip off his trousers and undershorts. He stood before the group stark naked, as though he had just stepped out of a shower, still puffing on the cigar, still yammering.

"Prior to this incident, I was living with my wife..."

A jailer handed him a special undershirt, with a flap that could be unbuttoned at the left shoulder, so the attending physicians could pull it back to listen for a heart beat after the job was done. He pulled it on over his head, holding the cigar clear so as not to get ashes on it.

"I have one consolation...when I do take that walk...I know that the Lord knows that I'm speaking the truth. "

At 11:35 Ciucci stepped into a pair of blue, rubber-lined, knee-length shorts, leaving his legs bare so an electrode could be applied directly to the skin. No slit pantleg like in Hollywood.

"The ones who conspired with their underhanded tactics to obtain their conviction will have to live with it for the rest of their lives," he rattled, a little less cocky than he had been in the beginning.

At 11:36 p.m. the Rev. Aidan Potter, Franciscan chaplain at the jail, entered the cell in his flowing, brown cassock with a rope belt, dangling in knots from his waist. Visibly upset at the media intrusion, the priest hissed angrily, "Have you men no decency? Can't you leave this poor soul alone to make his peace with God?"

"Fuck you, Father," Brennan growled, holding onto the bars with one hand and shaking an Irish finger at the astonished cleric with the other. "We're only doing our job. You've had seven fucking years to save this man's soul. If you haven't succeeded by now, by God, you haven't been doing your job."

As Potter glared red-faced at the newsmen, Warden Johnson, who had remained in the background, stepped forward. Johnson did not approve of the bizarre press conference either, but he was not about to argue with his boss, Sain, in front of the press. "I think you fellas have got enough to write about by now," he said, quietly but firmly. "It's really time for you to go back in and take your seats, so we can start getting things ready."

Nobody argued with Johnson. Brennan, who was taking the impending event personally, extended his arms through the bars and clasped Ciucci's hand in his. "I can't help you now, Vince," he wept, tears streaming down his cheeks.

As the newsmen trooped obediently out of the cellblock, Potter stood facing the condemned man, his head bowed in prayer. Twenty-eight faces turned and regarded the reporters curiously as they filed back into the insufferably hot witness room and found places on the long, wooden benches facing a corrugated aluminum screen.

At 11:54 an electric switch was thrown, and the screen rolled up to reveal the ugly, black chair in the center of the brightly-lit death chamber, behind a six-by-seven-foot protective glass panel.

The glass had been installed some years earlier after an electrocution went awry. The unfortunate victim had not been properly strapped into the chair, and when the juice hit him his legs snapped straight out with such force that his shoes went flying into the audience.

Sain now signalled Johnson, "We're ready." The warden put his hand gently on Ciucci's shoulder and said, "It's time." Ciucci took one last drag on the cigar, squashed it out on the floor and nodded.

A black mask was placed over Ciucci's eyes so he

would not see the ominous chair or the witnesses to his execution. He walked blindly between his guards who, holding firmly onto his arms at the elbows, guided him down the short hallway into the death chair, followed by Father Potter. As he took the last 17 steps he would ever take his voice could be heard reciting Hail Marys and Our Fathers.

As soon as Ciucci was positioned in front of the chair he was pushed firmly down into a seated position. With swift, rehearsed precision metal clamps snapped in place over his forearms and legs to pin them against the arms and legs of the chair, as a stout leather belt was tightened across his chest to hold him upright.

At the same time, one electrode was affixed to a saline-soaked sponge just above his right ankle while a black hood containing the other electrode was pressed tightly down against a small wet sponge on the top of his head.

Warden Johnson and his guards had been practicing the maneuver for the past 10 days, with one of their own group, who was the same stature as Ciucci, playing the role of the "prisoner."

In an earlier day, before Johnson became warden, a careless guard had not adjusted the upper electrode properly, and it arced when the switch was thrown, burning the man's head off. There would be no slip-ups under Johnson. If he had to kill a man, it would be done as humanely and efficiently as possible.

The press had long perpetuated a charade that there were four switches in the control room, only one of which was wired directly to the chair. That way none of the four volunteers who pushed the red buttons ever knew who actually delivered the lethal voltage.

They tried that once, but one of the volunteers chickened out at the last second and only pretended to press his button, so nothing happened as the condemned man sat quivering in the chair, waiting for the jolt to blast out his eardrums. On this day Jack Johnson, and no one else, would do the deed. It was a chore he detested, and would not assign to any other individual.

Johnson stood now, his hand poised on the control, watching Ciucci through a one-way glass. Every eye in the witness room was also riveted on the blindfolded figure sitting bolt upright in the stark black chair before them. He looked like a skinny-legged little boy in the short pants he'd been given to wear to die in. His adam's apple moved up and down as he swallowed nervously, and the white undershirt on his chest rose and fell slowly in response to his final breaths of life.

The only sound in the room was the scratching of pencils on note paper.

Then it hit. The muscles in Ciucci's neck burst into knots, his back arched, his fingers snapped into tight fists, and his body strained against the braces as 1,900 bone-cracking volts crashed through his system from head to toe.

How electricity kills is not fully understood, but experts believe the first high-tension jolt knocks out the medulla of the brain, which controls breathing and other automatic functions of the body. At the same instant the muscles of the body, including the heart muscle, go into violent spasms.

Four seconds later the body relaxed slightly as Johnson threw the switch to the bottom for the remainder of the minute — 900 volts for fifty-six seconds. This is the "burnout." It brings the man's blood to a boil.

At the end of one minute Johnson rammed the switch to the top again, giving Ciucci six more seconds of 1,900 volts. Then he pulled the lever down for another fifty-six seconds of burnout. Water trickled down from the chair in which Ciucci sat, a whisp of smoke spiraled upward from the top of his head, and steam rose from his reddened thighs.

Timing at this point was critical. A prolonged

application of juice would cause the skin to split, just like a hot dog on an electric spit behind the bar in a neighborhood tavern. The warden released the pressure on the button at the right moment, however, and the body went limp.

Petacque, who had spent the last two minutes staring at the concrete floor because he did not want to watch a man die, raised his head now and jotted some notes on the small pad he held in his lap, as he observed Ciucci's still form in the chair.

A jailer entered the room and unbuttoned the undershirt at the left shoulder, as two physicians stepped in and pressed their stethescopes against Ciucci's unmoving chest. The instruments left little white circles, like the marks produced by pressing one's skin after a severe sunburn. The doctors nodded. At 12:09 a.m. Friday, March 23, 1962, Vincent Ciucci had officially paid his debt to society.

The witnesses stared transfixed at the lifeless body in the chair as Father Potter stepped forward to administer the final absolution, and the aluminum screen rattled down.

Those who had just watched a man die shuffled uneasily to their feet. Nobody could think of anything to say. The silence was broken by Brennan, who let out a groan as his supper came up all over the front of his navy blue suit and he toppled off the bench onto the hard floor.

Two guards brought in a stretcher and hefted Brennan onto it. As they lugged him past City News Bureau reporter Mike McGovern, Brennan reached out and grabbed McGovern's arm, looked up at him pleadingly and growled, "If you write one word about this, you little son-of-a-bitch, I'll get you if it's the last thing I ever do."

The *Daily News* reporter assigned to write the "color" story lagged slightly behind while the other witnesses slowly made their way through the underground tunnel back to the Criminal Courts Building, to retrieve their wallets, keys, combs, loose change and other personal belongings. Ciucci's body had already been placed on a gurney, covered with a sheet, and wheeled out into the corridor to await the meatwagon.

The reporter paused at the long, narrow cart, pulled back the sheet and studied the face of the man who had been yammering at the press a scant half hour before. There was a deep, red burn, the size of a silver dollar, in the very center of the top of his shaved head where the electrode had sat. That was the only mark on him.

Otherwise, he had been rather neatly cooked, courtesy of the "People of the State of Illinois." He was now only a number.

Vincent Ciucci became the 169th person legally put to death in the County of Cook since Chicago was incorporated as a town in 1833. The pioneer who charted the course for all future executions was a ne'er-do-well named John Stone.

BOOK II

THE ROPE

The headings on the succeeding chapters reflect the headlines that appeared in newspapers of the day.

1

EXECUTION OF
JOHN STONE

JULY 10, 1840

Chicago's first legal execution, the public hanging of 34-
year-old John Stone, was carried off with all the hoo-rah and
trappings of a festive holiday in the young prairie town of
4,479 men, women and children. Stone had arrived in the
United States from Ireland in 1819 at the age of 13. Before
making his way to Chicago in the fall of 1838, he'd been
imprisoned as a horse thief in New York, and also served
time in Canada for robbery and being an accomplice to
murder.

Over the next year and a half Stone, who worked
haphazardly as a woodcutter, earned a reputation as a loafer
who spent much of his waking hours hanging around the
billiard hall upstairs at Couch's tavern at Dearborn and Lake
Streets. He came to the attention of Sheriff Isaac R. Gavin in
the spring of 1840 after Lucretia Thompson, a farmer's wife,
was found raped and murdered.

All signs pointed to Stone. He had once wise-cracked
about the attractive young woman's virtue; a shred of cloth
torn from his flannel shirt was found near her body; and the
suspect was seen burning his clothes after the murder. On
such circumstantial evidence Stone was convicted of

murder, and sentenced to hang by the neck until dead.

On Friday, July 10, 1840, still protesting his innocence, he was taken, chained and handcuffed, to a spot on the lake shore three miles south of the court house, where a gallows had been erected in the area of what is now Burnham Park. The *Daily Chicago American* gave this eye-witness account of the event:

"At the request of the Sheriff, nearly two hundred of our citizens on horses, and about 60 armed militia, assembled at the public square, near the jail between 12 and 1 p.m., as a guard to accompany the prisoner to the place of execution, and to preserve order during the ceremony. They were under the direction of Col's. Johnson, Beaubien, and Capt. Hunter, who volunteered their acceptable services on the occasion. Col. Johnson appeared in full uniform, and much credit is due to him and Capt. Hunter for their active and successful services in maintaining quiet and order on the occasion. The prisoner was conveyed in a coach with four horses, accompanied by the Rev. Mr. Hallam, of the Episcopal Church, the officiating clergyman, and some of the officers of the law. The procession reached the place of execution at about half past one, and the execution took place about a quarter after three. The prisoner ascended the scaffold dressed in a white loose gown, and with a white cap on his head, as is usual in such cases. He evinced much firmness on the gallows under the circumstances of the case, and in the presence of the clergyman, the Sheriff, and thousands of spectators (among whom we regretted to see women enjoying the sight) he persisted to the last in the assertion of his innocence—which declaration was publicly made in his behalf by the Sheriff, together with his acknowledgement as requested, of the satisfactory manner in which he was treated in the jail."

As the noose was being placed over the condemned man's head, a nervous Sheriff Isaac Gavin said haltingly, "Well, this is it, I guess. Do you have anything more you want to say before the sentence is carried out?"

"I swear to you, sheriff, I'm an innocent man," Stone repeated desperately. "I have never been to the Thompson house, and I never saw Mrs. Thompson on the day that she was murdered. I believe that there were two of them—two men—who did the murder that I've been wrongly accused of."

"If you didn't kill Mrs. Thompson, who did?" Gavin pressed. "You know the two individuals? Give me their names."

Stone shook his head. The last words he uttered were, "Even if I did know their names, I'd swing before I would have their blood upon me."

And swing he would. The newspaper account continues:

"The Rev. Mr. Hallam, Isaac R. Gavin, the Sheriff, and Messrs. Davis and Lowe, Deputies, attended the prisoner on the scaffold. The Sheriff seemed particularly affected, even unto tears. After the beautiful, solemn and impressive services of the Episcopal Church, for such occasions, were performed by Mr. Hallam, and the appropriate admonitions bestowed, the death warrant was read by Mr. Lowe—the knot soon after adjusted—the cap pulled over the face of the prisoner, and he was swung into another world. After he had hung until he was 'dead, dead,' a wagon containing a coffin, received his body, which was delivered to Drs. Boone and Dyer, pursuant to the order of the Court, for dissection. It is supposed that he died of strangulation, and that his neck was not broke in the fall, which was about four feet."

Indeed, the first public hanging was a botched affair, with the unfortunate John Stone twisting and writhing at the end of the rope, gagging and choking for several interminable minutes, while the lakefront crowd gaped in amusement.

2

EXECUTION OF WILLIAM JACKSON

JUNE 19, 1857

The public execution of William Jackson, 17 years later, didn't go much better than John Stone's. Even worse, one might say, considering the fact that the platform collapsed while he was swinging above it by his neck.

The 30-year-old Jackson, a Presbyterian carpenter who had come up from Kentucky, was a pleasantly handsome fellow, standing 5 feet 10 inches tall. He had dark blue eyes, brown hair, a reddish beard and a hair-trigger temper. He clubbed a man named Roman Morris to death with his walking stick on the road near Libertyville, and fled over the state line to Wilmot, Wisconsin. He was captured, returned to Chicago, and sentenced to be hanged.

It had rained for several days and the courthouse square was a quagmire on the day of the execution, scheduled for Friday afternoon, June 19, 1857.

The crowd began to gather early in the morning, and guards were posted to keep the growing throng back from the building. By 10 o'clock, according to one report, streets around the building were so crowded "with people of every age, sex, color and condition" that teams of horses and pedestrians had to force their way through.

The prisoner was brought out shortly before noon and hustled into a closed carriage that had been brought up to the jail entrance.

A platoon of Chicago Dragoons led the carriage, containing Jackson, his lawyer, a clergyman and a deputy sheriff, north on Clark Street to Lake Street, and then west to an area known as the Bull's Head. Two other wagons, containing the sheriff, coroner, two physicians, a group of newspaper reporters and a coffin followed, with a second platoon of Dragoons slogging through the mud at the rear.

Hundreds of carts, wagons and carriages of every description, jammed with men, women and children of all ages, followed the procession through the mudchoked roads to Reuben Street (Ashland Avenue), where a gallows had been erected midway between Polk and Taylor Streets.

There it was necessary for soldiers to clear a path through the throng, estimated at 5,000 to 6,000 to get to the scaffold, which consisted of two upright timbers connected at the top by a crosspiece.

A rope with a noose at one end was draped over the crossbar, hanging about five feet above the floor of a square wooden platform in the center of the structure. The other end of the rope was attached to a 257-pound cast iron weight suspended over a pit by a stout cord.

Excited mothers and fathers boosted their small children high over their heads so the youngsters could get a better look as the condemned man, his eyes red from weeping, calmly mounted the platform and took a position between the sheriff and a clergyman. After the minister led the assemblage in prayer, Jackson shook hands with the sheriff, his lawyer and the preacher and said good-bye.

"Oh! Lord God, save and receive me!" he declared, as his necktie was being removed. His arms and legs were pinioned, and a white shroud was draped around him. The noose was then adjusted about his neck, a black cap was drawn over his face, and he was left standing alone on the platform before the hushed crowd.

Sheriff Wilson then cut the cord holding the cast iron weight aloft and Jackson was jerked to Jesus.

As he swung above the crowd, kicking his feet spasmodically, too many onlookers clambered aboard the three-foot high platform for a better look, and it collapsed from their weight. "Fortunately," the local press reported, "no one was injured."

As the spectators gawked at the macabre sight, a gust of wind whipped the black cap away from Jackson's eye-bulging face, "which was distorted and discolored," giving all a memorable look at the dying man.

Local officials let him hang for about a half hour before he was cut down and pronounced dead by an attending physician. Sheriff's deputies then placed the body in the waiting coffin, which was turned over to the coroner for burial.

"After the removal of the body, the crowd dispersed in a very quiet manner, in strange contrast with the boisterous and rowdyish scenes which marked their course to the place of execution," the *Daily Journal* reported.

Jackson was one of six Middle-Western murderers hanged that fateful day. In downstate Edwardsville George W. Sharpe and John Johnson also died at the end of a rope, and across the river in St. Louis, Jacob Neuseline, Israel Shoultz and W. La Point were dispatched in a triple-header.

3

EXECUTION OF
ALBERT STAUB
THE MURDERER OF LAUERMANN

APRIL 20, 1858

The last public execution in Cook County, the hanging of Albert Staub, took place ten months later.

A German, Staub was born in Zurich, Switzerland, where he obtained a job as an accountant in a commercial house after graduating from college. He came to Chicago in the summer of 1857, and worked briefly as a bartender before landing a job as a farmhand in Blue Island. There he got into a heated political debate with Peter Lauermann, who he claimed tried to shove him off a farm wagon. Lauermann was shot dead, and Staub was consigned to the gallows at the age of 22.

On April 20, 1858, a new scaffold was erected on Reuben Street, near what is now Ashland Avenue and the Eisenhower Expressway, in a drizzling rain and a sea of ankle-deep mud. Staub was driven to the hanging grounds in a carriage, followed by five coaches carrying the sheriff, his deputies, the county physician, coroner, newspaper reporters, and sheriffs from other counties.

Several thousand men and boys followed the morbid procession, many taking shortcuts through muddy fields and knee-deep puddles, according to the *Chicago Tribune,* "determined to gratify their depraved tastes by witnessing the death of a fellow creature." Authorities attempted to cut them off by raising the Lake Street bridge over the Chicago River after the wagons had crossed, but they raced to other crossings and worked their way west to the appointed spot.

Pickpockets roamed the crowd of eight to ten thousand that had gathered around the gallows, including scores of women and children, who were not about to let the drizzle dampen their enthusiasm to watch a man dangle at the end of a rope.

The red-faced prisoner, tears mixing with the rain on his face, climbed unsteadily upon the scaffold, and had to be helped to the center of the platform by sheriff's deputies. Before being wrapped in the traditional white shroud he shook hands with the sheriff, the Methodist minister in attendance, and his lawyer. Shouts of "Get off the scaffold!" and "Get out of the light!" were heard from excited spectators, straining to get a better view.

Unexpectedly, Staub asked for permission to address the crowd, and spoke to them in German for several minutes. His final words, as interpreted by a reporter, were, "I wish to speak a few words to my German countrymen. You all see what the temptings of the devil have brought me to, and I wish you to be warned by my fate. Keep away from bad company, and let liquor alone. Do not covet the money of others, and do not let your wish for money lead you into crime. I implore you to get religion, to go to church, and to pray to God, for there is more rejoicing in Heaven over one sinner who repents than ninety-nine that need no repentance. Be warned by me, and do not commit sin. Amen."

The rope was then adjusted about his neck, and the black cap placed over his face. At 11:40 a.m. the trap was sprung, and Albert Staub was "launched into eternity." He struggled briefly and his muscles twitched as he hung above the crowd, where his body swung in the rain for the next 30 minutes.

At ten minutes after twelve Dr. Cheeney, the county physician, ascended the ladder to the scaffold and examined the lifeless body. He then turned to Sheriff Wilson and declared, "The body there hanging of the prisoner is now a lifeless corpse. The sentence of the Court has been by you fully and skillfully carried out."

The "lifeless corpse" was then lowered and carried to a waiting wagon provided by the coroner.

The *Daily Tribune* commented the following day:

"If hanging is to be the punishment for murder, by all means let us imitate the action of older States and have our executions private."

4

EXECUTION OF
MICHAEL MC NAMEE
FOR THE MURDER OF HIS WIFE,
JANE MC NAMEE

MAY 6, 1859

Following the hanging of Albert Staub, the State Legislature abolished public executions in Illinois. The new law stipulated that "such punishment shall be inflicted within the walls of the prison of the county in which said conviction shall have taken place, or within a yard or inclosure adjoining such prison." It limited spectators to the judges, prosecuting attorney, and clerks of the courts of the county, along with two physicians and twelve reputable citizens to be selected by the sheriff, up to three "ministers of the Gospel" selected by the condemned man, and any members of his family whom he wanted to watch him die.

Michael McNamee, a 32-year-old native of Fermanagh County in Northern Ireland, was the first person to go to his maker under the terms of the new law. McNamee had beaten his wife, Jane, to death in front of the couple's children during a drunken orgy above the North Side stable where they lived.

May 6, 1859, was the date set for Cook County's first

triple hanging, with Michael Finn, convicted killer of Nathaniel Vial, Henry Jumpertz, the slayer of Sophie Werner, and McNamee all scheduled to go to the gallows at 3 o'clock in the afternoon. Jumpertz won a new trial, however, leaving McNamee and Finn to swing in tandem.

A double-trapped gallows had been constructed in the high-ceilinged corridor on the main floor of the east wing of the courthouse. The hinged trap, wide enough to accommodate three men standing side by side, had been cut in the floor and was secured by a sliding bolt. When the bolt was pulled, the trapdoor would flop open, and whoever was standing on it, would drop into the basement at the end of a rope. The rope was looped over the same overhead beam that had been used in the gallows on which Staub and Jackson were dispatched.

Trains brought in groups of morbid curiosity seekers from Joliet, Freeport, Kenosha and Michigan City, hoping to "see the hanging." They arrived only to find the courthouse closed to the public for the day, and curtains draped over the insides of windows, to bar spectators in the yard from seeing what was going on inside.

McNamee's six-year-old son, Andrew, who had sat on his father's knee during the trial, and his four-year-old daughter, Mary Jane, were permitted one final visit in his basement cell on Wednesday afternoon. Little Andrew clung sobbing hysterically to his father's legs when it was time to go, and had to be forcibly pried from his last embrace.

Meanwhile a bitter flap developed over who would actually witness Finn's and McNamee's demise. Sheriff Gray, in selecting "twelve reputable citizens" from the hundreds who had applied, included one reporter each from the *Democrat, Herald, Journal, Staat Zeitung* and *Times,* but precluded representatives of the *Tribune* and the *Press.*

The left-out newspapers claimed this was an act of revenge, because they had earlier reported that the sheriff permitted "abandoned females" to visit one of the condemned men.

"The sun which is to rise this morning for the last time on one poor wretch in our city who is to expiate by a fearful fate, the crime of wife murder, ushers in a day which has for weeks past been invested with an unusual degree of interest and anxiety in this community," the *Press* proclaimed on page one. "If our readers lack in tomorrow's issue any portion of the proper details of a matter exciting so general interest, they will know where to locate the blame."

Friday dawned unseasonably warm, and many men in the city broke out their white suits and straw boaters from winter storage.

At 6 a.m. a temporary altar was set up in the jail corridor, and the sacrament was administered to McNamee and Finn, who were cellmates. McNamee seemed resigned to his fate, but Finn wept uncontrollably during the ritual.

In mid-morning Governor William H. Bissell granted the 24-year-old Finn an eleventh hour reprieve while he considered executive clemency, leaving McNamee to go it alone.

High Mass was said for the condemned man at 11 a.m., and he was administered extreme unction. After the service McNamee ate a hearty dinner—his first, and last, meal of the day.

Shortly after 2 p.m. Finn embraced his cellmate and wept like a child. "Mac, you're a good boy," he sobbed, draping his arms around McNamee's neck. "You've been kind to me while we've been together in this place, and I'm prepared to die as you, and to go with you, and I almost wish I could."

After Finn was ushered from the cell, McNamee prayed in solitude until 2:30. Four Roman Catholic priests then entered the cubicle and dressed him in a black, loose-fitting ankle-length robe, edged in white. A cross was embroidered on the front of the robe, across his chest, and on the back were the letters "I.H.S." in white.

At ten minutes to three the mournful procession proceeded from McNamee's cell, up the stairs from the basement jail, to the scaffold on the main floor. Before mounting the platform McNamee handed his lawyers a letter which said in part:

"I am about to die, and of all men I understand best the merits of my case. I have been told that my wife died of the abuse she received at my hands; but I do not hold myself guilty of murder, for I was so drunk that I had lost the use of my reason and knew not what I was doing...I have never ceased to pray for her, and hope that our loving God has had mercy on her, as I hope to receive mercy likewise."

McNamee, a fair haired man with a light complexion, then took his position in the center of the trapdoor. Asked whether he had any last words, as his arms were pinioned against his body, he replied, "I have nothing more to say than what I have said." A black hood was draped over his face. The noose was then adjusted about his neck in what was known as the French method.

This consisted of a thick, doubly-sewn leather belt about four inches wide, that was buckled tightly about his neck. The belt contained two eyelets, through which the hanging rope was passed. The purpose of the stiff collar was to dislocate the neck the moment the rope snapped taut, causing instant death rather than slow strangulation. It did not work as planned, however.

The bolt was pulled just as one of the priests had begun to intone, "Our Father, which art in Heaven..." The trapdoor clanged open, and there was a "twang" as McNamee dropped eight feet and the rope snapped tight. Unfortunately, the eyelets at the end of the straining cord gave way, the leather collar parted, and the tightly bound McNamee plunged fifteen feet more to the basement floor with a sickening thud.

The spectators gasped in horror as the hooded, black-robed figure lay motionless on the floor below, the rope swinging idly above the open trap. Four deputies clambered down the basement stairs, retrieved the unconscious man, and carried him back up to the gallows.

The badly bruised McNamee regained consciousness as the trapdoor was being reset. The black hood was removed, and he was asked, "Can you stand alone?"

The dazed McNamee apparently misunderstood the question and replied gamely, "Yes, I can stand that and twice that."

At 3:10 p.m. the rope was put back around his neck, this time in the form of a conventional noose. He said his good-byes again, and the black hood was once more lowered about his face.

Again, the clang of the falling trap, the plunging body, the sharp twang of the straightening rope, and the kicking and struggling of the condemned man as he swung by the neck in mid air. As McNamee fell through the trap the second time the knot in the noose slipped aside and his neck was not broken as intended. He dangled there, before the horrified witnesses, for more than 14 minutes before his Irish heart stopped beating.

At 3:45 p.m. the corpse was lowered and the rope removed from his chafed neck. McNamee's body was placed in a black walnut coffin, and turned over to his waiting sister, who had journeyed from Philadelphia to claim him.

The *Press,* which had been barred from the gruesome exhibition, took great delight in pointing out that the sheriff had sorely bungled the hanging.

5

THE MURDERERS HANGED
DECEMBER 15, 1865

A bitter Civil War would be fought in America, and President Lincoln would be assassinated, before there was another execution in Cook County. And when it was carried out on Friday, December 15, 1865—just ten days before Christmas—it became Chicago's first double header.

The recipients of the rope were a pair of hired killers named Jerry Corbett and Walter Fleming, otherwise known as the "Sand Ridge Murderers." The pair, who ambushed Patrick Maloney for a fee of $16 each, were Chicago's first known hitmen. They were convicted for the fatal shooting of Maloney in his home at a place known as Sand Ridge, near the Six Mile House, on November 20, 1864. Maloney's last word, as he fell mortally wounded in the doorway, was his wife's name, "Honora."

The Irish-born gunmen, who had both come to America at an early age, had been hired by a neighbor, with whom Maloney had been feuding.

The *Chicago Tribune* labeled the impending executions "Heaven ordained" and declared, "Who so sheddeth man's blood, by man shall his blood be shed."

The ponderous timbers and heavy bolts were brought out of storage and the gallows from which Michael McNamee had so pitifully been hanged was painstakingly reassembled.

The hole in the floor, three feet seven inches wide and five feet three inches long—big enough to accommodate two men—was covered by two hinged trapdoors which met in the center. Each was held in place by an 18-inch bolt.

A stout cord attached to the ends of the bolts ran up through the floor and looped near the gallows frame, where Deputy Sheriff James Connelly would yank it at a signal from the sheriff. The twin ropes dangling from the crossbeam above were adjusted for a six-foot fall. Each had been laboriously soaped, so as to slip snugly around each man's neck when the noose tightened.

On the evening before doomsday, Fleming, 35, accompanied by a deputy sheriff, made the rounds of the basement cells, shaking hands and cheerfully bidding good-bye to fellow prisoners, while the 26-year-old Corbett remained in his dingy, whitewashed stone cell and prayed by candlelight.

Both men slept soundly, awakening at about 6 a.m. on the appointed day. At 8 o'clock Corbett was let out of his cell to say his good-byes to the other inmates, as Fleming had done the night before. At 9 a.m. the sacrament of extreme unction was administered to the two prisoners in their cubicles.

Corbett had a French lithograph of the Virgin Mary on the wall of his cell, and Fleming's wall was adorned with a portrait of Raphael's Madonna. Each man's cubicle contained a small table, on which lay several crucifixes, vials of holy water, and religious books. The jail windows were so heavily coated with winter ice that little light could find its way through, making it necessary to burn candles throughout the day, giving the tiny cells the appearance of miniature chapels.

For the next hours Corbett sat on his bunk engrossed in prayer, while Fleming chatted amiably with several Sisters of Charity who had participated in the religious service.

Early in the afternoon the white muslin shrouds in

which the men were to be buried were brought to their cells and shown to them. Corbett showed little interest, but Fleming turned one of the garments over in his hands and examined it curiously.

After the Sisters left at 1:30 p.m. the two men were placed in a cell together. Corbett lit up a cigar that had been given to him, while Fleming puffed contentedly on a clay pipe. While they smoked, the two men dressed in the best clothes they had for the occasion—neatly creased trousers, clean white shirts, collars and ties. Each also wore a metal crucifix about his neck. From time to time the sound of laughter could be heard, as one of them uttered something that amused the other.

At twenty-five minutes to three the condemned men were led from the cell, and walked firmly, supported on either side by members of the Catholic clergy, up the stairs to the gallows. Arriving under the scaffold they were seated in chairs near the drop while Sheriff Nelson read the death warrants.

"Do you have anything to say before this sentence is carried out?" he asked Corbett.

"Nothing, only I thank you, and all others connected with the jail, for the kind treatment of me," Corbett answered. "I forgive all my enemies, and hope to meet them and my friends in Heaven; for I believe I shall go there as soon as I die. God bless you all."

When Fleming was asked whether he had any last words, he rose from the chair and said in a calm voice, "No, only I want to thank the sheriff and all in the jail for treating me so well. I forgive all who have ever injured me. God be with you all. I am going to Heaven!"

The white robes were then draped over each of the men, and they were positioned over the drop as the nooses were adjusted about their necks. Before the white hoods were placed over their heads and their arms tied at their sides, they shook hands with the priests and lawmen assembled on the platform.

Through the hoods covering their faces Corbett and Fleming could each be heard uttering the words, "Jesus, Mary, Joseph, save me..." at ten minutes to three, as the bolts were pulled and the floor beneath them gave way.

For a full three minutes after the six-foot drop the two men struggled violently. They then hung quietly for about two minutes, before their bodies went into apparent convulsions. Fleming's legs were drawn upward, almost as if he was trying to assume a fetal position. Then they dropped suddenly downward, only to be raised and lowered two more times before he finally gave up the grim battle for life.

Corbett struggled even longer before a final shudder enveloped his body, and he, too, hung in silence.

After the two men had been suspended for six minutes a pair of waiting physicians pronounced each of them dead. The bodies were permitted to swing for 20 minutes more, for good measure, before they were lowered and placed into the plain black coffins that had been prepared for them.

The *Tribune* reported: "The two guilty, sin-stained souls, weighed down by many hideous crimes, have been plunged into the dark river between time and eternity."

6

IT IS DONE

MARCH 14, 1873

The Cook County Courthouse where McNamee, Fleming and Corbett were hanged by their necks until dead met its own demise in the Great Chicago Fire of 1871. As the city rose from the ashes, a new criminal court and jail were built and by March 14, 1873, the jail was ready for the hanging of George Driver.

Driver, a skilled carpenter from Scotland, had fatally shot his 32-year-old ex-wife when she ordered him out of her home on November 20, 1872. He was convicted after his children, William, 14, Mary, 13, Isabella, 9, and George, 11, tearfully testified that they had witnessed the frightful act.

No need to build a new gibbet. One had already been prepared a year earlier for Andrew Perteet, a "colored" man who slit his wife's throat, but he won a reprieve. Since then the timbers had been stored under the courthouse steps at what is now Dearborn and Hubbard Streets. Now all the sheriff and his carpenters had to do was reassemble it. It did not go as well as they had hoped, since many of the unseasoned boards had warped, and had to be forced into place.

As the sound of the hammers reverberated throughout the jail at Dearborn and Illinois Streets, Driver's four children, his murdered wife's sister, Kate, and a lady friend congregated outside the iron door to his narrow cell. It must have been nothing short of pandemonium as they tried to have their last visit, with one of the women and the youngest child weeping uncontrollably, while two Presbyterian ministers, a Catholic priest, several Sisters of Charity, and a host of newspaper reporters all pressed around the door to catch his final words.

One reporter wrote, "He merited his dreadful doom and, as he said, would hope for nothing to avert it."

Young William grew restless during the session and wandered over to inspect the gallows, accompanied by a neighborhood chum. During the two-hour visit Sheriff Timothy M. Bradley was handed a telegram from Governor John L. Beveridge in Springfield. It said tersely: "I decline to interfere in the Driver case."

Advised of the message, Driver said in his crisp Scottish accent, "My children, the last hope is gone. Your father will die. Be good children. Go to Sunday school. Don't go with bad companions. Go to church regularly. And, above all things, let whisky alone." He then gave his oldest daughter his Bible, in which he had inscribed on the flyleaf, "George Driver's last present to his dear children."

After his visitors had departed, Driver, puffing on a short briar-wood pipe, sat on the edge of his bed and wrote a last letter to his aged mother in the Orkney Islands. The missive completed and sealed, he asked for a shave. Wanting to do it up right, his jailers summoned a German barber from Clark Street.

Driver was then taken to the cell of another condemned man, Christopher Rafferty, who had killed a policeman. "Well, Chris, I've come around to see you for the last time. Prepare yourself to go where I'm going," Driver smiled.

"I ain't afraid," Rafferty replied.

"Your body goes, but your soul will live," Driver continued. "You think on this, mind you. You are a young man yet." The two men shook hands, and Driver returned to his cell to make his final preparations.

Members of the audience removed their hats and stepped back respectfully as he marched to the makeshift scaffold and ascended the platform at precisely 2 o'clock. He sat in a chair provided for him while a Presbyterian clergyman led those present in prayer. At the conclusion of the prayer, Sheriff Bradley read the death warrant and asked, "Driver, have you anything to say?"

"Yes, a little," he answered, rising from his chair. As the minister and a deputy sheriff bent over to assist him, he waved them off saying, "Oh, I can get up alone. Never mind me."

Driver then delivered a short speech against the evils of drink, ending with, "Give up drink—all liquor. You see where I am standing now. Within a few minutes I will be where neither you nor I know, but I hope God is with me, and will take my soul."

He was then dressed in the customary white robe and hood, his arms were pinioned, and the noose was positioned about his neck. As he stood over the trapdoor he repeated, "Oh, Lord God, have mercy on me. Be with me, oh my God. May my soul rest in thy bosom, oh Lord."

Sheriff Bradley pulled the pin and the trap fell at 2:14 p.m. The drop was only about four and a half feet, but Driver's neck was dislocated by the fall. There was a slight jump forward, and a motion of the head. The body twirled slowly around for several minutes, and then was still. Three physicians stood ready to pronounce him dead.

At 2:18, however, his pulse was still beating. At 2:20 his heart and pulse continued to beat. At 2:22 his pulse fluttered and his heart beat began to weaken. At 2:23 the hanging man still exhibited a pulse. At 2:25 he was finally declared dead. Driver was then cut down, placed in a coffin, and carried through a mob of more than 3,000 curiosity seekers in the courthouse yard to a waiting hearse.

That same afternoon, John Marion Osborne was hanged

in downstate Knoxville for slashing the throat of a farmer's wife, Adelia Mathews, in Yates City, near Galesburg.

That hanging did not go well at all. As young Osborne swung at the end of the rope, slowly strangling after a five foot drop, he struggled violently. As one witness reported, "His legs moved up and down like the legs of a swimmer. The hands clutched nervously at the air. The spectacle was most horrible."

7

AT LAST

DECEMBER 12, 1873

Cuba was in the headlines, and war clouds with Spain loomed on the horizon as Cook County prepared the gallows to accept its first black man. It was not to be, however. Andrew Perteet, a portly 59-year-old paper-hanger, cheated the local executioner by taking his neck elsewhere to be stretched.

A free-born Negro, Perteet had come to Chicago from his native Georgia.

On the evening of September 16, 1871, his muddy clothing torn and spattered with blood, he had barged into Police Headquarters and declared, "I want to be locked up." When police went to Perteet's home at 43 E. Polk Street they found out why. His 44-year-old wife, Martha, lay dead on the kitchen floor. Her throat had been slashed with a razor.

Perteet pled insanity, but a jury wouldn't buy it. He was convicted of murder and sentenced to be hanged on January 12, 1872.

The scaffold was erected in the courthouse, but two days before it was to be put to use Perteet won a new trial, and a change of venue to Will County. He was tried in Joliet one year later, on January 13, 1873. He was again found guilty, and Judge Josiah McRoberts ordered him hanged on February 14—St. Valentine's Day. He won several stays of execution until December 12—two years and three months after his wife's murder.

On his last day he downed a breakfast of soup, bread and eggs in the Joliet prison. He passed up dinner, settling for a glass of water.

While dressing for his execution, Perteet discovered a button had come off his shirt, and requested a piece of thread to repair it. As he buttoned the shirt around his massive neck an attendant commented, "Isn't that rather tight?" "Not as tight as it will be," Perteet remarked, without cracking a smile.

Perteet then put on the white shroud, which had been brought to his cell. Finally he tied a white handkerchief around his forehead, and asked for a second, with which he tied up his jaw, as was customary when laying out a corpse. He then said good-bye to a group of friends who had gathered outside his cell, and followed Sheriff George M. Arnold downstairs to the prison dining room.

A gallows had been erected in the dining hall, a lofty stone room about 30 feet long and 12 feet wide. There was no platform. Only a pair of upright posts, with a rope tied in a noose dangling from a beam they supported. The other end of the rope passed through a hole in the floor, where it was attached to several sandbags weighing 500 pounds.

Members of the audience doffed their hats as Perteet walked under the scaffold and took his place. In a deep bass voice he joined the spectators in singing a Methodist hymn, before a final prayer was said for his soul.

After Sheriff Arnold read the death warrant he asked, "Mr. Perteet. Have you anything to say?" The doomed man shook his head negatively. The sheriff then declared, "Nothing remains, then, but the last act."

"I die, trusting in the Lord Jesus," Perteet muttered.

"Where are them straps?" called out the sheriff's father, who was assisting in the execution.

"Never mind, father! This is my duty," Arnold

protested, stepping forward. He then grabbed the leather straps and pinioned Perteet's arms at his sides, and tightened one around his ankles, as the prisoner stood motionless.

"It could not be said that he was pale," the *Tribune* reported, curiously.

The rope was placed around Perteet's neck, and as the black cap was being lowered over his face, he told the sheriff, "My whiskers are caught in the rope." Arnold adjusted the rope to make Perteet's last moments more comfortable. Neither man said another word.

At 1:59 p.m. the sheriff pulled a lever releasing the sandbags, and Perteet was jerked six feet into the air by his neck. There was no movement as he bobbed up and down as the rope stretched and contracted. At the end of seven minutes Dr. Benjamin C. Miller—the same physician who had examined Perteet's wife after she was murdered—officially pronounced him dead. The body was permitted to hang for another 40 minutes, before it was cut down and turned over to Dr. Miller for a post mortem examination.

Among other things, Dr. Miller determined that Perteet's neck, which had previously had a circumference of 19 inches, had shrunk to 14, due to being squeezed by the rope. He also examined Perteet's brain, and reported that he found no indication of insanity.

After the autopsy Perteet's body was reassembled, placed in a coffin, and buried in the prison yard.

8

RAFFERTY HANGED
FEBRUARY 27, 1874

George Driver's doomed friend, Chris Rafferty, lived for eleven more months before his name was finally called. The Irish-born Rafferty, a 25-year-old brickyard worker, will be remembered in history as Chicago's first cop killer.

On August 3, 1872, he fatally shot officer Patrick O'Meara who had tried to arrest him in a South Halsted Street saloon for assaulting another man. Rafferty fled, and was later arrested walking the Sanitary and Ship Canal tow path to Joliet.

Rafferty was tried three times—once in Chicago, and twice in Waukegan, where he had won a change in venue —and found guilty on all three occasions. He was originally scheduled to hang on December 26, 1873, but won a stay of execution only hours before he was slated to swing. A new date of death, February 27, 1874, was scheduled after a fourth trial was denied.

Rafferty, who came to Chicago at the age of 10, was extremely popular among the local Irish. But Governor Beveridge refused to commute his sentence, despite a plea from 14 members of the State Senate, 40 members of the House, the mayor and 20 aldermen from Chicago, and 300 interested citizens of Waukegan.

His execution had been moved to Waukegan after

police picked up a rumble that a band of Rafferty's friends from Bridgeport were planning to storm the county jail and set him free.

The unique hanging mechanism rigged in the Lake County Courthouse consisted of a long rope coming down through a hole in the ceiling in the front of the courtroom. The other end of the rope passed through a pulley fastened to a rafter in the roof. It was attached to an anvil, two enormous dumbells, and about 300 pounds of scrap iron. The weights were suspended eight feet above the attic floor by a cord, which ran down a stairwell to the main floor.

Rafferty awoke at 5 a.m. on the day of his death, and asked his jailers for some lukewarm water, with which he bathed himself. Then he blackened his boots to a fine lustre, shaved, put on a clean shirt, adjusted the gold studs, and donned a neatly creased black suit. It isn't every man, after all, who gets to deck himself out in the raiments he will die and be buried in.

Two clergymen remained in his cell praying with him until 8 a.m., when he was served a breakfast of two fried eggs, two large pieces of buttered toast, and a half dozen crackers.

After downing his last meal, he was visited by a woman named Mrs. Gallagher, who lived across the street from the jail and had struck up a friendship with him. She was permitted a 15-minute stay, and left sobbing. Later in the morning Rafferty was visited by his father, his brickyard foreman, and several friends from Bridgeport who had taken the train to Waukegan.

The press from throughout the country converged on the Northern Illinois town, including several young men from Milwaukee who tried unsuccessfully to pass themselves off as reporters so they could watch. One reporter wrote, "Never did a more lovely day dawn upon such ghastly work. It was too mild for winter, but the unmelted snow lying around the Courthouse square reminded that spring was yet far away."

At 12:30 p.m. Sheriff G.H. Bartlett entered Rafferty's cell and told him gently, "Chris, the hour has come. Are you ready?"

"I am ready," the prisoner replied in a steady voice.

Flanked by two Catholic priests, he then followed his keepers out of the jail and up the stairs to the courthouse. Clutching an ebony crucifix, he marched to a point beneath the dangling noose and took a seat provided for him. As the priests offered a prayer, he coughed twice while his eyes surveyed the throng assembled in the courtroom to witness his demise.

From somewhere in the crowd a voice was heard to remark, "He's going to die game."

After reading the death warrant Sheriff Bartlett turned to Rafferty and asked, "Do you wish to say anything?"

"I have nothing to say, sir," Rafferty replied firmly.

The prisoner was then asked to stand. Rafferty handed his crucifix to one of the priests, who held it to the condemned man's lips so he could kiss it while his legs were being bound together and his arms tied behind his back. After he was firmly bound the sheriff and his deputy reached behind Rafferty to shake his hands and bid him good-bye.

As Rafferty stood in the white muslin shroud that had been draped over him, one witness remarked, "He looks as collected and serene as if he was going to bed." He sighed audibly as the noose was adjusted around his neck, with the knot just below his left ear, and a white cowl was placed over his head.

At seven minutes to one the priests offered a final prayer. At the utterance of the word "Amen" Sheriff Bartlett cut the cord suspending the weights in the attic, and Rafferty was jerked five feet into the air by the rope around his neck. He bounced like a yo-yo as the stout line stretched, and fell about three feet, with his shoes coming to within eight inches of the floor.

When he was jerked skyward the knot below his ear slipped around to the back of his neck, causing him to strangle instead of dying instantly of a broken neck as intended. Rafferty drew up his legs and gasped feebly, and then was still.

As he continued to hang, Dr. O.S. Maxon lifted the shroud, took out his watch, and counted the dying man's pulse aloud. "Seventy," the doctor called out after the first minute. "Sixty-four," after the second; "Sixty," after the third; and so on, until after 10 minutes and 30 seconds, there was no pulse left to count.

The body was then placed in a mahogany coffin and carried two blocks, through a mob of 700 spectators, to the Church of the Immaculate Conception for funeral services.

On the same day that Rafferty died, convicted slayer William Keene was hanged in Jacksonville, N.Y., for the murder of a man named Valentine.

On November 26 of the following year, lovers Alice Harris and Tony Hellum were hanged in Monroe, Louisiana, for the murder of Mrs. Harris' husband, on the same day that two other convicted slayers were hanged in Mississippi.

The *Chicago Times* of November 27, 1875, reported the two double executions under the headline: JERKED TO JESUS.

9

WE WERE SIX

JUNE 21, 1878

The colorful tents and gaily decorated wagons of the renowned Adam Forepaugh Circus brightened the city's lakefront in June of 1878, but a lot more attention, it seems, was centered around the Courthouse Square, where an entirely different kind of side show was in the making.

The provocative headline above, which appeared on page one of *The Chicago Tribune,* alluded to the fact that on June 21 no fewer than six unfortunate felons were being hanged across this broad land of ours. Two of them, the *Tribune* pointed out, were "contributed by Chicago alone."

They were George Sherry, 22, and Jeremiah Connelly, 28.

Sherry, the first native-born white man to end his life on the Cook County gallows, was born in Cincinnati to Irish parents. He came to Chicago in 1876, and got a job as a ham-skewer at a packing house in the stock yards.

Connelly was brought to this country from his native Ireland as a boy. He worked as a deck hand on Great Lakes steamers until 1877, when he decided to settle in Chicago and got a job working at Sherry's side at B.P. Hutchinson's.

On the night of January 19, 1878, the two on a drunken rampage, stole a knife from a butcher shop, and fatally stabbed a 30-year-old painter, Hugh McConville, as he walked with his niece at 37th and South State Streets.

Both were caught in a nearby saloon, quickly tried, and sentenced to hang.

When a local reporter asked the Irishman how he felt, on the day of his death, he was quoted as replying, "Purty well, av coorse, under the circumstances, you know."

Sheriff Charles Kern stopped by to ask the two how they felt about the clothes they were to be buried in. Connelly examined the black dress coat lying on his bunk and opined, "It'll do." But Sherry was a bit more particular. "These won't do at all," he said, pointing to his ragged attire. "I've made arrangments for my body to be shipped back to Cincinnati, to be viewed by my friends, and I don't want them to know how poor I am.

"I guess I'll have to order you a new suit," Sheriff Kern agreed.

Meanwhile the sheriff's carpenters were erecting the gallows in the northeast corner of the new county jail building at Dearborn and Illinois Streets, using screws so that no hammering would disturb the inmates.

While Connelly was downstairs getting his last shave, Sherry was spiffing up in the new suit the sheriff had brought in. When Connelly returned Sherry greeted him with, "Hello! The boy looks slick, don't he?"

The two were then weighed. The 5 foot 8 inch Sherry, a burly, broadshouldered man with short brown hair and blue eyes, registered 161 pounds. Connelly, a good looking man who stood 5 feet 6, had curly dark brown hair and blue eyes, tipped the scale at 147. Both had gained weight in confinement.

Their last meal consisted of fried whitefish, potatoes, bread and butter and tea. Sherry ate quite heartily, but Connelly just picked at his bread and sipped a little of the tea. As they ate they could hear the clatter of horses' hoofs and the rumbling of wagon wheels in the jail yard, as the two hearses arrived to carry them away.

Sherry's brother-in-law, Martin Twohey, and several

friends from Cincinnati, and Connelly's brother, sat with the condemned men in their cells until 8:30, when all visitors were asked to leave while priests administered the last rites of the Catholic church to the prisoners. "Don't make any unnecessary haste," Sheriff Kern told the clergymen. "There's no need to rush this thing."

The air was raw and the sky overcast, and a cold drizzle whipped in off Lake Michigan as a group of 20 reporters was admitted into the jail, and took their seats at a long table facing the gallows. Sheriff Kern and his deputies were busy checking the two nooses, and tugging on the two ropes to make sure they were already stretched to their fullest.

Eight pallbearers who had been selected to carry the coffins to the waiting hearses stopped by the two men's cells and bade them good-bye, along with one of the physicians who would pronounce them dead. "We expect to be in the better land today. Don't cut me up," Sherry admonished the doctor.

At 10:07 a.m. the sheriff told the men, "It's time." The two, wearing tiny bouquets of fresh flowers in their buttonholes, fell in line behind the sheriff and his deputies, clutching their rosaries, with the priests at their sides.

Connelly and Sherry were seated beneath the ropes while Sheriff Kern read the death warrants. They were then requested to stand, while deputies adjusted their handcuffs and bound their arms and legs with leather straps. Connelly sighed audibly during the process, while Sherry stood in silence. Out in the audience a witness identified as Emil Jennings screamed hysterically and fainted, and was carried out by two policemen. Three other would-be witnesses became sick to their stomachs, and rushed from the room.

Stepping between the two men, Sheriff Kern said, "If you have anything to say, now is the time to say it. Any statement you may wish to make you can make freely. This is your last chance." Both men merely shook their heads.

They were then enveloped in the traditional white

muslin gowns, with the bottoms weighted so they wouldn't fly up during the pair's rapid descent. The nooses were fitted about their necks, and the white hoods placed over their heads.

At 10:21 a.m. the sheriff declared, "All ready," and rapped on a wooden partition behind the scaffold. The executioner, who was hidden from view, sprung the trap. The two men dropped with such force that the cracking of their necks could be heard as the stout ropes struck up a humming vibration. Another witness passed out, and had to be carried from the chamber.

Both men's necks were broken. They twitched spasmodically for two or three minutes, and were still. At the end of ten minutes both were pronounced dead. Their bodies were then allowed to dangle for another ten minutes, before being lowered to their coffins.

It was the first execution in Cook County that went off without a hitch.

In his final hours Sherry had penned a poem, to be delivered to his sister in Cincinnati after his death. It said in part:

> *I bid you farewell my sister, likewise to this world of sin.*
> *But tis hard, tis hard, my sister, to part from friends and kin.*
> *To be led like a brute to the slaughter, to die by the hangman's hand.*
> *To perish like a guilty felon, condemned by the laws of the land.*

Meanwhile, in downstate Paris, Illinois, 26-year-old Charles (alias John) Burnes, a red-haired man with a bushy red mustache, marched grandly up the stairs to the gallows, to be hanged for the murder of a farmer named Elijah Burdwell.

Neatly dressed in a dark suit, Burnes wore one white glove and carried the other in his hand, and puffed on a cigar as he mounted the scaffold. At the top he bowed and kissed the hand of a woman identified only as Mrs. Gilbert. He then deposited his cigar butt on the railing, drew on the other white glove, stood at attention while he was tied up, attached to the rope, and dropped to eternity before a crowd of 200 onlookers.

At Chillicothe, Ohio, Perry Bowsher went to the gallows without saying a word, for the fatal shooting of Edmund McVey, 77, and his wife, Ann, 72, the keepers of a local toll gate, during a robbery attempt.

At the same time, in Frederick, Maryland, Edward H. Costley, 26, a "bright mulatto" from Boston, was hanged for the murder of his cousin, Solomon Costley, whom he ambushed with a shotgun and robbed of $40.

And in Little Rock, Arkansas, Jacob Levels, "colored," paid with his life for the murder of another black man.

"No cooler man ever stepped on a death-engine," one eye-witness reported. "He ascended the steps as firmly and with as little emotion as a man would walk up to a banquet."

Asked if he had any last words before the trap was sprung, Levels declared, "Only one thing: Prepare to meet the glory!"

Back on Chicago's lakefront, the Forepaugh Circus was gearing up for a glorious six-day run.

10

THE BLACK CAP

SEPTEMBER 15, 1882

In the early morning hours of February 3, 1881, Police Officer John Huebner was patrolling in the 500 block of Dixon Street, when he came upon a burglary in progress in a nearby grocery. When fellow officers arrived, the policeman was lying mortally wounded on the sidewalk. "I downed one of them, but one of the other two shot me," he gasped before he died.

Eleven days later police arrested a man who gave his name as James Tracy, based on a tip from an informant. A jury took only three minutes to find him guilty, and just three more to sentence him to be hanged.

On the day of his death Tracy spent his last hours in the jail library, autographing cards, which he passed out to those who visited him to say good-bye. Each card bore his name, the date of his sentencing, July 8, 1882, and the date of his death, September 15, 1882. Tracy also presented Sheriff O.L. Mann with a list of names of those whom he wished to invite to his final "taking off," plus the names of three police officers he did not want to attend.

Meanwhile the scaffold on which George Sherry and Jeremiah Connelly had gone to their reward was set up in the jail yard and tested with a 200-pound bag of sand. It was then taken apart and reassembled in the jail.

Two hours before Tracy was to die he was served his last meal of six fried eggs, buttered toast, coffee, tea and several stalks of celery. He also asked for a dozen raw oysters, and would not sit down to eat until they were delivered.

Chatting amiably with friends and a reporter while he enjoyed his dinner, he revealed that he was a Civil War veteran, and that Tracy was not his real name. He adamantly refused to disclose who he really was, however. The reporter quoted him as saying, "I am resolved not to make known my identity. I may have folks alive somewhere, and do not want their reputations sullied by my ignominious fate." Whether he really said that, or the reporter was showing off his own vocabulary, has been lost in history.

As Tracy was being made ready for the stroll to the gallows, a jailer named Rehm suggested, "Don't you think you'd better take off your coat before going in there?"

"Naw," answered Tracy. "I'm afraid I'll catch cold."

He then told a friend, James McCann, "After it's over, I want you to see that I get a decent burial in Calvary Cemetery. Don't let my body fall into the hands of the doctors."

As Sheriff Mann read the death warrant to the condemned man in his cell, Tracy pinned a small religious emblem bearing the inscription, "Cease! The heart of Jesus is with me," over his heart. He was then led to the gallows, where Sheriff Mann, his hands quivering, addressed him in front of the witnesses:

"Mr. Tracy, you have just heard the death warrant read to you in your cell. Before proceeding to execute its provisions, an opportunity is given, if you wish, to make a statement."

In a firm, clear voice, Tracy responded, "I don't propose to make any statement further than to say I die innocent of the charge. I will be in the presence of my Maker in a few moments, and any man, under circumstances like these, if guilty, would acknowledge his guilt. But, innocent as I am, I have no fear of the hereafter. I die an innocent man. Truth is mighty, and it will prevail. I am ready."

After taking a long draught of water from a glass handed him by a deputy, the man called Tracy stepped onto the trapdoor. After his arms and legs were belted tightly together, a bailiff stood on a chair and lowered the shroud over him. Sheriff Mann, with trembling hands, then adjusted the noose, with the knot at the left side of the man's neck. The black cap was then placed over his head.

At 2:03 p.m. Sheriff Mann pulled a knotted cord projecting from the wall, to signal the executioner, and the trap opened, dropping Tracy about five feet. The body spun around for about a half a minute, and then hung motionless before the hushed audience. At 2:21 p.m. he was declared dead.

In accordance with his last wish, Tracy's body was not autopsied. Two doctors were permitted, however, to conduct an experiment to determine the effects of electricity on a human cadaver. They reported that an electrical charge caused the dead man's eyes and mouth to open.

After the experiment Tracy's body was placed in a coffin and buried in Calvary Cemetery, as he had requested.

On that same afternoon in downstate Metropolis a black man named Samuel Reddin was hanged for the murder of a shopkeeper, Adolphus Zimmerman, a Jew. Reddin's last words, before the black cap was put over his face, were, "My last look on earth."

And in Charleston, South Carolina, a Negro named Nathan Bonnet, accused of invading a white citizen's home, was taken from the jail and lynched by an angry mob, which then used his body for target practice.

11

JACOBSON'S EXECUTION
SEPTEMBER 19, 1884

In the fall of 1884 newspapers across the country were criticizing the former sheriff of Buffalo, New York, for personally hanging two condemned murderers instead of following the practice of hiring an anonymous executioner. A decade earlier Sheriff Grover Cleveland had pulled the trapdoor on Patrick Morrissey and John Gaffney with his own hand. The press now posed the question: "Can a man who has thus hanged criminals from choice and for money be elected President of the United States?"

The question was answered by the voters who, two months later, elected Cleveland to be our 22nd President.

Back in Chicago, after a hiatus of two years and four days, the scaffold was being readied for the first Scandinavian to lend his neck to the rope. The execution of Isaac Jacobson was scheduled for promptly at 12 noon on Friday, September 19, 1884. On Thursday Sheriff Seth Hanchett dispatched a deputy to a South Water Street hardware to purchase a new length of rope for the occasion.

Jacobson, a 54-year-old Finlander, had been convicted of fatally shooting his employer, George Bedell, the operator of a carpet cleaning shop, in an argument over $1 wages. A policeman, who was riding by on the Clark Street streetcar, jumped off and arrested him with the smoking gun in his hand.

The day was bright and clear, with the temperature hovering in the middle 60s, and a slight wind blowing from the southeast as Jacobson prepared for his last day on earth.

After a fitful night he was served breakfast of ham and eggs, spring chicken and strong coffee. He ate the chicken and sipped the coffee, but only picked at the rest. He then took a last walk around the jail with Sheriff Hanchett and the Rev. Charles Koerner, a Lutheran minister. "Sheriff, I hope there isn't any hitch, and everything goes off as quickly as possible," he told Hanchett.

The scaffold was a basic model, with an upright pillar supporting a beam extending out over the trapdoor, the beam held firmly in place by an angular brace.

About 250 spectators were packed into the jail's north corridor, where the device had been erected. These included some 50 newspapermen, the 12 official witnesses, aldermen, public officials, police of various rank, visiting sheriffs, assorted politicians and citizens with clout. All removed their hats at the sound of footsteps of the approaching death march as the clock struck 12 noon.

The gray-haired, bewhiskered Jacobson was ashen faced and obviously apprehensive as he mounted the platform behind Sheriff Hanchett and the Rev. Mr. Koerner, with a jailer and deputy sheriff at his side. He wore an ill-fitting brown suit, and twisted the brim of his slouch hat nervously in his hands as he seated himself in a chair placed over the trapdoor.

"Have you anything to say why the sentence passed upon you by a court of law should not be carried out?" the sheriff inquired.

Jacobson looked in annoyance at the noose, hanging by his left side, and shook his head negatively. Tears welled in his eyes and dribbled down upon his brown coat as Rev. Koerner offered a final prayer. Jacobson's hat fell from his lap, and he rung his hands nervously as he turned his head upward toward the vaulted roof. Sheriff Hanchett bent over and wiped the tears from the condemned man's face, as he quietly asked him to stand.

Jacobson got up and shook hands with the sheriff, minister and his jailers, without uttering a word. His wrists were then tied behind his back, and a strong leather strap was belted across his chest, holding his arms at his sides. His ankles were bound together, and the white shroud was draped around him. As the noose was placed around his neck, he called out, "Good-bye all! God bless us!"

His voice could be heard asking God for forgiveness as the white cap was placed over his head, and the audience waited in hushed silence for what would happen next.

At a signal from the sheriff there was a loud click as the bolt was pulled, and the trap fell, dropping Jacobson to his death at 12:08 p.m. It was quick, as he had wished. There was no movement save one convulsive heave of the chest as the body revolved slowly at the end of the rope. Six minutes later he was officially pronounced dead.

His body was placed in a coffin, which was sealed and turned over to two Scandinavian friends. A rhubarb developed after the lid had been screwed down, when Dr. T.J. Bluthardt, attending physician, declared, "I forgot to determine whether the man's neck was broken." Over the friends' objections, the coffin lid was unscrewed so the doctor could make his examination.

A reporter who observed the sorry performance said, "The dead man's face looked ghastly. It was bloodless and yellow. The ears were already blue, the eyes were half closed. There was no expression of pain upon the features. The neck was broken, and the small rope had cut a mark in the flesh."

After the body was returned to Jacobson's friends, for burial in Oakwoods Cemetery, a mob described by the press as "anarchists," led by August Spies of the *Arbeiter-Zeitung* and Albert Parsons, conducted a protest rally, in which they argued that Jacobson had been insane, and was only hanged because he was a working man.

12

THREE DANGLING CORPSES
NOVEMBER 14, 1885

The city's first triple hanging featured an immigrant trio described in the press as "the Italian stranglers." The newspapers of the day rarely failed to mention the ethnic backgrounds of killers or their victims.

The three, Agostino Gilardo, a 23-year-old soapmaker; Ignazio Sylvestri, also 23, a carter, who carried suitcases and trunks from the railroad stations to hotels; and Giovanni Azzaro, a 31-year-old shoemaker, had all come to this country from a small town outside of Palermo, Sicily. All three were married, and each was the father of a small child. None spoke English.

The victim of the so-called "Italian trunk mystery" was 20-year-old Filippo Caruso, a fellow Sicilian, who worked as a lemon peddler. Someone had slipped a noose over the poor devil's head and strangled him while he sat tilted back in a chair being shaved by Gilardo. His decomposing body turned up in a trunk two days later in Pittsburgh.

Police traced the trunk back to Chicago through a money order in the dead man's pocket. At the address listed on the money order they found the three suspects, who were identified as the men who purchased the trunk, and delivered it to the railway station. All three confessed, and were sentenced to hang.

Doomsday dawned cold and stormy. Several schooners that set out from Chicago that morning were forced to return to port in the 27-degree weather.

Before retiring for the night, Gilardo had ordered breakfast for all three, consisting of whitefish fried in oil, eggs fried in oil, broiled partridge, potatoes fried in oil, toast and coffee. Their last meal was served at 10:15 a.m.

After breakfast the three donned black suits provided for them, but all three refused to be shaved, washed or combed.

In his office, meanwhile, Sheriff Seth Hanchett examined three coils of rope: the one that had been used to hang James Tracy, still tied in the noose that was removed from his neck; the rope that was used to hang Isaac Jacobson, and a new coil woven from Italian hemp. Sheriff Hanchett chose the latter.

The gallows, with three ropes hanging from the cross beam, had been painted a dull black. An estimated 300 people had assembled in the death chamber. After the official witnesses and the press were seated, the sheriff threw open the doors to as many members of the public as there was room for—mostly members of the Italian community.

At 11:44 a.m., after the trio had made their last confessions to their priests, the sheriff met the condemned men in the jail library and read the death warrant. One of the priests, who spoke Italian, acted as translator. Five minutes later the procession, headed by Sheriff Hanchett, marched to the gallows. A deputy, carrying the white caps, shrouds and belts, brought up the rear.

Azzaro and Sylvestri stood ramrod straight and faced the crowd, while Gilardo, apparently on the verge of breaking down, kept his eyes tightly closed. After the men said their final prayers in Italian, the shrouds were placed around them, the nooses slipped down around their necks, and the white caps placed on their heads to shield their faces.

At 12:09 the sheriff signalled to the executioner, who was crouched unseen in a large box, and the trapdoor dropped out from under the men's feet.

Gilardo's and Sylvestri's necks snapped, and after a few convulsive twitches their bodies hung limply from the ends of the ropes. The noose on Azzaro's neck slipped, however, and the hangman's knot lodged under his chin. He drew up his legs and kicked, shuddered, quivered and gasped for five and a half minutes, while he slowly strangled to death.

After all three men were pronounced dead, their bodies dangled for another 25 minutes before being cut down, placed into coffins, and carted off to Calvary Cemetery.

13

A SCANDALOUS SCENE

MARCH 26, 1886

One of the most pathetic figures ever to go to the gallows was Francis "Frank" Mulkowski, a bewildered Polish immigrant who swore with his dying breath that he knew nothing about the crime for which he was being hanged.

Life had not been kind to Mulkowski. He had served 22 years in a Russian prison for the fatal shooting of a Russian during that country's reign of terror against the Poles in 1861.

Once he got out of jail he made his way to Chicago where, on August 22, 1885, he was arrested for the fatal beating of Agnes Kledzieck. There were no witnesses to the slaying. Mulkowski was convicted on circumstantial evidence, despite the fact that there was no blood on his clothing, and he claimed to have been somewhere else at the time the crime was committed. He was utterly baffled by the guilty verdict, and had to have it explained to him by a Polish speaking friend.

His last days behind bars were spent in abject bitterness. He spurned the traditional last meal, asking only for a couple of apples and oranges. He then turned his back to the jailor as he stood munching on them.

Sheriff Seth F. Hanchett had issued 200 passes for the execution, scheduled for 12 noon on March 26, 1886. As the hour approached, however, more than 1,000 rowdy, joking, hooting, cigar-smoking witnesses had elbowed their way into the jail corridor, all waving tickets to the event. One of the sheriff's bailiffs, it seems, had opened a little counterfeiting business on the side.

Sheriff Hanchett had bought a new coil of Italian hemp rope for the occasion, to go with the new walnut-stained gallows, which had been put together by a Halsted Street carpenter.

Mulkowski wore a stiff felt derby on his head and three days growth of beard on his chin as he prepared to leave this world. He refused to have a new suit of clothes made for his last public appearance, and marched to the scaffold in an ill-fitting gray suit, a bluish striped shirt without a collar or tie, and wearing heavy square-toed boots. His lawyer, John W. Byam, loaned him his Prince Albert coat.

Before leaving his cell for the last time, Mulkowski wrote his will in Polish. He bequeathed all his earthly belongings, which he itemized as two shirts, two pairs of pants, two hats, two coats, a watch and chain, eight dollars, and some cents to a fellow prisoner, William Rodgers.

Sheriff Hanchett stepped upon the platform and called for order at 12:08 p.m. as the prisoner was brought in. Oblivious of his surroundings, the condemned man stood on the trapdoor kissing his crucifix so passionately that the smacking of his lips could be heard among the spectators.

The victim's husband, Joseph Kledzieck, watched from a front row seat as Mulkowski's wrists were handcuffed behind his back, his feet bound together, and the shroud placed over him. The rope was then drawn about his neck and the white cap placed over his pallid, expressionless face.

Mulkowski stood, almost indifferently, as the signal was given and the trap was sprung. His shrouded body plunged downward and his neck snapped. His body moved convulsively for a few moments, and was then still. He was pronounced dead at 12:24 p.m., and five minutes later his body was cut down and placed in the pine coffin provided by the county.

"It was a gala day for the surrounding saloons, which filled up rapidly after the cadaver had been cut down," the press reported.

14

HOWLING LIKE A DEMON

JULY 16, 1886

James Dacey, a 39-year-old City Hall hanger-on and Demoratic vote chaser, was not thrilled when Alderman Michael Gaynor's candidate beat his own man in a special election May 14, 1884, to fill a vacancy caused by the death of Alderman John H. Ebley of the Ninth Ward.

Dacey was drowning his sorrow in Foley's saloon at 87 South Halsted Street the following evening when Gaynor came in and said, "Jim, let me buy a drink." Dacey answered by drawing a .38 caliber revolver, and putting a bullet in the alderman's head.

Gaynor had been a popular figure, and public feeling ran so high that authorities had to slip Dacey out of town and hide him in the Joliet jail. He was subsequently moved to Woodstock where, after being convicted and sentenced to hang, he was confined to the basement "debtor's cell" in McHenry County's 1857 jail.

Dacey was hardly a model prisoner. He spent his last night on earth and the morning of July 16, 1886, bound hand and foot and manacled to his cot.

The previous afternoon he had gone berserk, tore his clothing to shreds, and commenced howling in his cell upon learning that the governor had denied him a reprieve. When a Catholic priest entered the cell to try to calm him down, Dacey menaced him with a club, threw him to the floor and tried to choke him. A jailor, Richard Friend, thrust the muzzle of his revolver through the grating and shouted, "Stop it, Dacey, or I'll shoot!"

Once the priest was freed, jailors turned a hose on Dacey, spraying him for 20 minutes with cold water, which he deflected back at them with a tin pan. Two sheriff's deputies from Chicago and two Woodstock jailors finally wrestled the prisoner to the ground, shackled him and handcuffed him to his cot.

There Dacey laid, tossing and kicking, while screaming, cursing and howling, "I'll have blood before I die!" and "Cut my heart out and let me go to hell!" When a doctor was sent to examine him he hooted, "The tortures of Satan's furnaces there."

The doctor reported to authorities, "In my opinion, he is feigning insanity. I don't believe there is anything wrong with him."

The condemned man refused a last meal, taking only a glass of water, and puffing on a cigar while the priest, Father Clancy, offered prayers.

Because of rumors that cronies from Chicago might try to interfere with the hanging, eighty extra men were sworn in as sheriff's deputies to surround the jail opposite the town square. At 12:31 p.m. Dacey was carried into the jail yard, and marched up onto a gallows that had been erected for the occasion.

He blinked in the bright sunlight, and stared blankly before a crowd of 120 spectators, including the murdered man's brothers, Peter, Christy and Patrick Gaynor, and several of the jurors who had found Dacey guilty. As the noose was being adjusted around his throat he declared, "This is the happiest day since I came into the hands of (Sheriff) Udell."

The trap was sprung at 12:33 p.m., and at 12:45 Dacey's heart beat its last. His body was cut down and placed in a coffin aboard the 4:45 train for Chicago, where a doctor at Rush Medical College removed his brain for study.

The hanging of the Chicago prisoner was the first and only legal execution ever carried out in McHenry County.

15

DROPPED TO ETERNITY
NOVEMBER 11, 1887

In the spring of 1886 some 500,000 workers were on strike across America, demanding shorter hours and better working conditions. Management countered with scabs, blacklists, lockouts, armed guards, state militia and club-swinging, head-cracking police. In Chicago, where 34,000 able-bodied men were out of work, Haymarket was a riot waiting to happen.

On Tuesday evening, May 4, an uneasy crowd assembled in a light drizzle in Haymarket Square at Randolph and Desplaines Streets to denounce police brutality and the deaths a day earlier of two workmen protesting outside the strike-bound McCormick Harvester Works.

Some 1,200 to 1,300 people, many of them curiosity seekers, had gathered in response to a flyer distributed by August Spies, editor of the German-language newspaper *Arbeiter-Zeitung.*

Spies opened the meeting, climbing aboard a flatbed dray that would serve as the speakers' platform. He was followed by Albert Parsons, a spellbinding, blood and-thunder orator. Parsons then introduced the third speaker, Samuel Fielden, whose remarks were interrupted when the drizzle turned into a downpour and the crowd started to break for cover.

As they did so, a cordon of blue-uniformed police loomed in the darkness to the sound of marching feet. Captain William Ward, who led the column of 180 officers, approached the speakers' wagon and ordered the group to disperse.

Fielden offered no argument. "We are peaceable..." he began, as he and the others prepared to step down from the makeshift platform. He never finished his sentence. His words were cut off by an ear-shattering explosion in front of the police ranks.

One police officer was killed on the spot, and 60 to 70 others were felled by the blast. Seven of the injured policemen would later die of their wounds. The stunned lawmen instinctively opened fire on the crowd, killing three civilians and wounding uncounted more.

Hundreds of known or suspected anarchists were rounded up by authorities in the aftermath of the massacre. Thirty-one were indicted on various charges, and eight eventually were charged with murder.

They included Spies, the 30-year-old publisher who called the meeting; Parsons, the 37-year-old orator who could trace his lineage back to the Mayflower; the British-born Fielden, 39, a non-violent man known as "Good Natured Sam"; George Engel, 50, the German born owner of a toy store on Milwaukee Avenue; Adolph Fischer, 27, a German-born printer who worked for Spies; Louis Lingg, 22, the only bachelor in the group, who had come over from Germany just ten months earlier; Oscar Neebe, 36, a native-born American who worked as a tinsmith; and Michael Schwab, 32, a Bavarian bookbinder, who served as associate editor of the *Arbeiter-Zeitung*.

Why eight? The prevailing theory is that it was sheer retribution—eight anarchists for eight policemen. An eye for an eye—an anarchist for a cop.

During a highly publicized and electrifying trial, all

were found guilty of inciting to murder. All but Neebe were sentenced to death.

On the day before they were scheduled to die, Governor Richard J. Oglesby commuted Fielden's and Schwab's sentences to life imprisonment, along with Neebe.

Fielden, Neebe and Schwab were pardoned in 1893 by Governor John Peter Altgeld, who recognized that the evidence failed to support the anarchists' link to the bombing.

The governor's action came six years too late to help the other five, who had been sentenced to hang by their necks until dead.

The mass execution was scheduled for Friday morning, November 11, 1887, but it did not come off as planned. The handsome young Lingg cheated the hangman at the eleventh hour by holding a dynamite cap between his teeth and lighting the fuse with a candle, blowing his face clean away. How he obtained the lethal charge in his cell has never been determined.

The surviving quartet, Parsons, Spies, Engel and Fischer, were then led to the gallows in the old Cook County Jail at Dearborn and Illinois Streets at 11:30 a.m.

Their final moments were spent standing side by side, facing a throng of 170 witnesses, including more than fifty reporters, seated below the platform on wooden benches. Their bodies shrouded with white muslin, arms pinioned just above the elbows by thick leather belts tightened around their chests and wrists handcuffed behind their backs, the four mounted the gallows, where deputies bound their feet with leather straps.

Spies smiled slightly as he took his place behind the farthest noose. Fischer, his chest thrust out, stopped behind the second. Engel, an indifferent, almost stoic look on his face, was positioned behind the third. And Parsons, passively defiant, stood calmly behind the fourth rope.

As the white death hoods were placed over their heads,

and the nooses around their necks, the knots tightened just below the left ear, the muffled voice of August Spies pierced the eerie quiet of the barnlike room: "The day will come when our silence will be more powerful than the voices you are throttling today!"

"Hurrah for anarchy!" cheered Fischer through his muslin hood. "Hurrah for anarchy!" echoed Engel. "This is the happiest moment of my life," exclaimed Fischer. "Let the voice of the people be heard..." Parsons began, as Sheriff Canute Matson signalled the executioner, who severed a stout rope with a chisel, dropping the trapdoor under the anarchists' feet and cutting Parsons off in mid sentence.

The four white-robed figures dropped in unison, jerked at the ends of the ropes, and spun in a macabre death dance in midair for seven minutes and forty-five seconds until the last man stopped writhing. After their bodies were cut down, an examination determined that none of the anarchists' necks had been broken by the drop. All four died of slow strangulation.

It was not until a century later that a Hegewisch farmer named George Meng was identified by relatives as the actual bomb thrower. Meng, a known anarchist, died in a saloon fire in the 1890s.

The hanging of the Haymarket rioters was subsequently described as the most important single event in the history of the American labor movement. Their fellow anarchists carried on their work and formed the Industrial Workers of the World (IWW), which evolved into the CIO.

16

ZEPH WAS READY TO DIE

MAY 12, 1888

Zephyr Davis, whose parents had been slaves, came to Chicago from St. Joseph, Missouri, in 1887. A year later he would become the first black man to go to the gallows in Cook County, convicted of the murder six weeks earlier of Maggie Gaughan.

He spent the last day of his life sitting on the cot in the cell previously occupied by Louis Lingg, puffing on a cigar and reading the Bible. He seemed to enjoy being the center of attention as friends flocked in by the dozens to have one last chat with the condemned man. To each visitor he handed a card autographed: "From Cook County Jail, May 12, 1888. Zephyr Davis."

The *Chicago Tribune* reported:

"The five old colored women called the Mission Band also prayed and sung in their strange, weird, but affecting manner."

When a Tribune reporter asked Davis whether he had any statement to make, he replied, "I have nothing to say in any shape, form, or manner."

At 4 o'clock in the afternoon his mother, Sophia Davis, and brother called, acccompanied by their pastor. Sheriff Canute Matson conducted the prisoner, his mother and brother to the jail library for one last visit while the pastor offered a prayer, and the Mission Band sang hymns in the background.

When the weeping Mrs. Davis left the jail, she carried all of her son's personal belongings with her. "I don't want some dime museum to get hold of them," she told Sheriff Matson.

Rather than return the prisoner to his cell, the sheriff permitted Davis to spend his last night on a cot in the library. Before retiring at 1:30 a.m., he called for a pen and ink and some paper, and prepared a speech to be delivered from the gallows. A bailiff who had been assigned to guard the prisoner asked, "What are you thinking of, Zeph?"

"Old times, old times," he replied.

"Were they pleasant?"

"Pleasanter than these," he sighed.

A light rain was falling the next morning when Sheriff Matson read the death warrant to Davis at 10 o'clock. At 10:30 the door to the jail yard was opened, and assorted aldermen, city and county employees, ward politicians and newspaper reporters who had tickets to the execution pushed and crowded their way in and fought for seats.

"Gentlemen, please remove your hats and quit smoking until—in short, until you leave the jail," Chief Deputy Gleason shouted over the din.

Shortly after 11 o'clock Davis, accompanied by the sheriff, three jailers, and a black clergyman, the Rev. Mr. Henderson, mounted the stairs to the gallows and took a seat facing the witnesses who had assembled to watch him die.

He unconsciously tapped out the beat with his fingers on the arm of the chair as Reverend Henderson sang his favorite hymn, "Jesus, Lover of My Soul." As the hymn ended, Davis looked up at the cross-beam from which the noose was dangling and shouted:

Hide me, oh, my Savior, hide
Till the storm of life is past,
Safe into the haven guide;
Oh, receive my soul at last.

He then sat back in the chair and listened attentively as Reverend Henderson read the speech he had prepared the night before:

TO MY FRIENDS AND FELLOW-BEINGS OF THE CITY AND OF THE WORLD: I want to say before leaving you that I am sincerely sorry for the act for which I am to suffer, and for all other wrongs I have done. For the girl whose life I took and for her parents I am deeply and truly sorry, and would give all I have in this world if it could be called back; but since it is done and cannot be undone I am willing and ready to pay the penalty. I have nothing against anybody on earth, and I leave the world feeling love for all. I feel that by true, noble prayer, and I accept repentance. I have found forgiveness with God, and I ask the forgiveness of all mankind.

I ask all to be kind to my mother and my brother; they are not to blame for any of my conduct. I never went to school a day in my life and all I know about reading or writing I picked up myself, and therefore never had much education. I desire to say to all the boys with whom I have ever associated to take my warning and always try to do right.

I sincerely thank the officers of the law for the kind acts they have done for me, and I pray God to bless them all. I feel perfect peace with God, and do not fear to meet Him. Mr. Henderson has given me good instruction and has prayed earnestly for my

soul, and I feel that God has answered his prayer.
Hoping to meet you all in Heaven, I am ready to go.
        Zephyr Davis

After the speech was read, Davis rose from the chair and shook hands with everyone on the platform, smiling as if he were accepting congratulations for a job well done. He then placed his hands behind his back so he could be handcuffed. His legs were fastened together with a broad, black strap, and his arms were pinioned at his sides.

"Trust in God," Reverend Henderson told him.

"Yes, sir. I'm trusting in God," Davis replied, as the white shroud was draped over his body. He seemed to regard the process with interest as the noose was adjusted about his neck, and the white hood draped over his face.

"Are you ready?" Sheriff Matson called to a deputy at the foot of the stage.

"We are ready," the deputy responded.

Sheriff Matson raised his hand, and the front of the platform fell downward, dropping Davis as though he were on a fast slide until the rope stopped his progress. A deputy beneath the platform wrapped his arms around Davis' legs, protruding from the white surplice, and pulled down with all his weight until all movement ceased.

"A shapeless figure hung from the crossbeams, like a scare-crow in a cornfield," the *Tribune* reported.

17

PAINTER IS HANGED

JANUARY 26, 1894

The agonizing death of George H. Painter proved to be every sheriff's nightmare.

Three times he had been scheduled to hang for choking his fiancee, Alice Martin, to death. Three times in six weeks time he spent his "last night" in the death cell while the gallows was assembled in the jail corridor, and twice the governor had granted last minute reprieves. The third time would not be his lucky day. Governor John Peter Altgeld declined "to further interfere."

"Well, I suppose if that is so, I cannot help it," Painter said when he got the bad news.

He spent his last evening, the third time, playing cards with the sheriff's deputies on the death watch. He interrupted the game long enough to order a last meal of half a spring chicken, one dozen raw oysters, bread and butter, coffee, and a dollar's worth of cigars.

The temperature fell to a bitter 9 below zero during the night, and was still 5 below at 8 o'clock the next morning, the appointed time for Painter's execution. At 7:48 a.m. Sheriff James H. Gilbert stepped to the door of his cell and said, "All is ready."

"Well, so am I," Painter replied.

As he was being marched to the gallows he paused and

said, "Wait, I must smoke a cigar." The group waited while he lit up a cigar from the batch he had purchased the night before, then continued down the corridor.

Painter was the first to reach the platform, followed by Sheriff Gilbert and the Rev. A.P. Moerdyke and two deputies. It was the same gallows on which Zephyr Davis met his doom six years earlier. As the condemned man's wrists and ankles were being bound, Reverend Moerdyke offered a final prayer. A jailer removed the half-smoked cigar from Painter's lips, threw it on the floor, and asked him if he wanted to make a statement. Turning his head toward the jailer he said, "Morris, I can't talk with these false teeth in my mouth. Take 'em out, please." The jailer obliged, after which Painter cleared his throat and faced the crowd.

"Gentlemen (long pause). Gentlemen, I see some friends here today—some good friends. Oh, God, forgive them. A friend of mine who would come here to see me die—it hurts me. Gentlemen, if you are gentlemen, who could look at an execution—execution—there are few. The brotherhood of humanity has taught better things. Men have sought death because they thought there was advancement in future life. Today I hate death. I don't want to die. I don't want to die. Listen. If I killed Alice Martin—in court (long pause), the woman I dearly loved, the woman I loved so much that I would almost commit a crime for her, I pray this minute, my last minute on earth, that the eternal God will put me into eternal hell. Look here, gentlemen, if there is one man among you who is an American, I say to you on his soul—on his soul, I say, see that the murderer of Alice Martin is found. Good-bye. Good-bye. Good-bye."

The worst was yet to come.

Painter obligingly stretched his neck to make it easier for the jailer to adjust the shroud about his throat. The white cap was placed over his head, and the noose set in place. Everyone then stepped back, leaving Painter alone on the trapdoor. The sheriff gave the signal, and the trap opened.

Painter dropped, and there was a loud "snap" as the rope broke. The condemned man continued his free fall until he hit the concrete floor. His feet went out from under him on impact, and his head split open as it struck the concrete with a sickening thud.

As Painter lay motionless, blood oozing from the head wound, Dr. E.C. Fortner, the jail physician, knelt at his side and felt for a pulse. Painter was dead.

But he had been sentenced to hang, and the letter of the law would be carried out. A new noose was fashioned in the rope. His limp form was then carried back up onto the platform, laid across the drop, and the second noose placed around his neck. The sheriff again gave the signal, the trap opened, the dead body dropped, and this time the rope held.

The entire ordeal lasted sixteen minutes, from the moment the first rope broke, until his body was cut down. Death came just one month before his thirty-ninth birthday.

His body was removed to the Carroll funeral home on Wells Street, where he was laid out in a coffin. The next day thousands of morbid curiosity seekers filed past to get a look at the man who was hanged after he was dead.

18

HIGGINS IS HANGED

MARCH 23, 1894

It wasn't much he was asking, but in the end, 24-year-old
Thomas "Buff" Higgins, got his dying wish. He did not want
to meet his maker on the same gallows as that crazy Patrick
Prendergast.

Prendergast was not a popular man in Chicago, being as
he had assassinated the beloved Mayor Carter Harrison. An
obscure political hanger-on, he had worked on Harrison's
re-election campaign, and had asked to be appointed
corporation counsel. Harrison ignored the request. When he
arrived home on the night of October 28, 1893, after
delivering a speech at the World's Columbian Exposition,
Prendergast stepped from the shadows and shot the mayor
five times.

Higgins, on the other hand, a common burglar, had
fatally shot Peter McCooey, when McCooey awakened while
he was ransacking his bedroom.

Higgins and Prendergast were scheduled to hang side
by side at high noon on Friday, March 23, 1894. Higgins
appeared more upset over sharing the gallows with the
mayor's assassin than he was about having his neck
stretched. "I do not want to stand on the same scaffold with
him," he objected. So it came as good news to him when,
twelve hours before the trap was scheduled to be sprung,

Prendergast was granted a stay of execution for a sanity hearing.

Nor was Higgins surprised when the Supreme Court refused to grant him a reprieve. "Well, that's just what I expected," he told his jailers. "So my neck will crack Friday."

After having breakfast and joking with his jailers, Higgins walked with Sheriff James H. Gilbert and two deputies to the scaffold carrying a crucifix close to his face in both hands.

He kissed the crucifix as he stood on the trapdoor beneath the noose, while his legs were fastened together. He kissed it once more as it was taken from him, and his hands were tied.

There was no dramatic address, as in the case of Painter. Higgins simply muttered, "Good-bye," as the white cap was placed over his head. Sheriff Gilbert gave the signal, and the drop fell at 12:07 p.m.

As the shrouded figure dangled from the rope, it was immediately surrounded by a group of physicians, who listened while Dr. E.C. Fortner called out the dying man's pulse rate, until his heart beat its last at 12:15.

19

ASSASSIN HANGED

JULY 13, 1894

Patrick Eugene Joseph Prendergast kept his date with the gallows three and a half months later, after a lengthy "lunacy proceeding" in which his lawyers argued that he was "a nut," obsessed with the idea of bringing a traction system to Chicago. For every doctor the defense dug up to testify that Prendergast was insane, however, the prosecution brought in one to testify that the prisoner was as normal as any man ever was.

It was the first time in Illinois history that insanity was introduced as a legal defense.

When this failed, his lawyers tried to delay the inevitable by alleging that Prendergast was not asked, during his trial, whether he had anything to say before the death sentence was pronounced. Prosecutors dug up court records that indicated Prendergast read a prepared statement that took nearly fifteen minutes.

The last day of Prendergast's life was a hot one, with the temperature in the 90s. He had been taken the night before from his cell in the county jail to the same room in the adjoining Criminal Courts Building where George Painter and Buff Thomas spent their last hours. Jailers had brought in a cot with clean, white linen, a rocking chair, and a table to make his stay comfortable.

Asked whether he was receptive to visitors, Prendergast pulled in the welcome mat, asserting, "No, there is no one I care to see, except my attorneys. They are the only ones who can do me any good now, and if any one of them calls, show him in. I do not wish to see anyone else, and I do not desire to be bothered by callers."

His last meal consisted of ham and eggs, fried potatoes, bread and butter, pie and coffee. He ate heartily, after which he lit up a cigar and blew smoke rings into the air. As the final moment approached, he removed his necktie and collar, to make the hangman's job easier.

The march to the gallows, which had been set up in the jailhouse corridor, began at 11:43 a.m., with Sheriff James H. Gilbert leading the way. In addition to the usual wooden benches for witnesses, a telegraph instrument had been installed to report the event.

Prendergast walked uneasily, dragging his feet, and looking straight ahead as he mounted the gallows. The witnesses rose and took off their hats as the procession entered the room. His last words, to a Catholic priest as the noose was being adjusted around his neck, were, "I had no malice against anyone."

A jailer then pulled a cord, leading into a sentry box behind the scaffold in which the anonymous executioner was concealed, to signal that all was in readiness. The executioner cut a rope that released the trapdoor and Prendergast dropped to eternity at exactly 11:48 a.m.

"He went to his death like an ox going to the shambles," one newspaper reported.

After being pronounced dead he was cut down and placed into a plain wooden coffin, bearing a plate that read "At Rest." He was buried in an unmarked grave in Calvary Cemetery.

On that same day, in Livingston, Montana, Robert A. Anderson was hanged for the robbery-murder of one Emanuel Fleming; and in Fort Benton, Montana, John H.

Osnes went to the gallows for the murder of a fellow Norwegian, Ole Lilledall, during another robbery.

20

HARRY LYONS HANGED

OCTOBER 11, 1895

A ferocious storm enveloped all of Lake Michigan on October 10, 1895. The schooner Otter, bound for Chicago with a load of lumber, was driven ashore at Sturgeon Bay. Off Holland, Michigan, the schooner H.M. Avery, loaded with laths and shingles, lost most of its cargo as waves swept over its deck. The schooner Naiad, being towed by the steamer Allegheny, broke adrift and washed ashore at Kewaunee, Wisconsin. And the schooner Minnie Mueller was hurled onto the beach at Pentwater, Michigan, with a full load of corn.

In Chicago, Harry "Butch" Lyons prepared to meet his maker.

Lyons was convicted of murdering Albert I. Mason, a scenic artist. He died after being struck on the head with a revolver during a robbery attempt at Van Buren and Clinton Streets on the night of February 9, 1895. Before he died, Mason identified Lyons as his assailant.

During Lyons's trial, one of the jurors, J.O. Weber, went insane and had to be confined in an asylum. Lyons was sentenced to death on September 25, and the sentence was carried out just over two weeks later, a far cry from today's justice system, in which the appeals process drags on for years.

The scaffold was assembled in the northeast corridor of

the jail on the evening of October 10, and the rope tested with heavy bags of sand.

Lyons spent a sleepless night, writing letters, smoking cigars, and chatting uneasily with the sheriff's deputies assigned to the death watch. After a last breakfast of beefsteak, eggs, bread, butter and coffee, Lyons declared:

"Well, I am ready for whatever comes. I have got the worst of it thus far and I suppose I shall get the worst of it to the end.

"When I am hanged, I will be killed as an innocent man. I suppose that it is useless to protest that I did not murder Albert R. Mason, but as sure as I sit here I never injured a hair on that man's head. Why, we were friends...But what is the use of talking about the case? It has gone against me and I must suffer for a crime I never committed."

No one was admitted to the execution without a ticket. Sheriff James Pease limited the number of witnesses to sixty-one, including jail officials, physicians, deputy sheriffs, two visiting sheriffs from other counties in which hangings were scheduled, and two newspapermen from each of the city's daily papers.

Ten seconds after the noon whistle blew in the courthouse yard, the macabre procession consisting of the sheriff, the condemned man, three deputies, two priests and the county physician, reached the scaffold in the corridor. Lyons, clutching a black crucifix before his pale face, kissed the emblem and stepped onto the trapdoor. He then handed the crucifix to one of the priests, and closed his eyes.

His eyes clenched shut, he recited a prayer, along with the priests, as straps were adjusted about his arms, body and ankles, and the noose was tightened around his neck.

At 12:03 p.m. the drop fell, and ten minutes later Dr. E.C. Fortner pronounced Lyons dead of a broken neck.

The *Chicago Tribune* reported:

"Every detail of the arrangements for the execution was carried out to perfection."

21

HENRY FOSTER EXECUTED

JANUARY 24, 1896

At 6 p.m. on January 23, 1896, Colonel W.F. Dose, private secretary to Illinois Governor John Peter Altgeld, who was out of the state, opened the following telegram addressed to the governor:

"Preparations are being made to execute Henry Foster, a colored youth, tomorrow morning. An effort is being made to present facts to you which it is hoped will cause you to commute his sentence to life imprisonment. We have petitions asking a commutation of sentence to life imprisonment which, together with other facts, we wish to present to you. Will you kindly stay his execution for thirty days in order that we can present the case fully to you upon your return? Yours in behalf of the colored people of Cook County.

"Johnson & Alexander, Counsel, No. 21 Quincy Street, Room 407"

Colonel Dose wired back:

"Stay of execution cannot be granted except upon full statement of facts, showing good cause for Executive interference. Nothing has been presented to the Governor which would justify him in interfering with the court's judgment. In fact, your telegram containing a bare request for a stay received here hardly twelve hours before time fixed for execution is the first intimation the Executive has in the matter."

Foster was scheduled to be hanged at 12 noon on January 24 for the murder of George Wells. Wells was shot to death when he emerged from a saloon at State and Taylor Streets at 4 o'clock in the morning on October 4, and attempted to interfere while Foster was robbing a man named Henry Workmeister.

The condemned man's lawyers made one final plea to Governor Altgeld, and one hour before the hanging they received another telegram from Colonel Dose saying, "The Governor declines to interfere."

Several hours earlier, when Foster was asked what he wanted for his last meal, he told his jailers, "Fried chicken, and lots of it."

A crowd of about 1,000 curiosity seekers had gathered outside the jail yard as final preparations for the execution were made. At 11:15 a.m. the official witnesses and members of the press were led into the north corridor, where the same scaffold on which "Butch" Lyons died had been erected.

Among the witnesses was Gecrge W. Wells, Jr., son of the murder victim. "I saw my father die, and I want to see the man that killed him die," he explained.

At 11:50 a.m. Sheriff Pease and several deputies went to Foster's cell, where he was praying with the Reverend J.M. Townsend, and told him his time was up.

"I am ready," Foster replied.

The procession mounted the scaffold at 11:57, with Foster reciting the Lord's Prayer.

"Do you have anything further that you would like to say?" the sheriff asked.

"Gentlemen, I did the deed," Foster responded. "I killed George Wells, and I do not want anyone to suffer for it. But the Lord has forgiven me of all my crimes. All I have to say is, I did not want to die. This may be a lesson to someone. I see a lot of you around here who may have young boys coming up, and this may prevent them from coming where I am today."

Turning to Eugene Tousley, the jail elevator operator, Foster continued, "You may have a boy and I want you to watch him and see that he does not come to where I have today. I am ready to die."

Raising his hand and looking toward the ceiling, he cried, "May the Lord forgive me."

Foster then shook hands with the sheriff and the deputies who surrounded him on the trapdoor. He declared, "I am trusting in Jesus," over and over as his arms and legs were strapped, the white robe placed around him, the noose tightened, and the cap adjusted over his face.

This done, the two deputies who had been holding him steady stepped back, the sheriff nodded, and the trap was sprung.

The powerfully-built, 173-pound prisoner dropped through the opening. Despite the fall of seven feet, however, his neck was not broken, and he dangled at the end of the rope for a full eleven minutes until the last breath left his body.

22

PAYS FOR HIS CRIME

MAY 15, 1896

Alfred C. Fields, a handsome, twenty-six-year-old black man who worked as a bellhop at the opulent new Lexington Hotel, the future headquarters of Al Capone, set a legal precedent in the state of Illinois.

He became the first person to get the death penalty after pleading guilty to the crime of which he was accused.

Since coming to Chicago from Winchester, West Virginia, four years earlier, Fields had roomed with Ellen Randolph and her husband, Beverly, a Pullman car porter, in the Randolph home at 2458 South Dearborn Street. He was engaged to marry a girl named Lettie Adams.

Fields's future swirled down the drain on February 20, 1896, however, when he and his twenty-seven-year-old landlady quarrelled over the fact that he had fallen behind in his rent. Fields ended the argument by bashing Mrs. Randolph's brains out with a flatiron and a lemon squeezer. He then laid her body on the bed, took $25 from her purse, and set the house afire.

After stashing the money in his locker at the Lexington, a few blocks away, Fields returned to a neighborhood saloon and watched firemen put out the blaze. He was arrested at the scene.

His execution on May 15, 1896, was to have been part

of a triple-header, with convicted slayers Joseph Windrath and Nic Marzen joining him on the gallows, but his would-be companions won last-minute reprieves, leaving Fields to go it alone.

"While outside was the hum of preparation and the sound of feet on iron steps, Fields sat as quietly in the jail dispensary as though he had just been sent in with a message and was waiting for an answer," The *Chicago Tribune* reported. "Like all other condemned men, who have somehow managed to keep what is called their nerve up to the last, the colored boy ate a good breakfast in the morning, and smiled as he chatted with his guards."

As final preparations for the execution were being made, police from the Chicago Avenue station had to be called to disperse the milling crowd that had gathered outside the jail.

Fields, dressed in black, with a white satin ribbon given to him by his sweetheart pinned to the lapel of his coat, walked erect and unshackled to the gallows between two deputies.

Asked whether he had any last words, he declared, "Well, I suppose that on this occasion I ought to say something, but I don't know what to say. I have confessed to the minister and gained spiritual comfort. I bid you all good-bye, and hope to meet you in a better world."

He smiled and repeated, "Good-bye, all," as his arms were pinioned and the rope was adjusted about his neck. The shroud and white cap were set in place, the deputies stepped back, and at 12:25 p.m. the trap fell.

As with Butch Foster, Fields's neck did not break, and it took him fourteen minutes to die by strangulation.

The *Tribune* reported:

"Whether it was the religious faith, a strong nerve, or a weak mind, incapable of grasping the situation, the spectators were hardly able to determine, but the majority of those who witnessed the execution attributed the condemned man's coolness to the latter cause."

23

SHAMS ON THE SCAFFOLD
JUNE 5, 1896

Joseph Windrath's eleventh hour reprieve—literally just seven minutes before he was to have hanged with Alfred Fields—did not last long. On June 5, 1896, he, too, went the way of the rope.

Windrath had been granted a stay of execution for three weeks, for the purpose of a sanity hearing, after his lawyers argued that he had gone mad while in custody. When his lawyers, J.R. Burres and Hugh Pam, told him of the reprieve, he shouted, "I'll put him in the bad box, put him in the bad box, put him in the bad box! Where is the hat?"

Doctors, who subsequently examined him, determined it was all an act, however—a role which he continued to play right up to the second the trapdoor dropped.

Windrath had been convicted of the murder of Carey B. Birch, treasurer of the West Side Street Car Company during a robbery in the carbarns at Milwaukee and Armitage Avenues on the night of June 23, 1895. Windrath professed his innocence, but his partner, Julius Manow, confessed and bore witness against him.

The "nut act" began immediately after he was found guilty. He spent long hours in his cell, shrieking, "Hang Manow!"

He refused to talk to his wife, Barbara, when she visited

him in jail on the night before his execution.

"Don't you know me, Joe?" she asked.

"Hang Manow," he muttered. "Put him in the bad box."

Earlier in the day she had gone to Springfield to personally plead with Governor John Peter Altgeld to spare her husband.

It was cloudy the next noon, with thunderstorms threatening, as a weeping Barbara Windrath stood in the crowd milling outside the jail, carrying a small child in her arms, while two others tugged at her skirts.

When the Rev. John P. Dore of Holy Name Cathedral called at his cell to administer the last sacrament, Windrath grabbed the crucifix and held it like a revolver, shouting, "That's what I'd do with that!"

"My son," said Father Dore, trying to soothe him. "Will you not..." The priest never finished his sentence. Windrath sprang at the cleric and attacked him, and had to be restrained by deputies.

A short time later he was carried to the gallows by two deputies, before the smallest group of witnesses who had gathered up to that time to view an execution. In addition to the twelve physicians, then required by law, there were only a handful of news reporters and several lawmen. As the procession entered the room, a sheriff's deputy signalled the witnesses to remove their hats.

"Put him in the bad box," Windrath said, glowering down at the group. He continued his muttering, even as the rope was adjusted about his neck, and the white cap put over his head. His last words, as the trap was sprung at 12:01 p.m., were, "Put him in the..."

He dropped to his death in mid-sentence. An autopsy showed he died of a broken neck.

24

MANOW MEETS HIS FATE
OCTOBER 30, 1896

Joseph Windrath's partner, Julius Manow, also went to his death, despite his guilty plea which, he claimed, had been given in exchange for a promise of leniency.

His dying act was to clear Windrath, asserting, "I wish to state right here that Joe Windrath never had a hand in that affair, and that he died an innocent man."

Manow, a native Chicagoan who had served two prison terms for burglary, died a bitter end, insisting that prosecutors had promised him a life sentence if he would withdraw his plea of innocence and enter a plea of guilty in Carey Birch's homicide.

"I was as much bunkoed into this plea as the greenest granger ever was with a shell game. I had no more show than a fly who gets into a spider's web. Judge Horton was the spider in this case," he asserted.

On the verge of collapse, Manow was removed from the regular cellblock and placed in the death cell near the gallows at 3:30 p.m. on October 29, 1896. His only request was for a deck of cards. "I shall not sleep much," he told Father John P. Dore, the priest from Holy Name Cathedral, who spent a half hour chatting with him. Dr. E.C. Fortner, the county physician who would pronounce him dead, sat up with the prisoner for part of the night, playing cards with him.

After Fortner left, the condemned man dozed restlessly on his bunk, and awakened repeatedly to ask his guards, "What time is it?" He made every effort to keep awake, as though trying to cram every minute of life into his remaining hours. "I'll expect to get enough sleep soon enough," he told his guards.

The last day of his life dawned cloudy, with a trace of showers, and the temperature climbing only to 50 degrees. His last visitors were his sister and Windrath's widow, Barbara, who stopped by his cell at 6 o'clock on the morning of October 30.

When a group of clergymen arrived to offer prayers he dismissed them, telling his jailors, "They can't save my neck, and they can't do me any good now.

"I intend to go like a man."

With Sheriff James Pease's permission, Manow walked to the gallows with his hands free, a privilege that had been accorded to only one other recent prisoner, Buff Higgins, two years earlier.

With his dying words he reiterated that he had been double-crossed by the judge and prosecutors, who sent him to the gallows after he had agreed to plead guilty. "I believe the word of a confessed murderer is better than that of a murderer who has not yet confessed," he said.

Manow declined the services of a minister as he stood on the trapdoor, and nodded to the deputies to proceed. He closed his eyes while his arms and legs were strapped together, and the white hood placed over his head.

The trap was sprung at 12 o'clock sharp, and Manow dropped through the opening. The twelve physicians who surrounded the body to watch for evidence of life determined that the fall had failed to snap his neck. It was fifteen minutes before his heart stopped beating. Three minutes later, when all signs of life vanished, his card-playing partner, Dr. Fortner, stepped forward and pronounced him dead.

25

M'CARTHY'S LIFE IS OUT
FEBRUARY 19, 1897

At 8 o'clock in the morning on February 19, 1897, a guard paused before Cell No. 23 in Chicago's old Cook County jail on Dearborn Street, and called through the bars, "Hello, Dan! How do you feel?"

"I feel as if I was going to die," the cell's occupant, Daniel McCarthy, responded matter-of-factly.

McCarthy, a twenty-seven-year-old wife killer, had no cause to feel otherwise. He had been up since 6:30 a.m., when his brother, Thomas, stopped by to tell him that there did not appear to be much hope for a reprieve. Governor Tanner had said he would "review the case," but that was all.

This was yet another instance in which the defendant had pleaded guilty, and still got the death penalty. McCarthy had prepared a written statement but, on second thought, tore it up.

"I guess I'll just try and take it easy," he said, as the hours passed. His brother nodded. There was little else to do. Thomas left at 10:30 and joined the crowd outside, as jailers made final preparations for the new year's first hanging.

Two priests, the Reverend John P. Dore and Father Scanlan, joined the prisoner in his cell as Sheriff Pease came in and read the death warrant, as required by law.

McCarthy listened intently, then shook his head from side to side when asked whether he had anything to say.

At 11:55, led by the sheriff and followed by the priests and two deputies, McCarthy calmly mounted the gibbet. A waiting deputy told the thirty assembled witnesses, "Hats off!"

McCarthy shuddered noticeably as the leather straps were tightened around his legs and arms, and the noose lowered over his head. He stood mute. There would be no last words to be recorded for posterity.

At 11:59 Sheriff Pease nodded, and the trapdoor fell. McCarthy shot downward for five feet. A slight moan was audible as he reached the end of his rope with a jolt. His chest heaved convulsively, and his bare neck, partly visible beneath the white hood, took on a bluish tinge as he slowly strangled to death. Twenty minutes later, he was pronounced dead.

Meanwhile, in St. Louis, Dr. Henry Rohlfing, pathologist at the Missouri Medical College, disclosed that an autopsy on the brain of Arthur Duestrow, who was executed there, revealed that Duestrow was insane and never should have been hanged.

26

TWO DIE ON THE GIBBET

MAY 28, 1897

It was a clear day for a hanging as Chicago's official weather observer, L. Manasse, an optician, recorded a noon temperature of 53 degrees outside his office at 88 E. Madison Street.

Not since the Haymarket rioters were hanged ten years earlier had there been a multiple execution in Cook County. There would be one again this day, when the State of Illinois exacted its punishment from John Lattimore and William T. Powers.

Swinging by a rope, side by side, would be just about the only thing the two black men had in common. They had been convicted for separate crimes.

Lattimore was sentenced to death for the murder of Louis Marvic near Summit, Illinois, on November 28, 1896; and Powers was consigned to the noose for the slaying of John J. Murphy, a South Side saloonkeeper, at 735 Root Street on December 29.

Chicago's black community was abuzz on the fatal day, after a rumor circulated that Lattimore had picked what could be the winning number in a South Side policy game. The *Chicago Tribune* reported:

"It is a negro superstition that any number selected by a colored man about to die on the gallows will prove a winner to those who play it."

The rumor apparently started after Lattimore had slipped a note to one of his guards, Wesley Plummer, to be passed on to a woman who would call for it within a week. The note read:

Chicago, May 27, 1897.—Mrs. H.T.: I will tell my minister and he will have the number put in this note for you as I did promise you. J. LATTIMORE

In giving Plummer the note, Lattimore had told him, "Wesley, in about a week, maybe sooner, a woman will call at the jail and inquire for you. She will hand you a bit of paper bearing the initials 'H.T.' Will you go with her to my grave, or arrange it so she can find the grave?"

"I will," Plummer promised.

"Thank you, old man," Lattimore replied, shaking the jailer's hand.

"Who is this woman?" Plummer inquired.

"Don't ask me now, Wesley. She will tell you who she is," the condemned man told him.

After spending their last evening praying and singing hymns with two Baptist ministers, the Reverends John Ford and A.L. Harris, the two prisoners retired just before midnight Thursday. Powers slept right on through to 5:45 Friday morning, when he awoke and asked a guard named Goebel, in German, "What time is it?"

Lattimore, on the other hand, spent a restless night. He finally got up from his cot at 2:30 a.m., got fully dressed, and read from his Bible.

When Powers awoke, he too got all decked out in his Sunday-go-to-meeting clothes. In the absence of a mirror, he used a burnished tin cup to see his reflection so he could comb his hair.

"Well, old fellow, how do I look?" he asked Goebel.

"First rate," the jailer replied.

"Do you think I look good enough to take a stroll down State Street?"

"You certainly do," Goebel smiled.

"Well, I'm ready to go. Come on," Powers laughed, enjoying his own gallows humor.

For his last meal, Powers requested a breakfast of frogs' legs, ham and eggs, mushrooms, french fries, celery and coffee, topped off with a fine cigar. Lattimore's last meal consisted of fried fish, oatmeal, custard, strawberry shortcake, ice cream and coffee.

Both men ate heartily, seeming to enjoy the novelty of ordering anything their hearts desired. After breakfast Lattimore joined Powers in singing, "Nearer, My God, to Thee," until Lattimore complained that Powers was singing too fast.

Their last visitor was Powers's brother, George, who spent an hour with the men. He was sobbing quietly as he left the jail.

Shortly before noon a South Side undertaker named Jacobson pulled up in a horse-drawn wagon containing two coffins. As Jacobson applied for admittance to the jail, a woman who identified herself as Rosina Marvic appeared and asked permission to witness Lattimore's execution.

"I want to see the murderer of my husband hanged," she declared. The woman left in tears after Sheriff James Pease refused to let her into the jail.

While Mrs. Marvic was denied tbe opportunity of seeing her husband's killer pay for the crime, Lattimore was also denied his dying wish.

As the two men stood on the gallows, with the nooses around their necks, and the white caps about to be lowered over their heads, Lattimore turned to a jailer named Whitman and made a strange request: "Take off my shoes."

"What is it?" the astonished jailer asked.

"Take off my shoes," Lattimore repeated. "Take off my shoes."

"No," Whitman told him. "I can't stop now. I'll attend to that later."

Whitman and another deputy, named Hall, continued with their ghastly chore, tightening the leather straps about the two men's knees. The Rev. Mr. Harris began reciting the Twenty-third Psalm as the caps were drawn down over the men's faces.

"Take off my shoes," Lattimore insisted, one more time. Those were his dying words.

The trap fell, and the two white-robed figures plunged downward until the ropes stopped their fall. Lattimore's neck snapped and he died quickly. Powers died by strangulation. It took thirteen minutes.

Eighteen minutes after the trap fell the two bodies were cut down and placed in the waiting coffins. They were then taken to the funeral parlor at 2805 South State Street, where a large crowd of curiosity seekers, both black and white, filed past the caskets to view the bodies of the two men, still dressed in the suits in which they were hanged.

Arrangements had already been made to bury Powers in Oakwoods Cemetery. Lattimore, it appeared, was bound either for the potter's field or the dissecting table, since no one stepped forward to claim his body. At the last minute, however, two Baptist ministers, the undertaker, and Wesley Plummer, the jail guard who had come to know the doomed prisoners, chipped in and bought a plot so Lattimore could be buried at Powers's side.

27

CHRIS MERRY IS HANGED

APRIL 22, 1898

Suddenly, the United States was at war with Spain! A fleet of battleships, monitors and cruisers, under the command of Rear Admiral W.T. Sampson, was off the coast of Key West, steaming toward Havana.

At the same time, in Chicago, preparations were underway for the hanging of a burly vegetable hawker with the Dickensian name of Christopher Merry.

Merry was anything but. A huge man, described as "powerful as a gorilla, coarse and calloused and cruel," he beat and choked his wife, Pauline, to death in their cottage on Hope Street on November 19, 1897.

After the murder was solved by Jim O'Shaughnessy, a reporter for the *Chicago Chronicle,* Merry told Police Captain John Wheeler, "I didn't mean to kill my wife. She was handy to have around. It was just a family quarrel and I hit a little too hard."

Once Merry was in custody his own mother came forward to testify against him. "He beat me almost daily, for no reason," she told Captain Wheeler. "He loved to inflict suffering on others. I would willingly tie the rope around his neck myself."

Actually a double hanging had been scheduled for this rainy Friday noon, April 22, 1898. Nic Marzen, convicted of murdering Fritz Holzhueter, had originally been scheduled to hang alongside Arthur Fields on May 15, 1896, but won a last-minute reprieve. On this day he was scheduled to swing from the gallows with Merry, but again fate intervened. Hours before he was to have walked to the scaffold, the Supreme Court granted him a new trial.

On the evening before his death, Merry said his last good-byes to his elderly mother and three-year-old son, Chris Jr. His mother, holding her little grandson by the hand, left the jail in tears.

Merry retired at 10 p.m., but awakened at 3 a.m. and began to pray. Then he drifted back asleep until 6 a.m., when he was roused for breakfast. His last meal consisted of ham, boiled eggs, toast and tea, after which he puffed on a cigarette and chatted with Jerry Roeder, one of the death-watch guards.

His last visitor was Father John Dore of Holy Name Cathedral, who would accompany him to the scaffold. At 11:48 a.m. Sheriff James Pease and Chief Deputy Charles Peters told the prisoner it was time to go.

Merry's bravado deserted him half-way to the gallows, his knees buckled, and he had to be supported by two deputy sheriffs. Once he was positioned on the trapdoor, facing the sixty-five assembled witnesses, a guard stood on each side to keep him from falling off the platform.

As the leather straps were being tightened around his legs, and a jailer prepared to bring the noose down over his head, Merry whispered in a hoarse voice, "Can you put it over the hood, instead of under it?"

"No, Chris. I can't do that," the jailer answered.

As soon as the knot was adjusted and the hood in place, the two deputies who had been steadying Merry stepped back and, at 12:01 p.m., the trap fell. Merry died hard, and moans could be heard coming from under the hood for nearly ten minutes, until Dr. Francis W. McNamara finally pronounced him dead.

The body was cut down at 12:20, and an examination by the twelve attending physicians indicated Merry had died of slow strangulation—the same as his murdered wife.

28

DRUGGAN AND JACKS EXECUTED
OCTOBER 14, 1898

A powerful pre-season snowstorm borne on a north wind battered the Chicago area on the night of October 13, 1898. Banners and festive decorations that festooned the downtown area in preparation for a Peace Jubilee were whipped away, and electric light bulbs strung across State and Dearborn streets broke loose and crashed to the pavement. Heavy, wet snow clung to the red, white and blue bunting draped around the County Building, causing the colors to run together and the decorations to tear.

Passengers in the city's open streetcars were blinded by the pelting snow, motormen were unable to see the street ahead, and traffic cops, caught without their rain coats, were soaked to the skin.

Friday, as the city dug out, was a terrible day for a hanging.

Two condemned killers were scheduled to go to the gallows at high noon. It would not be a double bill, as in the case of John Lattimore and William Powers, or any of the earlier multiple executions. Sheriff James Pease, who was in charge of arrangements, decided that there would be two separate hangings.

John Druggan and George H. Jacks would march to the scaffold one after the other.

Jacks and a friend, William J. Willows, had decoyed Andrew F. McGhee into a vacant flat at 2030 Indiana Avenue on the night of February 26, and bludgeoned him to death in a $26 robbery. Willows turned state's evidence and got fourteen years in prison. Jacks got death.

Druggan, just turned twenty-one, entered Robert Gudgeon's saloon along with four friends on the night of January 11, and announced a holdup. When Gudgeon failed to put up his hands fast enough, Druggan shot him dead. Druggan's companions were all sentenced to prison and Druggan, the triggerman, was consigned to the rope, even though he had pled guilty.

Jacks nearly collapsed when told that the governor had refused to interfere in the execution. "I can't believe this is true," he moaned. "If the worst comes to the worst, I suppose I shall have to stand it. But...I am not ready to go. I did not expect it and have many things I desired to fix up. I have some business matters to attend to."

On his last night on earth, Druggan's father, mother, two sisters, brother and his grandfather were permitted a final visit. As they prepared to leave, the youth's mother fainted and had to be carried from the death cell. After his family left, Druggan began to laugh hysterically, and so unnerved Jacks that he had to be moved to another cell.

Jacks then wrote a letter to reporters, in which he denied ever having seen McGhee, and insisted that Willows was the murderer. Druggan, meanwhile, confessed to Father John P. Dore, saying the slaying of Gudgeon was "a sudden impulse," and not premeditated.

Only a handful of sheriff's deputies, news reporters, Father Dore, and the jury of twelve physicians were permitted to witness the executions.

Druggan mounted the gallows first. The trapdoor dropped at 12:01 p.m., and his body shook convulsively for seven minutes before it was still. Thirteen minutes later he was pronounced dead. After he was cut down, placed in a coffin and carried away, a new rope was adjusted and the platform replaced.

As Jacks stepped onto the trapdoor, he mumbled responses to a prayer recited by Father Dore. He was dropped to his death at 12:37 p.m.

Post mortem examinations showed that both men died of strangulation.

29

HOWARD HANGED FOR MURDER
FEBRUARY 17, 1899

London was agog over the engagement on February 17, 1899, of the Earl of Crewe to Lady Margaret Etrenne Hanna, youngest daughter of the Earl of Roseberry. In Kansas City, Jesse James, Jr., was going on trial for train robbery; and in Madison, Wisconsin, legislators were pondering a bill to prohibit tight lacing of ladies' undergarments as a hazard to their health.

Back at home, "Spring Weather Here To Stay," one newspaper proclaimed, as Chicago prepared for the grand opening of the Hotel Edwards, a residence for working girls, on Lexington Avenue.

Over at the Cook County Jail on Dearborn Street, a gallows had been erected in the third floor corridor to receive the neck of Robert Howard, a black youth convicted of murdering Frank C. Metcalf.

It would be the first hanging under the direction of newly elected Sheriff Ernest Magerstadt and, as far as anyone could determine, the first time a man had been condemned to death as an accessory to murder while the accused killer was still at large.

Metcalf, a machinist, was slain in an alley behind the firehouse on Taylor Street during a robbery attempt on the night of November 9. The actual killer, Albert "Snakes"

Nixon, had never been caught.

Howard denied his role in the slaying to the very end, in talks with the Rev. Abraham L. Harris and his guard, Wesley Plummer. Two hours before he was to meet his fate he was baptized.

Howard's last request, to die with his boots off, was granted. As he mounted the gallows at noon, accompanied by the sheriff, several deputies, and two clergymen, Reverend Harris and Reverend Revardy C. Ransom, he turned to his guard and said, "I don't want to die with my shoes on." Sheriff Magerstadt stopped the procession at the top of the stairs so Howard could kick off his shoes.

Before the death cap was placed over his head, as he stood poised over the trapdoor, the sheriff asked, "Is there anything you would like to say?" Howard shook his head negatively. The sheriff stepped back, and the trap was sprung.

Doctors determined that Howard was rendered unconscious by the fall, and died almost instantly, although his neck was not broken.

No one appeared afterward to claim the body. At nightfall it was removed to the Cook County Morgue, to be turned over to a medical college.

30

MURDERER BECKER IS HANGED

NOVEMBER 10, 1899

All August Becker wanted before he died was a cold bottle of beer—good German that he was.

The garrulous Becker found himself on death row for the murder of his wife, Rachel, in their home at 5017 Rockwell Street, on January 29, 1899. Police said he cut her body into pieces, and boiled them, in an effort to conceal the awful deed. He needed her out of the way, they suggested, so he could marry her sister, Ida Sutterlin—which he did just two weeks later. After he was arrested for his first wife's murder, Ida divorced him.

His date with the gallows was set for November 10. At 3 o'clock in the morning he was wide awake in his cell, taking care of business. First he made out his will, then he mapped out a plan for his last public appearance.

"I want one thing distinctly understood," he told his guard, James Diesei.

"What is that?" Diesei asked, curiously.

"That I am to be allowed at least one hour—maybe one and a half hours—to talk. I want to roast George Sutterlin. I have a good deal to say. After I have finished, I want you to hand me up two bottles of beer. That's all I ask."

The deputy nodded.

"I have a few friends left in Germany. I will write to

some of them," Becker continued.

"I think I will write a few lines to my former wife, Ida Sutterlin-Becker," he added sarcastically. "No doubt she would be pleased to hear from me. She was such a dutiful wife when I was arrested for a crime I did not commit. She called to see me only once, and then I had to send for her. I guess I'll just write to her and tell her a few things about her father."

The previous evening, after his last supper, Becker sent his compliments to the cook, but added he wished he had something to wash the meal down with.

"I wish I could have some beer. I have been asking for beer ever since I've been here, but no attention is paid to my request. I like beer. Can't I have a bottle?" he begged.

When his request was denied, he sent a message to Michael Emil Rollinger, another convicted wife killer, who had been scheduled to hang with him, but won a delay of one week. "I hope you have better luck than I do," Becker told him.

In his will he listed an estate of $8,500, mostly in property. He left $2,000 to his physician, and bequeathed a like amount to his ex-wife, Ida. The rest went to relatives in Germany.

Upon completing the will, Becker called Sheriff Ernest Magerstadt, and had it notarized. "If by any chance I'm not executed, I want the will returned to me," he emphasized.

Becker then took a short nap, and spent his remaining hours gazing at the sky from his cell window. His self assurance left him when Sheriff Magerstadt stopped by his cell at 11:30 to read the death warrant, and he had to be steadied by two Roman Catholic priests, who administered the last sacrament.

"Is there anything I can do for you?" the sheriff asked, sympathetically.

"Yes," Becker replied. "I'd like two bottles of beer."

Magerstadt granted him his dying wish. Becker gulped

them down, licked his lips, and said he was ready. The march to the gallows began at 12:03 p.m., led by the sheriff and his chief deputy, Charles Peters, with two priests, Fathers Reithymeier and O'Brien, next in line, followed by Becker, walking between two deputies.

As the noose was tightened around his neck, Becker proclaimed his innocence for the final time.

"This is the last chance I will have," he announced. "Gentlemen, my name is August Becker. I am an innocent man. My father-in-law, George Sutterlin, killed my poor good woman."

Those were his last words. The trap fell at 12:06 p.m. Becker was declared dead seventeen minutes later.

Elsewhere in Chicago, "The Great Ruby" was playing at the McVickers theatre, and the University of Chicago and Northwestern University were gearing up for their annual football game.

31

MICHAEL ROLLINGER IS HANGED
NOVEMBER 17, 1899

Michael Emil Rollinger, convicted of choking and then burning the body of his wife, Antonia, in the bedroom of their Racine Avenue home on December 16, 1898, agonized throughout the week's delay he had won, over whether Governor Tanner would stop the hanging. When November 17, 1899 arrived, with no word from Springfield, the condemned man shrugged, "Well, I suppose that settles it."

On his last afternoon, after being transferred from the cellblock to the death chamber, Rollinger sent for the Austrian Consul and arranged to have some of his keepsakes sent back to friends in his homeland. Rollinger, who went by his middle name, then called for a pen and paper, and prepared the following announcement:

> *To the Public: There are several witnesses here in Chicago who know I can prove that I am innocent. I have a witness who will testify that he spoke to my wife between 6:30 and 7 o'clock the evening of Dec. 16, 1898. EMIL ROLLINGER.*

The witness he referred to was a waiter named John Miller. Rollinger's previous attorney, Edmund Furthmann, had interviewed Miller, and determined that he could not be sure of the time he had spoken to Mrs. Rollinger.

Rollinger slept late the next morning—his last. When he awakened, his first words were, "Any word from Springfield?"

After being told by his lawyer, William Stanton, that the governor had declined to interfere, he prepared for the end. As he stood on the gallows at high noon, he turned to the crowd and declared:

"Gentlemen, I say I am an innocent man. Some lawyer—my lawyer—I will not mention his name, he told me he would take my case to the Supreme Court. He took all my money, but he did not take my case to the Supreme Court. Another lawyer, Mr. Stanton, went to Springfield last night, but it was too late. Gentlemen, I not only lose my own life, but it kills my children and my mother. I am an innocent man. I wish you good-bye. Don't look on me with a bad face when I am gone. That's all I have to say."

As the white cap was being lowered over his face, he repeated the prayer for the dying, as it was read by two Catholic priests. The words of the prayer could still be heard coming from under the hood as the trap was sprung. There was a crack as the prisoner's neck snapped. Death was almost instantaneous.

The *Chicago Tribune* reported:

"It was the most successful execution in the matter of producing instant death since the execution of 'Butch' Lyons."

The second man in a week to swing for the crime of uxoricide, Rollinger would be the last person to be executed in Cook County in the Nineteenth Century.

32

DOLINSKI AT LAST DIES
ON THE GALLOWS

OCTOBER 11, 1901

George Dolinski and Anton Lisl had a lot in common, not the least of which, both men worked as florists, and they were married to sisters. In a crime that rocked Chicago's large Polish community, Dolinski was convicted of murdering Lisl so he could have his brother-in-law's young wife.

Three months before the slaying, Dolinski sent his own wife and their three children to Poland, so he would be free to continue the affair with his wife's sister. When Mrs. Dolinski did not hear from her husband, she wrote to Chicago police, fearing something had happened to him. Only then did she discover that he was in jail, charged with Lisl's murder.

The tragic story began on the night of October 29, 1900, when Lisl was set upon, stabbed and shot to death as he took a shortcut home from work through the woods skirting Bohemian National Cemetery on Chicago's far Northwest Side, in what was then the suburb of Irving Park.

Dolinski was arrested on circumstantial evidence: his watch and chain were found near the body; his clothing was torn and spotted with blood; and police found a note from his paramour detailing her husband's shortcut home.

Despite her husband's affair with her sister, Mrs. Dolinski returned from Poland and stood by him. Despite Dolinski's protestations that he knew nothing about his brother-in-law's murder, he was convicted and sentenced to hang.

After two earlier reprieves, Dolinski was finally scheduled to die at high noon on Friday, October 11, 1901. It would be Cook County's first execution in the Twentieth Century.

Dolinski spent a restless night, sitting on the edge of his cot, with his face buried in his hands. "If I only knew that my family would not be in want, I could die in peace," he moaned. "My wife, the poor woman, her health is not the best."

Early the next morning Mrs. Dolinski and the couple's three children arrived for a final visit. Dolinski patted the baby's cheeks, and chatted with the other two. As the condemned man's wife was leaving, word came that the Supreme Court had refused to interfere in her husband's execution. She screamed and collapsed to the floor, and had to be sent home in a cab.

Mrs. Lisl also called at the jail, but she was denied permission to visit the man a jury said had killed for her.

Dolinski then made his last confession to Father Vincent Rapouz of St. John's Polish Catholic Church. The march to the gallows began exactly at noon. Opie Read, the world famous writer, assigned to the execution by Hearst's *Chicago American,* wrote:

"If silence could have color it would have been black. A white robe lying on a chair made all things look ghastly. A cricket crept out of a cell and chirruped, and its notes were like needle points in the air."

A bailiff, circulating among the reporters, commented, "I don't know why this is sadder than any other hanging, but it is."

One reporter, who had witnessed the hanging of the Haymarket anarchists, got up and said, "I'm going to get out of here. I can't stand it." He could not leave, however. The death party was entering the room.

The deputy ordered the witnesses to remove their hats. Dolinski, clad in a shabby black suit, and with a rosary around his neck, walked between jail guards Kanute Thimes and John Finley, firmly holding his arms.

Opie Read wrote:

"Out came an emaciated, miserable thing. Once they had called him a man. Now he was not to be classified. His mouth was open. He was dazed.

"Someone touched him, to move him further up on the trap, and he looked up as if stung. He was bow-legged, and when they put the straps about his ankles he cringed as if in a vise. When they strapped his arms he looked up with all hope gone out of his eyes. When they put the white robe upon him he gasped. And then came the ringing voice of the law..."

It was the voice of Sheriff Ernest Magerstadt. "George Dolinski, is there anything you have to say why the sentence of the law should not be executed upon you?"

"I...I..." Dolinski stammered. "I have got this to say. I am not guilty of killing that man. I...I..."

A priest held a prayer book to Dolinski's lips, and he kissed it. Thimes then adjusted the white robe, and Finley pulled the white cap over the man's head.

At 12:03 p.m. the hangman, concealed in a square brown box at the rear of the scaffold, yanked a rope and the trap was sprung. Dolinski dropped to eternity.

He was pronounced dead at 12:14 p.m. Now, both sisters were widows.

33

LOUIS THOMBS IS EXECUTED: SAYS "INNOCENT" TO LAST

AUGUST 8, 1902

Louis Thombs, also known as Toombs, was convicted for one of the more heinous homicides Chicago had witnessed to date.

Thombs was caretaker aboard the steamboat *Peerless,* moored in the Burlington slip in the South Branch of the Chicago River, during the winter of 1901-1902. He had hired a young woman named Carrie Larsen as the ship's cook. He apparently did not approve of her cooking, because on her first day on the job, according to police, Thombs strangled the young woman, and sunk her body through a hole in the ice.

The chief witness against him was a young river rat named Robert Keising, who had been allowed to sleep aboard the ship. Keising told Canalport District police that Thombs had forced him to help dispose of the body. Thombs was convicted and sentenced to death on Keising's testimony.

On his last night on earth, Thombs played cards with his jailer, George Hitzman, until nearly midnight. "If I am going to the scaffold tomorrow I will be as brave as any of them, you can bet," he said, as he studied his cards. "I don't care for myself, but I feel sorry for my poor wife."

His wife, Minnie, had been permitted an hour-long visit with the condemned man that afternoon, and left in tears.

The temperature was in the low 80s as the noon hour approached on August 8, 1902, and Thombs readied himself for the final walk. "I did not commit this crime. My life has been sworn away by Keising," he complained to his lawyer, Ivy Rogers. "If Keising had been pressed as hard as I was, I would not be sacrificing my life today."

Thombs was given one last moment to state his case, as he stood on the trapdoor with the rope around his neck.

"I am about to pay the penalty for a most atrocious crime. I am innocent. My only hope is that the lapse of time will purge my wife and child of the disgrace that is now being brought upon them," he told the hundred or so assembled witnesses.

The white cap was then placed over his head, the trap dropped, and he paid the penalty.

As was becoming the practice, a large crowd had gathered outside the jail in Illinois Street to watch the body being removed after it was cut down.

34

PESANT DIES ON THE GALLOWS
APRIL 15, 1904

Louis Pesant spent most of his last night on earth sitting on his jail cot with his head in his hands, as if deep in thought.

He was scheduled to be hanged between 10 a.m. and 2 p.m. on April 15, 1904, for the murder of a woman named Mary Spilka. Pesant had confessed that he kicked and beat the woman to death in her home at 368 West Eighteenth Street, after which he stole her life savings of $227.

On the afternoon before the scheduled hanging, Pesant was taken from his jail cell and given a shave. As he returned to his quarters he stopped opposite the cell of another condemned killer, Harvey Van Dine, reached through the bars to shake his hand, and said, "Good-bye, Harvey."

Van Dine, one of a trio of so-called Car Barn Bandits, grasped Pesant's hand warmly and said, "Good-bye, old man."

Pesant was walked to the gallows shortly before 11 a.m. the next day. His last act was to kiss a crucifix, held by a Roman Catholic priest, as jailers tightened the straps around his arms and legs.

At a signal from Jailer John S. Whitman, Pesant dropped through the trap at 11:18 a.m. Seventeen minutes later he was pronounced dead of a broken neck.

A ne'er-do-well in death, as in life, his execution rated only three paragraphs in the newspaper.

35

CAR BARN BANDITS
DIE ON GALLOWS

APRIL 22, 1904

In the new century's first triple-header, Louis Pesant's jailhouse friend, Harvey Van Dine, went to the gallows himself just one week later, along with Peter Neidermeier and Gustav Marx.

Van Dine, Neidermeier and Marx, who were hanged on April 22, 1904, were just about the worst kind of people anyone would fear to meet. They had been charged with eight murders, including those of two tavern patrons, Otto Bauder and Adolph Johnson; saloonkeeper Benjamin La Gross; James Johnson, a streetcar motorman, and Francis Stewart, a cashier, in a car barn robbery; Detectives Joseph Driscoll and John Quinn, in separate gun battles; and L.J. Sovea, the brakeman on a train they hijacked in Indiana while fleeing police.

And those were just the murders for which they were hanged. The twenty-four-year-old Neidermeier boasted of having killed twenty-three men, including a railroad worker in Louisiana, and wounding seventeen others. He offered to provide police with all the details if they would pay him the $16,500 in reward money on his head. Marx claimed to have killed eight men, including a miner in Camp Goldfield near Victor, Colorado.

Van Dine was the only member of the trio to show remorse, and asked forgiveness for what he had done.

Marx was the first one of the group to end up in custody, when he was picked up on suspicion. His partners planned to storm the jail and get him out, but police got wind of the scheme and chased them to the Indiana Dunes. There, fifty policemen surrounded the suspects and captured them after a day-long gun battle when they shot the railroad man and tried to steal his train.

In one of the bizarre angles that followed the trio's arrest, Marx's lawyer, George Popham, cut a deal for his client to get life in prison in exchange for testifying against his partners. Marx refused. "If Pete and Harvey swing, I want to go, too," he declared. "I don't want to live and hear them curse me for squealing, and to see their ghosts in that dark cell."

Then an astrologer, Mme. Seera, predicted that Neidermeier would cheat the gallows by taking his own life before he was scheduled to hang. This was abundantly clear to Mme. Seera, because on Friday, April 22, Saturn, the most evil of all the planets, would return to the exact degree and minute, in the same sign of Aquarius, as at the moment of Neidermeier's birth.

The stars bode bad for the other two defendants, especially Van Dine, who was born on Friday, arrested on Friday, convicted on Friday, and sentenced to die on Friday.

Neidermeier did his best to make the seer's prediction come true, by butting his head against the bars of his cell while screaming, "I'll never hang!" Guard Louis Leonetta eventually entered the cell and subdued the prisoner.

All three men were visited by their mothers on their last night on earth. Van Dine's brother, Frank, and his girlfriend, Mamie Dunn, were also permitted to see him.

As the visitors left, Van Dine gave his fiancee a prayer book that Neidermeier had given him earlier. In it he inscribed, "A present from Peter Neidermeier to his old friend and comrade, Harvey Van Dine, April 10, 1904, and willed in return, as a gift of love, to Mamie Terese Dunn, my sweetheart, April 21, 1904, from Harvey."

When a Roman Catholic priest came to the men's cell the next morning to offer a prayer as they were being made ready for the gallows, Neidermeier rejected him. "I'll die as I lived, as an atheist," he answererd. "I'll die game. I don't need any priest to help me die."

As he arose from his cot, however, the color drained from his face and his knees buckled. He had to be placed on a hospital gurney and wheeled to the scaffold, where deputies seated him in a kitchen chair placed over the trapdoor.

Neidermeier was the first to go, after his arms and legs were bound and the white shroud and cap adjusted. The trap was sprung at 10:36 a.m. and he dropped through the opening, chair and all. He was pronounced dead of strangulation twenty minutes later.

Marx was next. He walked calmly to the gallows at 11:15, flanked by two priests, and carrying a crucifix, which he kissed repeatedly. As the white cap was drawn over his face, his muffled voice was heard to say, "Holy Mary, pray for me." The drop fell a moment later, at 11:34, and he died instantly of a broken neck. His body was removed fourteen minutes later.

Van Dine mounted the platform at 11:54, wearing a white rose in his lapel and carrying a crucifix. His last words, as the trapdoor fell out from beneath his feet, were, "Forgive my sins and have mercy, my savior..." He was pronounced dead at 12:13 p.m. His neck, too, had been broken.

Doctors G.F. Lydston and Joseph Springer, who examined the bodies afterward, reported that the measurements of the heads and faces of all three bandits "displayed evidence of degeneracy."

The next day, showing the strain of presiding over four hangings in a week's time, jailer John Whitman put in for an extended vacation.

After her son's execution, Sophie Van Dine pledged the remainder of her life to help others less fortunate than herself. She became known as the "angel of the county jail," subsequently served as a probation officer, and ultimately became a volunteer worker at the Oak Forest Infirmary.

Eighteen years after her son's death on the gallows, a reporter for the old *Herald and Examiner* tracked her down at the hospital and reported:

"Tiny arms yearn toward the motherly woman who moves daily through the children's ward...that ward given over to the babies of lunatics, morons, brutes and fiends."

36

WIFE MURDERER IS EXECUTED
SEPTEMBER 30, 1904

Frank Lewandoski, 48, was hardly a doting husband. After an absence of two years he had returned home, got into an argument with his wife, Frances, who was fourteen years his senior, and cut her throat.

Then he ran to a neighborhood saloon at 586 Dixon Street, slashed his own throat, and fell to the floor unconscious after gasping, "I have killed my wife and myself."

Mrs. Lewandoski's son, Matthew, 21, found his mother when he returned home after going out for a bucket of beer. She was taken to St. Mary's Hospital, where she died a short time later. Lewandoski was also taken to St. Mary's, where doctors patched up his neck for the hangman.

Lewandoski's date with the gallows was scheduled for September 30, 1904. He spent his last evening reading from a Catholic prayer book in his native Polish, then fell asleep and spent a restful night.

He was up at 5:30 the next morning, dressed with care, and had breakfast. Then he visited with two priests from St. Stanislaus Polish Catholic Church until Sheriff Thomas E. Barrett and Jailer John Whitman, back from his leave, entered the cell at 10:15 to read the death warrant.

It was a clear bright morning, with temperatures in the high sixties, as Lewandoski marched to the gallows between two priests, and took his position on the trapdoor.

"I go to my death washed of my sins," he declared firmly. "I know I am forgiven, and I meet death bravely."

Whitman gave the signal. The trap was sprung, and Lewandoski dropped through the opening. Seven minutes later he was pronounced dead.

Witnesses described the hanging as "one of the most successful in years."

37

MURDERER OF POLICEMAN IS HANGED IN COUNTY JAIL

JANUARY 20, 1905

Russia was in the throes of a revolution, Czar Nicholas was in hiding, and Chicago was toughing its way through a bitter cold snap on January 20, 1905, when John Johnson, a black, 34-year-old wagon driver, paid the price for the murder of a Chicago policeman.

Johnson and a friend, Louis Tilford, had been engaged in a drunken brawl when Policeman Dennis Fitzgerald stepped in to break them up. The two turned on the police officer and kicked and beat him unconscious, after which he was fatally shot with his own gun.

Johnson was standing over the mortally wounded lawman with the smoking revolver in his hand when reinforcements arrived. He was tried for Fitzgerald's murder and sentenced to death. Tilford got fourteen years in prison.

"I got the worst of the trial," Johnson remarked bitterly. "Tilford got fourteen years and is as guilty as I am. Up to the time of this trouble I was a hard working teamster and had never been arrested. The fact that I was hopelessly drunk should have saved me from the gallows."

It did not, however. It was a tradition in Chicago that carried well into the 1960s: Kill a cop, you die!

On his last night, Johnson sat up until two hours past midnight with the Reverend F.M. O'Brien of Holy Name Cathedral. When the priest left, the comdemned man told him, "Good night, Father. I will not be afraid when the hour comes."

Sitting on his bunk, contemplating his fate, Johnson commented to his guards, Thomas Caspers and James Lenahan, "You know, I did not kill Officer Fitzgerald. I had the gun in my hand all right, but I had just picked it up." Then, turning to the night jailer, Jenks O'Neill, he said, "Don't wake me up until it's time. You won't have much more trouble with me. I must travel the lone journey in a short while. I don't expect any one to stay the execution."

Johnson slept until 9 o'clock the next morning. Then he got up, dressed in a black suit, ate a light breakfast, and announced, "Well, I'm ready. I'm not afraid to go. I have prayed for forgiveness and believe I will be saved."

He walked to the gallows without emotion, accompanied by Father O'Brien and flanked by jail guards. Standing on the trapdoor, Johnson took one last look out over the room, filled with nearly one hundred doctors, police officers and newspaper reporters. As the jailers were strapping his hands at his sides, he told John L. Whitman, "Wait a moment! Mr. Whitman, take the letter out of my pocket and give it to the priest."

Whitman removed the letter from the man's pocket, and asked him, "Have you anything to say?"

"Nothing," replied Johnson. "Everything I had to say is in that letter."

The noose was adjusted about his neck, the white cap lowered over his head, and at 10:41 the trapdoor dropped out from beneath his feet.

Johnson's body was left suspended for twenty-five minutes before it was cut down, although doctors determined that his neck was broken by the fall, and he died almost instantly.

The contents of Johnson's missive to the priest were never made public.

38

CONTEST TILL DROP FALLS
FEBRUARY 16, 1906

Robert Newcomb and John Mueller, each convicted of murdering three people, paid the supreme penalty in separate hangings, both on February 16, 1906. It was Cook County's first equal opportunity execution day. Newcomb was black, and Mueller was white.

Newcomb's victims included Walter Blue, who was shot to death, Mrs. Florence Poore, and Police Sergeant Peter Shine, who had attempted to arrest the suspect.

Mueller, a cook in Potter's, a downtown restaurant, fatally shot and stabbed his wife, Annie, and their two small children, Martha and Mary, then attempted to end his own life by slashing his throat with a razor and shooting himself.

On the night before the two men were scheduled to die, the gallows was assembled in the northeast corner of the old jail, and all other prisoners were moved to a different cellblock so they would not have to witness the execution.

A fellow death row inmate, Johann Hoch, shared a cigar with Mueller, slapped him on the back and joked, "Never give up hope. See how many times they've hanged me already, and I'm here yet. They won't hang me, either, and they won't hang you."

There was still hope for Mueller. His lawyers were trying desperately to prove he was insane. At the eleventh hour they introduced evidence alleging that his forbears in Austria for generations back had been imbeciles.

For Newcomb, there was no hope. "I have never had any hope that I would escape the gallows since I killed those people," he admitted. "I am ready; but I wish everyone would pray for me. I need it."

A number of Negro prisoners attended a chapel service held for Newcomb that evening, under the direction of jailer John Whitman. It was an unusual scene as the man who was about to die arose and addressed his fellow inmates.

"I know what brought me to this," he said. "I know it and you know it. Drink and bad places are responsible. You can see what it will do for a fellow, and I want you to promise to stop it when you get out of here. That's all I want to say. Good-bye to you all."

A number of the black prisoners were weeping as they returned to their cells.

Newcomb's last visitor was Edward Poore, husband of the women he had slain. He told Newcomb, "I forgive you."

It was clear and chilly outside, with the temperature at 10 a.m. registered at 23 degrees, as Newcomb was led to the scaffold. Sheriff Tom Barrett had decided to hang him first, giving Mueller's lawyers a few precious extra minutes to continue their battle to save him. As the final arrangements were being made, Sheriff Barrett received a telegram from Genoa, Illinois, a small town near Rockford. It said: STOP THE EXECUTION AT ONCE. After studying the telegram, the sheriff decided to ignore it, since no one had ever heard of the person whose name was signed to it.

The execution proceeded as scheduled. Newcomb was dropped to his death at 10:42 a.m., as he was reciting the Lord's Prayer.

Eight minutes later, at 10:50 a.m., Chief Deputy Charles Peters and Whitman entered Mueller's cell and read the death warrant to him. "Well, if there is no hope, I am ready," he said.

There was still hope, however. His lawyer, William H. Barnam, made a frantic appeal to Judge Ben M. Smith to delay the execution until Mueller could be examined to determine his sanity. Judge Smith refused to grant a delay past the scheduled date, but said that if the sheriff could have the prisoner examined at once, he would listen to what the doctors had to say.

As the noose waited for his neck, Mueller waited in his cell, where Dr. Hugh T. Patrick arrived at 12:25 p.m. "I have come to examine into your sanity," the doctor explained, as Mueller stared at him apprehensively.

Fifteen minutes later Dr. Patrick stood before the bench, where he told Judge Smith, "I find the man quiet and collected. He answered my questions coherently. He showed no abnormal depression or delusion. There were no indications of mental excitement. His memory, however, appears to be defective. I asked him about the crime, and he said the last thing he remembered was going to bed with the children. When he awoke he was in the hospital, bandaged. He had no further recollection of the crime."

Dr. F.W. McNamara, the county jail physician, concurred with Dr. Patrick's finding that Mueller was sane, and Judge Smith declared that he would not interfere with the execution.

Mueller was then marched to the gallows, accompanied by the Rev. F.M. O'Brien of Holy Name Cathedral. Mounting the stairs between two deputies, he steadied himself with his manacled hands against the railing. He was pale and trembling, and answered questions put to him by the priest in an almost inaudible voice.

As the straps were about to be tightened about him, and the white cap put over his head, Mueller took off his glasses and handed them to Whitman. "Give them to Sister Rose," he said.

The priest began his chant, and as Mueller repeated, "May God have mercy on my soul," the trap was swung out from under his feet at 12:42 p.m. He plunged through the opening with such force that his neck snapped. Five minutes later his heart beat its last, and he was pronounced dead.

Mueller's body was wheeled out into the corridor, where it was placed beside Newcomb's, waiting for the undertaker.

39

LAW WINS FIGHT;
HOCH IS HANGED

FEBRUARY 23, 1906

Johann Adolph Hoch, who laughingly predicted that the law would never put the noose around *his* neck, learned otherwise just one week after Newcomb and Mueller fell through the fatal trapdoor.

If ever a man deserved the gallows it was Hoch. Known as the "Bluebeard of Chicago," he was a nightmare come to life. Hoch wasn't even his real name. He was born Jacob Schmidt, the son of a preacher, at Horweiller-Bingen-on-the-Rhine, Germany, in 1854.

A metal worker who had studied pharmacy, he married Christine Raub, daughter of a wealthy family. Several years later he deserted his wife and four children, married a woman in a neighboring town, and used the wedding dowry to come to America in 1883.

His first stop was Wheeling, West Virginia, where he married a woman who owned a saloon. When she died a month later, he sold the tavern, left his clothes and a fake suicide note on the bank of the Ohio River, and made his way to Chicago.

There he opened a saloon of his own on Western Avenue, and married Martha Steinbrecher in December of

1895. When she died barely a month later, leaving a substantial estate, he sold the tavern and moved on.

In quick succession he took brides in Milwaukee, St. Louis, again in Chicago, and again in Milwaukee, either deserting them or burying them before moving on to the next.

In 1904, his busiest year, he married women in Milwaukee, Chicago and Philadelphia, before returning to Milwaukee where he walked down the aisle with Lena Hoch. When she died, three weeks after the ceremony, he took her name as well as her $1,500 bank account, returned to Chicago, and rented a home at 6430 South Union Avenue.

Unaccustomed to sleeping alone, Hoch placed a want-ad in the *Chicago Abendpost,* a German language newspaper, on December 3, 1904:

> *MATRIMONIAL—German, with his own income, wishes acquaintance of widow without children. Object, matrimony.*

The ad brought him Julia Marie Walcker, a candy store owner. Within five days they were married, she sold the sweet shop, and turned every cent she had over to her new husband. Five days later Julia fell ill, and on January 12, 1905, she, too, died. Four days later Hoch married her sister, Amelia. When he subsequently deserted Amelia and skipped with her $750 bank account, she went to the police.

Julia's body was exhumed, and found to be loaded with arsenic. Police tracked Hoch to New York, where he had just proposed to a boarding house hostess, Gerta Kimmerle. Hoch, "a little, fat man with a red, round face and a semi-bald, hair fringed head," was brought back to Chicago to face charges of bigamy and murder.

Chicago police, digging into the widower's background, verified thirty-four wives before they stopped counting. How many fell ill and died unexpectedly, and how many were simply abandoned, will never be known.

Hoch admitted to being a bigamist, but insisted he had never killed anyone. "I just had bad luck with unhealthy wives," he explained.

He was convicted and sentenced to hang for Julia's murder.

The reason the 52-year-old Hoch might have been optimistic when he told his cellmate, John Mueller, "They won't hang me," was because he had won three earlier reprieves. On February 23, 1906, however, his luck ran out.

Even then, Jailer John L. Whitman delayed the execution two and a half hours, until 1:30 p.m., while Hoch's lawyer, Harry Olson, fought unsuccessfully for another delay.

Curiously, Hoch's last visitor was his last wife, Amelia, his previous wife's sister, who had testified against him at his trial. Whatever attraction he had for members of the opposite sex remained with him until the end. As he sat in his cell, waiting to be led to the gallows, inmates in the women's cellblock, directly above his, serenaded him with "Lead Kindly Light," "Jesus, Lover of My Soul," and "Nearer, My God, to Thee."

When the time came, Hoch appeared to be the calmest member of the group as he marched to the scaffold between Whitman and Deputy Charles W. Peters, followed by a pair of Lutheran ministers, the Reverends J.R. Birkelund and August W. Schlechte. He took his position upon the trapdoor with military-like precision, clicking his heels together sharply, and standing ramrod straight as he faced the crowd.

"I would like to say a few words," he told Peters, as Whitman secured the straps about his ankles, knees and shoulders.

"Of course, go ahead," Peters nodded.

"Oh, Lord, our Father, forgive them. They know not what they do," he uttered in a loud, clear voice. "I must die an innocent man. Good-bye."

Reverend Birkelund then began reading the Twenty-third Psalm, "Yea, though I walk through the valley of the shadow of death..." as Whitman brought the noose down over the prisoner's head. Hoch obligingly tilted his head from side to side to assist in the process. As the slipknot was tightened, the white shroud draped about his body, and the cap placed over Hoch's head, Reverend Birkelund recited the Lord's Prayer. When he came to the final word, "Amen," the trapdoor swung out from under Hoch's feet and he dropped to his death at 1:34 p.m.

The customary group of physicians, who examined the body as it slowly swung to and fro, agreed that he had died almost instantly of a broken neck.

After Hoch's body was cut down, it was placed in a rough coffin, and turned over to the two Lutheran clergymen. His final wife, Amelia, whom he had deserted, drove up to the jail in a carriage to claim her estranged husband's possessions.

On the streets outside, squads of police dispersed the largest crowd that had gathered for an execution since the four Haymarket anarchists were hanged in 1887.

40

DIES ON GALLOWS,
STOLID TILL END

JUNE 22, 1906

With the possible exception of Frank Mulkowski two decades earlier, Richard G. Ivens was one of the most forlorn specimens of humanity ever to drop through the trapdoor with a noose around his neck.

Ivens, a twenty-four-year-old stable hand, had confessed to strangling Bessie Hollister, an attractive young choir singer, and concealing her body in the barn behind his father's carpenter shop at 368 Belden Avenue.

The wife of Franklin C. Hollister, a wealthy printing company executive, was reported missing on January 13, 1906, after she failed to show up for choir practice at the Wesley Methodist Episcopal Church. It was young Ivens, himself, who reported finding her bruised and battered body the next day, with a length of copper wire tightened around her neck.

Under police questioning, he admitted killing Mrs. Hollister when he encountered her on the street, and she resisted his advances.

Ivens almost did not live to meet the hangman. W.C. Hollister, brother-in-law of the slain woman, and a partner in the Hollister Bros. Printing Co., called at the North

Halsted Street station to warn police, "Keep a watch on my brother, Frank. Keep him away from Ivens or he'll kill him."

Police Inspector John Lavin immediately ordered the husband placed under scrutiny. But then, as Ivens was being led to a cell, W.C. Hollister drew a revolver and tried to shoot the prisoner. A detective leaped forward and knocked the weapon from his hand.

At Ivens' trial his lawyer, I.W. Foltz, introduced a unique defense:

"Ivens had a restless night, and since there had been a number of attacks made upon women before, he may have dreamed about these, and when questioned by the police and accused of the murder, the dreams came back to him and he declared his guilt."

The jury wouldn't buy it, and he was consigned to the gallows on March 24. Less than three months later the scaffold was assembled in the corridor outside his cell to carry out the sentence.

Ivens spent his last night playing cards with his jailers, and writing a farewell note to his mother and brother.

The 11 a.m. temperature on June 22, 1906, was a balmy 68 degrees as he walked almost aimlessly to the gallows, dressed in a dark gray suit and soft flannel shirt, with a black and red string tie. In his lapel he wore a button that said, "Love, Benevolence and Charity."

Sheriff James Pease and Chief Deputy Charles Peters led the procession, followed by the prisoner, walking between two deputies. Jailer John L. Whitman and the Rev. Walter T. Sumner, an Episcopal priest, brought up the rear.

Ivens appeared to be in a semi-stupor as he stood on the platform, oblivious to Whitman, who was tightening the straps around his arms, legs and shoulders, and adjusting the noose around his neck. He looked out over the audience of fourteen physicians and a handful of newspaper reporters as though they were not there, as the white cap was lowered over his face.

He had no last words.

Whitman stepped back and the drop fell at 11:03 a.m. Fifteen minutes later Dr. Francis McNamara, the jail physician, and Dr. H.I. Davis, county physician, agreed that the confessed slayer of Bessie Hollister was dead.

The young choir singer's murder so shocked Chicagoans that they demanded better police protection, and the city council doubled saloon license fees from $500 to $1,000, to generate enough revenue to double the size of the city's police force.

41

'I'D RATHER HANG THAN BE JOHN D,' SAYS SLAYER

OCTOBER 12, 1906

While Richard Ivens went to the gallows seemingly oblivious of his surroundings, Daniel Francis gleefully declared that he was looking forward to the experience.

"Today I feel happier than I ever did before in my life. I am simply waiting for the minute that they slip that rope noose about my neck and my feet will slip out from under me," he said, cheerfully. "I would not change places with John D. Rockefeller. I am better off than he is at this very minute, though I shall hang until I am dead. I would not even change places with President Theodore Roosevelt. What do they know about where they are going when they die? They know nothing about it. I know where I am going, and for that reason my place in the shadow of the gallows is better to me than if I could change places with them. "

Francis, described variously in the press as "the giant negro" or "the colored evangelist," was under sentence of death for the fatal shooting of his wife, Martha, as she held the couple's baby in her arms, and Mrs. Mary Scroggs, a woman friend.

He awoke at 5:45 on the morning of October 12, 1906—his last—and ordered a hearty breakfast.

"This is the last chance I'll have to see daylight a-breaking on earth," he told Jenks O'Neill, a jail guard. "I'm hungry. Not many more chances to eat. This must be a good breakfast."

"What do you want?" asked O'Neill.

"Bring me a porterhouse steak with mushrooms, baked potatoes, coffee, toast and—I guess that'll be all."

After breakfast, as he was being readied for the walk to the scaffold, Francis told his guards, "I forgive everyone who has anything to do with my execution, and you needn't have any misgivings about me. Down in Texas, where I was raised, there was a man once who went crazy because he was afraid he was being haunted by the ghost of a man who was hanged. I won't haunt any of you boys," he laughed.

A freak cold wave had swept through the Chicago area the previous day, dropping the temperature to 27 degrees, wilting flowers and killing plants. A south wind brought a return of warmer weather the next day, with the thermometer rising to 68 degrees as Francis began the death march shortly before 11 o'clock.

"I am ready and willing to die. God be merciful to me, a miserable sinner," he shouted. "Oh, death, where is thy sting? Oh, grave, where is thy victory? My faith has made me free!"

As he stood upon the trapdoor, and the hood was about to be lowered over his head, he uttered his last words, "This is the happiest day of my life. In a few minutes I will be enjoying the delights of Heaven. I am glad to die."

The floor fell out from under him at 11:01. The "giant negro" dropped through the opening like a bullet, his neck snapped, and he was dead before his massive body stopped spinning.

42

TEACHER'S SLAYER IS HANGED
DECEMBER 13, 1907

Friday the Thirteenth was the unluckiest day possible for Richard Walton, the eleventh black man to be executed for the crime of murder in Cook County.

Walton had been convicted of strangling Lillian Grant, a white kindergarten teacher, while burglarizing her home on September 18, 1907. He fled after the slaying, but was captured in Springfield a week later. He confessed to the crime, and two and a half months later he was having his last meal.

While not looking forward to the gallows, as did Daniel Francis, Walton was resigned to his fate. "I deserve to hang," he said stoically.

As lawyers fought to win a reprieve, Walton spent his last day issuing opinions on all manner of subjects, from Sunday closings, which he favored, to lynching, which he was wholeheartedly against. Between comments he munched on delicacies, sent by citizens opposed to capital punishment.

Two members of the Illinois Pardon and Parole Board, C.G. Eckhart and E.A. Snively, came to Chicago to interview the prisoner, his lawyer, the state's attorney, and the trial judge. Afterward they notified the sheriff that they would not interfere with the scheduled execution.

Walton's last words, before being dropped to eternity, were to thank jail officials for their kindness, and to declare that he bore no ill will against the judge or prosecutor. After his body was cut down it was turned over to his mother, who had come from St. Louis to take her son home.

43

WILLIAMS, WIFE SLAYER, DIES ON THE GALLOWS

OCTOBER 22, 1909

It was a cruel twist of fate that put Andrew Williams next in line for the gallows.

It started with a piece of good luck. Williams won $36 playing poker, and wanted to share his good fortune with his wife, Ophelia, who, with their three-year-old son, Johnule, had been staying at the home of her father, Police Officer John Hardy. Hardy had never liked Williams, ever since he eloped with his daughter.

Here is what happened next, as Williams related the incident to a reporter:

"I telephoned Ophelia that I was going to see her and the boy. I went, and was met at the door by my father-in-law, John Hardy. We quarreled, and Hardy and I fought a duel with revolvers. My wife stepped between us and was killed. The jury found that it was my revolver that killed her, and in accordance with that finding, I have to be hanged."

The fatal shooting occurred on March 11, 1908. Over the next year and a half Williams won three reprieves until, on October 22, 1909, his luck ran out.

A newspaper of the day reported:

"The scaffold was put in place early today and

Williams, in the death chamber, was receiving final religious consolation.

"If Williams is executed today—and the man has lost every vestige of hope—the County Jail will lose its model prisoner.

"Since the day of his arrest, Williams has been one of the meekest prisoners ever lodged in the County Jail. In many other ways Williams is one of the most remarkable men that ever was sentenced to the gallows in Chicago. Although a colored man, he is well educated.

"He attended high school in Topeka, Kan.

"He does not swear.

"He professes to be a Christian.

"He was never arrested before the tragedy in which his wife was shot dead while holding her infant son in her arms."

Williams spent his last night on earth playing cards with William O'Brien, one of his guards, while the gallows was tested by dropping a 250-pound sandbag through the trapdoor at the end of a rope.

"I don't think I am responsible for my wife's death but, nevertheless, I will go to the scaffold like a man," Williams told O'Brien. He retired at 10:30, and slept until 6:30 on the morning of his death. When he awakened he yawned, stretched, and sat up in bed.

"Hungry?" asked William J. Oadwine, a guard who had replaced O'Brien during the night.

"A little," answered Williams. "I'd like a little breakfast after a while."

He then dressed and gazed out of the window, where an early morning fog was lifting. "I hope to see the sun shining through here before I go," he told Oadwine.

After a breakfast of three eggs, steak, mashed potatoes, pears, oranges and a glass of milk, he asked for the morning papers. Williams carefully read the stories detailing preparations for his death. Then he turned to other news, stories about Commissioner John J. Holland suspended for jury rigging; vice lord Mike "de Pike" Heitler on trial for trying to bribe a police inspector to leave town; Turks killing hundreds of Kurds in battle; and the skeleton of a missing woman found in Islip, New York.

When the time came, and Chief Deputy Charles Peters read the death warrant, Williams bowed his head understandingly and stepped forward to take his place in the procession to the gallows. He was accompanied by the Reverend D.P. Roberts of Bethel M.E. Church.

Williams mounted the scaffold and, without being guided, took a position on the trap and put his hands behind his back. Straps were quickly adjusted around his ankles, thighs and arms, and his wrists manacled, while Jailer Will T. Davies placed the rope around his neck and lowered the white cap over his head.

Through it all Williams prayed audibly, and was still uttering words of prayer when Davies stepped back and the trap was sprung.

After Williams dropped through the trap, his body was allowed to hang for nearly fifteen minutes before County Physician Francis W. McNamara, who had officiated at fifteen consecutive executions, stepped forward and pronounced him dead.

Gentleman that he was, Williams died without a struggle.

44

FIVE SLAYERS DIE; HANGING RECORD

FEBRUARY 16, 1912

It had been two years, three months, and twenty-five days since the execution of Andrew Williams. During that time there were some 800 homicides in the Chicago area—an average of twenty-eight a month—yet through it all, the stout timbered gallows gathered dust.

All that changed on February 16, 1912, when no less than five convicted murderers—an all-time record—were dropped through the trapdoor on a single day. Two of them were brothers, and one was a teen-aged boy.

He was eighteen-year-old Thomas Schultz. The others were Ewald Shiblawski, twenty-one, and his brother, Frank, twenty-three; Philip Somerling, twenty-one, and Thomas Jennings, twenty-eight.

Schultz, the Shiblawski brothers, and Somerling were part of a gang of white youths the press called the "Boy Bandits." On the night of October 20, 1911, the four of them, along with eighteen-year-old Leo Sommers and nineteen-year-old Frank Kito, fatally beat and stabbed a truck farmer, Fred W. Guelzow, at Lincoln and Peterson Avenues, and stole his wagonload of vegetables.

They were caught the next morning, which was to have

been Ewald Shiblawski's wedding day, when they tried to sell the farmer's horses.

Jennings, a six-foot, 200-pound black man, had been convicted of fatally shooting Clarence D. Hiller, chief clerk of the Rock Island Railroad, during a home invasion. As he fled from the scene on the night of September 19, 1910, he left his fingerprints on a newly-painted porch railing. Jennings' trial marked the first time that an accused murderer had been identified and convicted on the basis of his fingerprints.

During a dramatic moment in his trial, Jennings' lawyer, W.G. Anderson, challenged police Captain Michael E. Evans, head of the new Bureau of Identification, to prove that a person could be identified through his prints.

Captain Evans left the witness stand, took a book from the lawyer, blew some dust over a page and brought out the lawyer's thumb print while the astonished jurors looked on. That clinched the case for the prosecution. The jurors returned a verdict of guilty, and Jennings was sentenced to be hanged.

While waiting for the sentence to be carried out, Jennings turned jailhouse preacher, and converted a number of his fellow inmates to Christianity. He had no relatives, and no one from the outside visited him in jail.

With the "Boy Bandits" it was quite the opposite. They spent most of their last day on earth visiting with relatives through the double screen on the fifth floor of the jail. The conversation was strained, at best. Nobody wanted to talk about why they were really there.

"Lake Michigan is frozen," the father of the Shiblawski boys commented to his youngest son, Ewald.

"It's been a cold winter. We felt it even here," Ewald agreed.

"That's right," nodded the youth's fiancee, Julia Kline, speaking in German. "We have all nearly frozen."

"They've been laying off men at the factory," the elder

Shiblawski continued. "Work is scarce."

Occasionally Julia, who was to have become Ewald's bride on the day he was arrested, laughed nervously.

Sommerling and Frank Shiblawski talked quietly with their wives, while young Schultz divided his attention between his parents and his little sister, Rosie, who sobbed uncontrollably.

The Reverend F.M. O'Brien of Holy Name Cathedral also visited the four condemned men, and administered holy communion.

After their relatives had left, Ewald Shiblawski asked for a pencil and paper, and wrote a short note to the widow of the man he had helped slay:

> *Mrs. Guelzow: I must die tomorrow for the murder of your husband and father of your child.*
>
> *I wish to God I had never done it and I ask you to forgive me, if you can.*
>
> *I had a fair trial. My lawyer, Edward B. Esher, did what he could and Edward S. Day, the assistant state's attorney, treated me fairly.*
>
> *I am guilty and before my death I ask your forgiveness for the great wrong I did.*
>
> *God knows that if I would live I would spend my whole life in trying to do for you and your child what I ought to do.*
>
> *I am sorry. I again ask you to forgive me if you can. I am truly sorry for what I did.*
>
> *Ewald (Walter) Shiblawski.*

The four young men spent most of the night playing poker for money, as if it mattered. At 11:15 p.m. they sent out for pork chop sandwiches, then resumed the all night card game.

Jennings spent his final hours with a minister, in prayer. Jack Johnson, the world heavyweight boxing champ, called at the jail and asked to see the prisoner, but was denied permission.

The Shiblawski brothers were the first to make the march to the gallows when morning came. Frank stood on the right, facing the witnesses, with Ewald on his left. Father Repinski of St. Stanislaus Catholic Church joined Father O'Brien in praying for the prisoners as Jailer Will Davies and his assistants tightened the straps and placed the hoods over the men's heads.

Davies then pulled a cord. The drop fell at 10:17 a.m., and the brothers fell through the opening together. Ewald Shiblawski was pronounced dead at 10:26, and Frank joined him in death at 10:30.

One minute after the trap was sprung Deputy Sheriff John R. Durso burst into the execution chamber with a court order calling for Sheriff Michael Zimmer and Jailer Davies to delay the executions pending a sanity hearing.

Chief Deputy Charles Peters telephoned the judge and told him, "The Shiblawski brothers have already been hanged. I am now going ahead to hang the other two men and will do so unless a formal writ is issued."

Sommerling and young Schultz were then brought in, and the grim proceedings continued. They were dropped through the trapdoor in unison at 10:49.

Jennings' execution was temporarily delayed while his lawyers made a last minute effort to have his conviction thrown out. They argued that the use of fingerprints in his trial was tantamount to forcing the defendant to testify against himself. At 12 noon Deputy Peters received a note from Judge Kenesaw Mountain Landis saying he would not intervene.

Peters then went to the death cell where Jennings was praying with Father O'Brien. As Jennings prepared for the march to the gallows he became so wobbly that two deputy sheriffs were forced to hold him up by his armpits. The two deputies helped him onto the trapdoor, and steadied him while the noose and white cap were being set in place.

At 12:15 the deputies stepped aside and the trap was sprung. Jennings plunged downward, and at 12:23 he was pronounced dead.

The body of Jennings, who had no family, was turned over to the medical examiner.

The bodies of the four "Boy Bandits" were taken to the Joseph Jarzembowski undertaking parlor at 1356 Noble Street, where police lines had to be set up to control the crowd of three thousand curiosity seekers who filed past to view the remains.

At one point a young woman carrying a two-week-old baby tried to force her way through the crowd, then dropped to her knees screaming hysterically, "Let me see my man! I got the right to see my man!"

After she was identified as Philip Sommerling's widow she was ushered in for a last look at her husband. Frank Shiblawski's young widow also appeared at the funeral home, and fainted when she saw her husband's distorted face.

Elsewhere in Chicago on that fateful day, a man named Edward C. Kraemer won a divorce from his wife after testifying in Superior Court:

"She knows every street car conductor on the North Side, and when I would get on a car with her they would say, 'Hello there, girlie.'"

45

SMITH PAYS STOICALLY FOR LIFE OF SLAIN GIRL

FEBRUARY 13, 1915

It would be three more years before the gallows was again put to use—this time for Roswell C.F. Smith, a young choir singer and confessed slayer of four-year-old Hazel Weinstein. The youngster had been dragged into an alley behind her home at 2634 West Madison Street on the night of July 7, 1914, sexually attacked and strangled.

A month after her husband's arrest, Smith's wife, Hazel May, sued him for divorce, citing the child's murder as her reason. Smith had bigger problems than his wife, however. He was convicted of the tot's death and sentenced to hang.

A newly formed group, the National Anti-Capital Punishment Society, immediately set out to save Smith's life. Calling capital punishment "a relic of barbarous times," the Right Reverend Samuel T. Fallows, pastor of St. Paul's Reformed Episcopal Church, charged that hanging him would be nothing less than "legalized murder."

An attorney for the group, George S. Remus, argued, "Insanity experts agree that moral perversion is equivalent to insanity. The state has no right to assume that it can punish a murderer by taking his or her life in return. It is a damnable situation."

Prosecutors argued that Smith was far from insane, however, and produced a report by Dr. H. Douglas Singer, director of the State Psychopathic Institute. He stated:

"There is no evidence of any insanity and from the information received from the prisoner and other sources, he knew the nature and consequences of his crime at the time it was committed."

On the afternoon of February 12 Smith's father, Roswell Sr., visited his son for the last time, talking with him at great length. His mother, who was estranged from her husband, visited him that evening, and they sat and talked for hours with their heads close together. After his mother left, Smith ordered a hearty meal.

The Reverend Benjamin Aldrich, pastor of the New First Congregational Church, where Smith formerly sang in the choir, spent two hours with the condemned man before he retired for the night.

"I have one hope," Smith said. "I hope that ten or twenty years from now, when I have been forgotten—I hope that Illinois will realize that taking a life in the name of the law is a disgrace to the law."

Smith awoke at 6:30 on the morning of his death, bathed, ate a light breakfast, and sent for Dr. Aldrich. "It's just you and I together until the end, now, doctor," he told the clergyman. A short time later, the march to the gallows began.

Smith, who had been acutely nervous throughout his confinement, suddenly seemed calm and ready to face his fate. His jailers said the condemned man believed he had convinced his mother and father to get back together.

Following Jailer Will T. Davies into the death chamber, he paid scant attention to the white robe and shroud as he mounted the green painted gibbet reciting the Psalms.

Even after the cap was placed over his head, Smith could be heard, chanting, "I will raise mine eye unto the hills, whence cometh my help..." until the trap fell and cut him off in mid-sentence.

As the booming, clanging of the trap echoed through the jail, other inmates commenced an eerie wailing, known as the "death howl," which they regularly set up whenever one of their own died at the end of the rope.

"The boy, he's gone," said his father, who heard the clamor from outside the jail where he was waiting to claim the body.

Eight minutes after the trap dropped, the prisoner was pronounced dead.

The elder Smith, groping blindly through tear-filled eyes, climbed up beside the undertaker on his wagon, to ride around to the back door of the jail, where he had been told he could claim his son's body.

Meanwhile State Representative John H. Lyle, who had attended the hanging, said he would introduce a bill in the State Legislature to abolish capital punishment in Illinois.

46

LINDRUM AND WHEED DIE
ON JAIL SCAFFOLD

FEBRUARY 15, 1918

World War I was raging across Europe three years later when the next execution in Chicago was carried out. It was a double header, featuring the necks of Edward "Blackie" Wheed and Harry Lindrum.

Wheed, a wild-eyed ex-convict who had served ten years at Leavenworth for counterfeiting, had fatally shot two Brinks guards, Barton Allen and Louis Osenberg, during a payroll robbery on August 28, 1917.

He was captured two days later after a withering gun battle in which he held off 250 policemen for two hours while they poured everything they had into his mother's small brick cottage at 2633 Thomas Street. Firing guns with both hands, from all four sides of the building, Wheed wounded three police sergeants before surrendering when the army of cops threatened to dynamite the house.

After his capture he also confessed to the robbery of the Halsted Street Trust & Savings Bank, in which Policeman Peter Bulfin was slain.

On the day before Wheed killed the two Brinks guards, Lindrum had shot Policeman Joseph Patrick Tiernan to death during a robbery.

Justice came fast for the two confessed cop-killers. Just five and a half months after their arrests they were swinging from the gallows.

It was cloudy and cold on February 15, 1918, as Chief Deputy Sheriff Charles Peters completed final preparations to carry out the sentence at 9 a.m.

Wheed, who had feigned insanity and spent his days snapping at imaginary flies, gave up the act and declared that he was resigned to his fate. "I shouldn't have killed those bank messengers," he mused. "Maybe my death on the gallows will even the score."

When Lindrum was told that his last appeal for executive clemency had been denied, the color drained from his face and he fainted. A jail physician had to resuscitate him before he could be marched to the scaffold, where a "medical jury" of twenty-four doctors had gathered to watch him and Wheed die.

By the time he had mounted the scaffold, Lindrum had gained his composure. "Be sure to get it tight enough," he quipped, as Peters adjusted the noose around his neck. Then, looking defiantly out at the witnesses, he declared, "I'm innocent." Those were his last words.

The cocky two-gun Wheed, on the other hand, who had held off 250 policemen in one of the fiercest gun battles in Chicago's history, tottered on the scaffold and went all to pieces. He was quivering and mumbling prayers as the trap was sprung, and he and Lindrum dropped to their deaths together.

47

ANDERSON IS HANGED FOR SLAYING OF POLICEMAN

JULY 19, 1918

By the spring of 1918 American doughboys were fighting their way across Europe while, in Chicago, a daring attempt was made to spring four convicted murderers from their death cells in the Cook County Jail.

The four included cop killers Dennis Anderson, Lloyd Bopp and Albert Johnson, along with Earl Dear, who had killed a chauffeur.

On the night of May 5, a botched attempt was made to blow out the side of the jail with nitroglycerin and dynamite. The first bomb failed to explode, and the blast from the second brought one hundred police officers racing to the scene before anyone could get away.

The ill-fated jailbreak would have been Dennis Anderson's last hope for survival. An ex-convict and burglar, he had been sentenced to die on the gallows on June 14 for the murder of police Lieutenant Patrick Lavin.

Despite his shady background, Anderson, twenty-one, had somehow landed a job as a railroad detective for the Chicago Junction Company, under Lavin's jurisdiction.

On October 21, 1917, Lavin came upon Anderson and three other men stealing tires from a warehouse on Canal

Street. Anderson spotted the lieutenant and gave the alarm. Then he pretended to chase his companions as they fled. Lavin caught one of the men and brought him back to a watchman's shanty, where he was holding him at gunpoint when Anderson walked in.

"Here, keep an eye on this bird while I call the wagon," Lavin said, handing Anderson his revolver. Without a word, Anderson picked up Lavin's weapon and shot the lieutenant dead.

On the day that Anderson was to have been hanged, his 14-year-old sister was scheduled to graduate from grammar school. When Chief Deputy Charles Peters learned this he telephoned Springfield, and the sympathetic Governor Frank Lowden granted the convicted killer a last-minute reprieve, so as not to ruin the child's graduation day.

Meanwhile Anderson's seventeen-year-old brother, John, was arrested for the murder of Edward Eggert, a South Side saloonkeeper, in an attempted robbery. That gave poor Bridget Anderson two sons to visit in the Cook County jail.

She had her last visit with Dennis on Thursday, July 18, on the afternoon before he was again scheduled to die. That evening jailers brought young John down from the boys' cellblock to spend some time with his older brother.

"Hello, Dinnie. How—how are you feeling?" the younger brother asked. Then they clasped hands, and engaged in nervous conversation.

"They won't be punishing me when they hang me," Dennis said. "It will all be over in a few minutes. But they'll be punishing my parents and relatives. I'm not afraid of death.

"Don't take a chance with a jury," he advised the teenager. "Go before a judge and tell the truth, and maybe you won't have to go through this."

On the morning of July 19, Anderson dressed in dark trousers and a striped white shirt, with sleeve garters above the elbows. He wore no vest or coat, and no collar. The lake mist still hung low over the North Side streets as he took a last look out his cell window at the sun, trying to break through. The prisoner was served a hearty breakfast, but declined to touch it.

"How do you feel?" one of the deputies assigned to watch him asked.

"Fine and dandy," Anderson smiled.

At 9:03, as witnesses took their seats facing the gallows, Jailer Will Davies walked in with a new coil of rope under his arm. The rope was tossed over the cross beam, and the noose was fashioned. The rumble of passing traffic echoed through the high windows, and there was a nervous giggling, whispering, and the striking of matches among the spectators.

At 9:30 the death march began, and a deputy ordered the witnesses, "Remove your hats!"

The shuffle of feet could be heard in the corridor as the death party approached. Anderson, his silver belt buckle catching the reflection from the tall window, mounted the scaffold with Father William O'Brien of Holy Name Cathedral at his side. The priest was reciting the litany as Anderson stepped to the center of the trap.

"Have you anything to say?," asked Sheriff John Traeger.

"No," Anderson mumbled, shaking his head. A strand of hair fell over his forehead, and he instinctively tried to brush it back, but his arms were pinioned at his side.

The sheriff repeated his question. "Have you anything to say?"

"No, sir," Anderson declared.

The prisoner wet his lips as Jailer Davies tightened the straps, adjusted the noose, and draped the shroud around his shoulders. He bent his head to kiss the cross held by Father O'Brien, as the white hood was lowered over his head.

Davies stepped back swiftly, and pulled out his pocket watch. The trap was sprung with a resounding boom, and

Anderson dropped through. As the noise echoed through the jail, the condemned man's younger brother fell to the floor of his cell, sobbing violently, "My God, poor Dinnie. Poor Dinnie."

Twelve minutes later the jury of physicians examined the swinging body and pronounced Dennis Anderson dead. The witnesses shifted uneasily in their seats as one of their number, a tall, suntanned man, got up and walked out of the room. It was John F. Lavin, the slain man's brother, who had come to see his brother's death avenged.

48

BOPP, SLAYER OF POLICEMAN, DIES ON THE GALLOWS

DECEMBER 6, 1918

On the night of September 12, 1918, two convicted killers, Lloyd Bopp and Earl Dear, overpowered guard John Kempter and broke out of the Cook County jail in a vain attempt to escape the gallows. They vowed, "We'll never be taken alive," but surrendered meekly when 200 policemen surrounded a flat in which they were hiding at 1310 Bryn Mawr Avenue.

Knowing that orders had been issued to shoot them on sight, the two heavily armed gunmen agreed to give up to two policemen friends, Tom Kane and Tom Sheehan, who were summoned to the scene by Lieutenant James E. Doherty of the Sheffield Avenue Station.

Doherty, visibly disappointed at the killers' surrender, holstered his revolver and sighed, "I'm out of luck."

With Bopp back behind bars, plans went ahead for his execution, which had been scheduled for December 6.

Bopp, a sallow-faced drug addict and auto thief, had been convicted of the murder of Oak Park Policeman Herman Mallow on June 14, 1916. He had twice been sentenced to death, and several times reprieved.

A twenty-three-year-old stringbean who stood 5 feet 11

inches tall and weighed only 130 pounds, the chestnut haired Bopp spent his last night in his cell, weak, shaken and bereft of all of his previous self-assurance. After confessing to the Reverend James Horsburg of Holy Name Cathedral, he paced the floor of the death cell and pleaded with his jailers for more heat.

"It's cold in this place. I'm freezing," he complained.

Once the heat had been turned up, he slept well on his last night on earth, and had to be roused by one of his guards at 7 a.m. "Gee," he said, rubbing his eyes. "The night went quick."

Shortly before 10 o'clock, as guards prepared Bopp for the walk to the scaffold, a visibly nervous Earl Dear—who was also awaiting execution—asked jailer Will Davies to summon the Reverend Earl M. Ellsworth of the La Salle Street Methodist Church to come and sit with him while his pal's neck was being stretched.

Though his face was chalky white, Bopp walked firmly to the gallows a short time later, flanked by Fathers Horsburg and Francis M. O'Brien. As the rope was being adjusted around the prisoner's neck, the two priests bowed their heads with him in silent prayer. Bopp's last act was to kiss a crucifix, held to his lips by Father O'Brien.

Shortly after 10 a.m. the trap was sprung, and Bopp dropped to his death.

A native of Sumner, Illinois, he would have celebrated his twenty-fourth birthday on Christmas day.

49

JOHNSON HANGS FOR THE MURDER OF POLICEMAN

FEBRUARY 28, 1919

Like Lloyd Bopp, who had tested the gallows before him, Albert Johnson was a convicted cop killer. He was also a rather demanding prisoner, whose last wish had to be denied for reasons of pure logistics.

Johnson, a Negro, had shot and killed Policeman Martin Corcoran in a gun battle at Broadway and Waveland Avenue on the night of June 6, 1917, after he had robbed a home on nearby Pine Grove Avenue.

He was to have been hanged on February 7, 1919, but Governor Frank Lowden granted a last-minute stay until February 28, while his lawyers sought to prove him insane. It was the first time the 1845 statute on "lunacy" had been used since the case of Patrick Prendergast in 1894. After deliberating several hours on the night of February 21, a jury in the court of Judge Robert E. Crowe declared that Johnson was sane, and preparations for his execution were resumed.

On the day of his hanging, a cold wave whipped into Chicago on the wings of a forty-five-mile-an-hour gale, ripping down utility poles and plunging temperatures from 46 degrees to just eight above zero in twelve hours.

In his death cell, Johnson spent his last hours entertaining the clergy, and accepting the prayers of every denomination available—just to be on the safe side. His dying wish, to be accompanied to the gallows by eight ministers, was denied by jailer Will T. Davies.

"Johnson accepted spiritual advice from every minister and priest who talked to him. He asked each one to stand on the gallows and give him solace in his last minute," Davies explained. "I have been forced to refuse six of the ministers this permission, for if I granted the man's request the gallows would be so crowded with spiritual advisers it would be impossible to spring the trap."

Although he had gone through a sleepless night, Johnson faced death calmly when the final hour arrived. As he was taken from his cell he gave Davies two notes, one to be delivered to his mother, and the other to his sweetheart.

The note to his mother asked forgiveness "for the sorrow I have caused." The message to his girlfriend said, "Trust in the Word and believe."

Johnson mounted the steps to the scaffold at 9:30 on the morning of the 28th. As he stood on the trapdoor, and the noose was being adjusted, he turned to Davies and said, "God bless you, Will. Don't let me suffer; do it quick."

Those were his last words. Davies did it quick. The trap was sprung at 9:36, and eighteen minutes later Albert Johnson was pronounced dead.

50

DEAR IS HANGED
PARENTS TAKE HIS BODY HOME

JUNE 27, 1919

Earl Dear, the man who had briefly escaped from jail with Lloyd Bopp nine months earlier, was without a doubt one of the most mysterious men ever to meet his maker at the end of a rope. No one, it seemed, knew who he really was.

Earl Dear was the name he used when he arrived from Pittsburgh four years earlier, but he claimed that was not his true identity. He was the scion of a wealthy Eastern family, he said, and did not want to embarrass them.

Dear, a drug addict and auto thief, was once arrested with a memorandum book in his pocket, showing payments to politicians, "fixers" and crooked prosecutors to keep him out of jail. He beat the rap so often that he acquired the nickname of "Immune."

On January 18, 1918, Earl "Immune" Dear tried to steal a car belonging to Dr. Philip Schuyler Doane, which was parked in the Loop. When Rudolph Wolfe, the doctor's chauffeur, tried to stop him, Dear shot him dead. Police arrived seconds later, as Dear stood over the slain chauffeur, smoking gun in hand. "Innocent as usual," was Dear's boastful remark as he was taken into custody. "You'll never settle me!"

A jury did "settle" him, however, and sentenced him to be hanged. He still believed himself "immune" from punishment, however, and boasted to jailer Will Davies, "They'll never knock me off."

Dear's last visit with his wife, Margaret, was almost casual, considering the circumstances. Dressed in a chic, blue tailored suit, blue hat, lace stockings and rhinestone-buckled pumps, with a fur draped about her neck, she appeared at the jail and announced her presence to Davies.

"Want to see her?" Davies asked the prisoner.

"Well, if she's here, I might as well," Dear shrugged.

At the end of the visit, as the soon-to-be widow prepared to leave, Davies asked the 26-year-old Dear, "Aren't you going to kiss your wife, Earl?"

"Well, if she wants to, I will," he drawled.

"You know, Earl, you know, you're the only one I ever loved," she cried.

"Yes," he agreed, almost indifferently.

"Kiss me, Earl."

He bent forward and mechanically touched her lips through the bars.

"Kiss me right—kiss me like you used to."

Dear kissed her again, for the last time.

"I'll never leave him," Margaret cried, and collapsed in a faint. Dear exhibited no emotion whatsoever as jailers lifted his wife off the floor and carried her away.

As the clock struck midnight on June 27, 1919, to introduce the day of his death, Dear rose from his cot and called to his guards, "Give me dope—please, please. Give me dope—anything, morphine, cocaine, opium!"

Sorry, old man," said Deputy Sheriff Paul Dasso. "But you know the orders. Will you have a cigarette?"

"Cigarette, hell!" Dear snapped. "What good will a cigarette do me?

When the Reverend Elmer Lynn William arrived to pray with the condemned man, Dear begged, "Please, get me a shot of something, Mr. William."

Reverend William went to Davies and said, "It's cruel to let him suffer. Can't you let him have something?"

"Give him religion," Davies said. "It's better than drugs. Let him see how it feels to face some of the naked realities of life without the false nerve."

"Listen, Dasso," Dear said, turning to the night guard. "If you ever meet the governor, tell him Earl Dear was innocent, will you?"

"I don't know the governor," Dasso answered.

"If I can't have some hop, gimme some coffee," Dear demanded.

A jailer brought the condemned man a cup of coffee. Sipping the hot brew, Dear complained, "Good God! I'm going mad. Sleep? How can I sleep? No, there's nothing to do but walk. I'll get no sleep tonight."

Shortly after 9 a.m., after a night of pacing his cell, Dear was told that the hour had arrived. In a last-minute show of bravado, Dear grabbed a rag and dusted off his shoes, smoothed down his custom-fitted green suit with his hands, and adjusted the knot of his rich, green necktie.

Davies, the white-haired jailer who had officiated at so many hangings, was already on the gallows, tugging at the yellow rope, and suspending his own weight from it to give it a last-minute test as the hundred or so spectators looked on.

At 9:22 a deputy stationed near the door called out, "Everyone remove your hats!"

The nattily-dressed Dear marched into the room, flanked by Reverend William and the Reverend Earl M. Ellsworth. The condemned man walked steadily, head up, and positioned himself in the exact center of the trap.

"Earl Dear, have you anything to say?" Sheriff Charles Peters asked gravely.

"No—I have nothing to say," Dear answered quietly.

Working rapidly, Davies and two assistants bound

Dear's legs with leather straps, adjusted the white shroud about his body, and tightened the noose around his neck. Holding his head high, the boyish looking Dear took one last look at the gray daylight streaking into the death chamber as the white hood was lowered over his head.

Davies quickly about-faced and took a giant stride, away from the trapdoor.

The Reverend Mr. Ellsworth, sensing the moment had come, quickly began reciting the Twenty-third Psalm. "The Lord is my shepherd. I shall not..."

With a loud crack of plank against plank, the trapdoor swung open at 9:25 a.m. Dear dropped through the opening and the rope twanged as it interrupted his fall. His shoulders shrugged slightly, then all movement stopped as the body slowly rotated at the end of the rope.

The deathly silence in the room was abruptly broken by a choking sound.

"My God! Did he do that?" a reporter asked.

A lean, gray cat snaked between the scribe's legs and padded slowly across the room, hacking and coughing. "He's been at every hanging over the past five years, and he always makes that damnable choking noise when he hears the trap fall," a guard explained, shaking his head.

Five minutes later Dear's body was lowered, and a physician put a stethoscope to his chest. "Still a few ticks left," he commented. "Give him a few minutes."

At 9:34 Dear's heart stopped beating, and he was pronounced dead of strangulation. His body was placed on a cart and wheeled to a waiting hearse for the trip to the county morgue.

A short time later the widow of the murdered chauffeur, Rudolph Wolfe, and the slain man's mother, Mrs. Frank Fischel, turned up at the morgue and demanded to see Dear's body. They were refused admittance, but were shown Dear's death certificate. Mrs. Fischel studied it, then nodded, satisfied that her son's murder had been avenged.

Dear's foster parents, Mr. and Mrs. Adam Dear, accompanied by his widow, Margaret, claimed the body and took it back to Pittsburgh for burial.

The secret of who Earl Dear really was accompanied him to the grave.

51

PAYS FOR LIFE OF JANET

OCTOBER 27, 1919

Six-year-old Janet Wilkerson was a brown-eyed tyke called "Dolly" by her neighbors along East Superior Street, because of her delicate features. On July 23, 1919, she simply disappeared.

Chicago police were baffled. Among those questioned was a gray haired janitor named Thomas R. Fitzgerald, known to neighborhood children as the "Candy Man." He was released after detectives were satisfied he knew nothing of the child's disappearance.

But Harry Romanoff, a reporter for the *Herald and Examiner* was not so sure. Giving candy to children fit the classic pattern of a sex moron, as child molesters were called in those days. Romanoff visited a notion store on North Clark street, where he bought the biggest doll in the place. Then he stopped by the East Chicago Avenue lockup as Fitzgerald was preparing to leave.

Laying the doll on a table, where it caught Fitzgerald's eye, Romanoff sighed, "Yes, it's little Janet's doll. Her mother wanted to get it out of the house. Don't you think it's time you got this off your conscience?"

Before Romy, as the reporter was known, left the station, he had a full confession. Clutching what he thought was the missing girl's doll, Fitzgerald told how he had strangled the youngster and hidden her body under a coal pile in the basement of an apartment building.

He then signed an affidavit, witnessed by the detectives, that he had confessed exclusively to the reporter for the *Herald and Examiner,* giving Romy the biggest scoop of his career.

Fitzgerald, 39, pleaded guilty to the slaying, and Judge Robert L. Crowe sentenced him to be hanged.

"You did right, honey boy," his wife, Martha, told him. "If you couldn't impress an intelligent man like Judge Crowe, it isn't likely you could have made much impression on a jury of twelve men."

On the day before he was scheduled to die, Fitzgerald took communion offered by the Reverend Joseph Phalen of Holy Name Cathedral. "Now my soul is clean and I am prepared to go," he said. "I feel it was God's will that my crime was committed, and that I must pay for it with my life."

On October 17, 1919, less than three months after little Janet disappeared, Fitzgerald paid the price. More than 1,700 people had put in requests to witness the execution, and it was standing room only in the death chamber at the old Cook County Jail.

A haze of cigar smoke hung over the room at 9:24 a.m. as a deputy sheriff faced the crowd and removed his hat—a signal for the witnesses to do likewise, as the death party entered the room.

Accompanied by Father Phalen, the Reverend James Horsburg and his jailers, the prisoner marched in, wearing a dark gray suit which hung loosely on his slender frame. His white shirt was collarless, and his arms were handcuffed behind his back. His bald head and gold-rimmed glasses caught the rays from the high windows as he mounted the stairs to the scaffold.

"Fitzgerald, have you anything to say?" asked Sheriff Charles Peters as the doomed man stood on the trapdoor.

"Nothing, thank you," answered Fitzgerald calmly.

The prisoner swayed slightly as the shroud was draped around his body and the rope lowered over his head. He raised his chin to help jailer Will Davies adjust the noose.

"Grace of the Lord..." prayed Father Phalen, as he held a crucifix at the man's lips.

The white hood was then placed over Fitzgerald's head, as a jailer tightened a belt around his legs.

"Holy Mary..." the priest's voice intoned.

Outside, a passing truck on Illinois Street backfired so loudly that several of the witnesses jumped nervously in their seats.

A deputy supporting Fitzgerald stepped back, a button was pushed, and the trapdoor fell. The white robed body plunged downward.

"Thy kingdom come. Thy will be done..." the priest continued.

Bang! Bang! Bang! The truck outside backfired loudly three more times.

Fitzgerald's body dangled at the end of the rope for exactly fourteen minutes as Father Phalen recited his prayers. At 9:40 a physician declared that there was no pulse or heartbeat. Two minutes later the body was cut down.

"Thomas Fitzgerald, sick brained slayer who sent horror stalking into every home in Chicago when he killed tiny Janet Wilkinson, was hanged today in the county jail," the *Evening American* reported.

52

SLAYER OF WIFE AND
MAN PAYS PENALTY

JANUARY 2, 1920

The 1920s had barely roared in when Raffaelo Durrage, alias Durazzio, roared out with the crash of the trapdoor and the twang of the rope.

Durrage had been convicted of murdering Onofrio Gargano and Gargano's wife, Mary, six months earlier, in the heat of summer.

The ground was covered with snow now. It was bitter cold, and the temperature hovered at 2 below zero at 3 a.m. on January 2, the appointed hour for Durrage's date with the gallows.

A public flap developed when Harry C. Laubenheimer, the first deputy sheriff, announced that 200 county jail innates would be permitted to witness the hanging.

"I know from experience that anyone who has witnessed a hanging never will kill deliberately," he declared. "It is the greatest lesson you can give a criminal."

The proposal was hotly criticized by Gertrude Howe Britton of Hull House, and Mary McDowell of the University of Chicago Settlement, who branded it "shocking" and "immoral." Governor Frank Lowden bowed to the social workers' pressure and ordered that no prisoners be brought in to view the execution.

Sheriff Charles Peters and Jailer Will T. Davies got around the governor's directive by simply not moving out the prisoners who were already quartered in the cell block where the hanging was to take place.

"If we are going to have capital punishment as a deterrent to crime, we should make it as public as the circumstances will permit," Davies argued. "Then, if we find it does not deter murderers, we ought to abolish capital punishment."

Durrage spent a short and restless night in his death cell, pacing back and forth and chain-smoking cigarettes. Davies had moved the death hour up to 3 a.m. to thwart any eleventh-hour attempts by defense lawyers to cheat the hangman.

The prisoner walked firmly and quickly to the gallows, between his guards, followed by two clergymen. He took his place in the center of the trap and stood without trembling while he was being bound and robed for death.

Then Davies asked in a loud voice: "Raffaelo, have you anything to say?"

The Italian did not answer. He gave no indication that he either heard or understood the question.

At 3:08 a.m. the trap was sprung, and Durrage dropped to eternity.

Father Giambastiani, an Italian priest, stood swathed in a heavy overcoat with a fur collar in the chilly roam as he chanted the Litany for the Dying.

"Raffaelo was glad to die," Father Giambastiani said. "He said that he was glad to die because, in his own heart, he knew that he justly deserved his fate. He was entirely repentant."

Asked afterward how many prisoners had viewed the execution, Davies remarked, "There were about 200 men in the tiers where the execution took place. Of course, I don't know how many looked at it."

53

KILLER GOES TO DEATH
CHARGING BETRAYAL

FEBRUARY 20, 1920

Twenty-two-year-old John "Smiling Jack" O'Brien was a cocky young smart aleck right up to the moment they put the rope around his neck and pulled the floor out from under him.

O'Brien had been sentenced to die for the fatal shooting of Detective Sergeant Richard Burke. He admitted shooting the policeman in a saloon on South Halsted Street, but said it was a companion, William "Sonny" Dunn, who fired the fatal bullet. O'Brien felt betrayed, claiming that Dunn's underworld associates had assured him that if he took the rap for Dunn, they would get him off by bribing the jury.

Visiting her son in jail was hardly an inconvenience for O'Brien's mother, Bridget, since two of her other sons, William, 17, and Martin, 19, were locked up in nearby cells on theft charges.

As Mrs. O'Brien wiped away her tears, on her last visit with Jack, he flashed his boyish grin and told her, "Be brave, mother, be brave." Then, patting her on the shoulder, he said, "Good-bye, mother. Don't worry about me."

She left the jail sobbing, "My boy! My boy!"

As jail carpenter James Stanhouse put the finishing

touches on the scaffold on the morning of February 20, 1920, O'Brien's two younger brothers were brought to the death cell and given ten minutes to bid Jack good-bye. They found him leaning casually against a radiator, with his hat on.

"Why the hat, Jack?" his brothers asked him.

"That's right. It's excess baggage," Jack laughed, and tossed it on his bunk. Mike picked it up and put it on his own head.

"You won't be needing this, Jack, so I might as well take it," he said. All three brothers laughed over that last bit of genuine gallows humor.

At the end of the visit, Will said, "Don't weaken, Jack."

"I won't," he replied.

"If you do I'll shoot you," Will laughed.

A jailer then asked O'Brien whether he wanted to give a statement to the press.

"With the ship sinking and the waves washing over the deck, there's nothing that can be said," was his answer.

O'Brien's last visitor was his lawyer, F.A. McDonnell, who asked, "How do you feel?"

"Peaches," O'Brien replied.

"Jack, I've done my best, and we're licked," McDonnell apologized.

"Well, I've carried the buck all along," O'Brien answered. "If I'm to be 'topped' for Sonny Dunn, I guess that's all there is to it. But he'll get what's coming to him, either in this or another world."

O'Brien's hanging was to have been a "private" affair, without the usual crowd of friends of the guards, local actors, aldermen, politicians, and visiting dignitaries. At the last minute, however, the entire February grand jury asked to be allowed to witness the execution.

The grand jurors had been asked to determine whether the sheriff should permit other prisoners to watch the hangings in the county jail, and they decided they should see one themselves before issuing a ruling.

O'Brien refused a last breakfast, taking only a cup of coffee with milk and sugar. He dressed in a blue serge suit, shined shoes, white shirt and necktie for his date with death. He was puffing on a cigarette when the guards came to his cell to get him.

"Put up the cigarette," one of the jailers ordered.

"Gee, I'd like a few more bats at that dizzy stick," O'Brien said, biting the cigarette between his lips as his wrists were handcuffed behind his back. He continued smoking during the death march, with the two cassocked and surpliced priests chanting at his side.

As he mounted the gallows, one of the jailers said, "Throw away that cigarette and listen to the priest."

O'Brien twisted his face into a snarl, took one last drag, and spat out the half-smoked cigarette. He then stepped onto the trapdoor, cursing his fellow gang members who had let him take the rap for Dunn.

As jailer Will T. Davies stepped forward to adjust the noose about his neck, O'Brien turned his head and quipped, "Don't get that rope too tight. It will be tight enough in a little while."

The trapdoor fell at exactly 10:44 a.m., and O'Brien's body dropped through the opening. The fall failed to break his neck, and it took him fourteen minutes to strangle to death.

Through it all, one of the priests intoned, "Be merciful; be merciful."

54

SLAYER OF 2 IS HANGED
FOR LOOP CRIMES

APRIL 16, 1920

There was hymn singing, praying and dancing in the "colored" cell block of the old Cook County Jail on Wednesday afternoon, April 14, 1920. Fellow inmates, led by a Negro pastor who had been jailed for operating a confidence game, were holding a combination revival and farewell service for William Yancy Mills.

Mills, alias Willie Williams, a 20-year-old roustabout and dock walloper, had been sentenced to hang for beating Anthony Brizzolarro, a merchant, and Isadore Ganski, a tailor, to death with a lead pipe.

The semi-literate dockman, who had worked the wharves of New Orleans and Baltimore before making his way to Chicago, put his last words down on paper the night before he was scheduled to die:

> *I'm still strong and not barthed because I no that I'm going to rest, and I hope this will be a warning to others. Someday this will come out because the truth may be crushed to grown but it will rise agin. I'm not blameing no body but myself because I no that I were not living the right life and also running with a bad*

class of people, so that why I'm here today. I'm innocent of this crime as and Infant baby. But however I have nothing agince no one. as Bill Sanders say he rather be in my shoes and to be in the one who prosicuted me. so buys let this be a warning and always rember your truly W.Y. Mills.

Two days after his party, on April 16, the burly Mills made his march to the gallows, accompanied by the Reverend A.L. Harris, pastor of the Harmony Baptist Church. Mills shuffled up onto the platform, his hands chained behind him, and looked curiously at the small group of professional witnesses that had gathered to see him hang.

It was the smallest crowd ever assembled for an execution in the county jail. Sheriff's deputies had to go to the press room to round up a group of newspaper reporters to make up the legally required jury of witnesses before the hanging could proceed.

A jailer had to nudge the prisoner to get him to step over to the center of the trap as he stood looking out over the group, and then glanced curiously at the rope hanging overhead. He looked straight ahead as jailers forced his outspread legs together so that they could buckle the leather straps.

Reverend Harris intoned, "The Lord is my shepherd. I shall not want," as the shroud was adjusted and the noose brought down about the condemned man's head.

"Have you anything to say?" asked jailer Lorenz Meisterheim.

"I want to thank everybody," Mills said. "Especially Reverend Harris. I'm at peace and I'm going home to my maker."

"Amen. Though your sins be red as scarlet, they shall be washed white as snow," the clergyman replied.

As the white cap was being lowered over Mills' head it

caught on his nose, and a deputy sheriff had to step forward and pull it down over his face. Meisterheim stepped back, and the trap dropped at 9:18 a.m.

"Our Father, who art in Heaven..." Reverend Harris prayed, as the body plunged through the opening.

Mills did not give up his life easily. He struggled for twelve minutes, until he was pronounced dead at 9:30, and his body was cut down.

55

GANG KILLER LOSES NERVE ON GALLOWS; REESE CALM

OCTOBER 14, 1920

A record thirteen hangings were scheduled over a three-day period in mid-October of 1920. Three condemned killers eventually went to the gallows—two on October 14, and one on October 15. The other ten were either granted reprieves or won new trials.

The two who died on Thursday, the fourteenth, were 22-year-old Frank Campione, who killed Albert Kubalanzo in a $6.50 pool hall robbery; and John Henry Reese, 40, who chopped his wife Mary's head off because she wouldn't stop nagging him. Campione was white. Reese was black.

Reese worked as a dining car waiter for the Michigan Central railroad. Campione was a member of the notorious Cardinella gang, believed responsible for at least four homicides and more than 250 holdups.

On the day before they were to die the two were placed in the same cell, to spend their last night together.

Campione, who had been feigning insanity and pretended he could not speak English, extended his hand to Reese and said, "Well, partner. We might as well be friends. I guess we're here for the same reason."

Before retiring for the night, Campione entertained

Reese and the deathwatch guards by doing card tricks.

Campione lost all his tough guy bravado the next morning, however, and doubled up in agony on his cot, blubbering for the jail guards to save him.

"It's time to turn to God, Frank," Reese told him. "Religion is a great help to a man in our fix."

"You go to hell!" cried Campione.

Father James Shields of Holy Name Cathedral called at the cell to try to comfort Campione, while the Reverend Boston Prince of Provident Baptist Church prayed with Reese. The hangings were scheduled for 8 a.m.

At 7:45 a sheriff's deputy carried a chair into the execution chamber. "Campione's quitting," he told the assembled witnesses. "They'll have to hang him sitting down."

He was followed by a deputy carrying two lengths of rope, coiled over one arm, and two white shrouds in the other. Another deputy brought in several leather straps. "That's to strap Campione in," he remarked. "He's quitting like a dog."

Eight o'clock came and went, but the execution could not be held until the sheriff and jail physician arrived. Both were late. It was not until 8:24 that two stout deputies standing on the scaffold removed their hats, to signal that the death procession had begun.

Campione stumbled into the room, moaning and clutching a pillow, supported by Father Shields and jailer Lorenz Meisterheim. His bushy hair was in disarray, and his ashen face darkened by a three-day growth of beard. His black shirt was open at the front and his sleeves were rolled up to display a tattoo on one arm.

Meisterheim and Father Shields had to push him along as he shrank back, whimpering, when he saw the two ropes looped over the cross bar on the scaffold. Two deputies dragged him under the rope on the right as Reese, dressed in a neat, dark suit, positioned himself confidently under the other.

"Are—they—really—going—to—hang—me?" Campione blubbered. Reese, standing erect under the cross beam, looked down at him in wonderment. "Don't—let—them. Save me," Campione begged, as he attempted to throw himself at the feet of the white-robed priest.

Father Shields began to pray as the groaning Campione doubled up, as if in pain, and wilted as the leather straps were tightened about his legs. "Jesus—Mary—Joseph," he sobbed. "My little baby! My wife!"

Three deputies held him as the shroud was draped over him. At one point it appeared they would have to place him in the chair to hold him still long enough to adjust the noose. Reese glared at him and shook his head in disgust.

"Have you anything to say, Reese?" asked Sheriff Charles Peters.

"I am going to my rest. God Almighty will take care of me," the prisoner said calmly. He then bowed politely, like a school boy reciting a poem.

"I'm—going—my—rest. Take—care—me," Campione muttered in terror, as he lurched sideways. He squirmed and cried as the noose was tightened about his neck. "Where are you, Mr. Meisterheim? Talk to me."

"Be brave, Frank," said the jailer, who was helping to hold him up. "It'll be over in a minute."

"Shake hands once more then," he cried, as Meisterheim touched his manacled hands. "Are they—really going—to hang me?" He was still whimpering as the white headpiece was lowered over his face.

Standing beside the cowering gangster, Reese held his head high to make it easier for the deputy to adjust the noose and lower the white cap.

"Stand back, Father Shields," a deputy cautioned.

There was a scurrying of footsteps as the priest moved away from the trapdoor, and the deputies who had been holding Campione up released their grip and stepped back.

Reese remained standing erect as Campione began to topple sideways.

The trap was sprung at 8:30, and the two cellmates dropped through the opening together.

Reese's neck snapped and he died almost instantly. His body was cut down eighteen minutes later. Campione strangled to death. It took twelve minutes before the jail physician pronounced him dead, and it was twenty-three minutes before his body was finally cut down.

Outside the jail, Chicagoans were enjoying one of the last summer-like days, with the temperature pushing 70 degrees.

56

SLAYER OF TWO
DIES ON SCAFFOLD

OCTOBER 15, 1920

The third hanging, that of Frank Zagar, took place the following day, October 15. A ruthless gunman, the 21-year-old Zagar had literally bragged himself onto the gallows.

He sealed his own fate during his trial six months earlier for the fatal shooting of Polidaris Serdakis, and wounding Spiros Kalzouros. After the prosecution had presented its case, defense attorney Eugene Moran called Zagar to the witness stand to establish an alibi. Zagar turned the tables on his lawyer instead.

"I bumped Serdakis off and shot his friend," he bragged to the jury. "And what's more, I croaked another fellow that same night."

The other holdup victim killed that night had been Paul Palipo.

"He was a mutt—wouldn't stick up his hands quick enough. I got $35 from him," Zagar boasted.

Asked about the other two victims, he explained, "Serdakis was slow too about throwing 'em up. And after I got his $10 he lowered his arms. So I just bumped him off."

"Why did you shoot the other man?"

"Oh, I just thought I might as well kill him too."

After he got done with his testimony the jury figured they might as well consign him to the gallows.

Zagar tried to keep up his swaggering pose to the very end. When his distraught mother called to pay him a final visit in his death cell, he refused to embrace her or his twelve-year-old sister, and called to a guard, "Say, take my old woman out of here."

When Father James Shields of Holy Name Cathedral came to pray with him, he cursed the priest and shouted, "To hell with that stuff."

Shortly after midnight on the day of his scheduled execution, a jailer named Kordeki brought Zagar a cup of coffee and a sandwich. "I wouldn't mind a little game of cards," Zagar told him. When Zagar beat Kordeki in a game of rummy he laughed triumphantly at his success, and said, "Let's have another game."

Zagar turned in for the night at 4 a.m., and was still stretched out on his cot when the sun streamed through the window of his cell three hours later.

The hanging had been scheduled for 8 a.m., but was already running nine minutes late when the spectators, including several members of the October Grand Jury, filed in and took their seats. They noticed two chairs on the scaffold—one draped with the death shroud, and the other with a strap buckled around it, in case Zagar got wobbly and could not stand up. The rope, its end tied in a noose, hung stiffly from the crossbeam.

"That's why so many of them strangle," said a guard, nodding toward the rope. "You can't get that Irish hemp any more. That's like silk and gives just enough. This kind is too stiff."

At 8:13 a deputy on the scaffold removed his hat and held up his hand. "Everybody put your cigars and cigarettes out and take off your hats," he droned. The death march had begun.

One minute later Zagar walked into the room,

handcuffed and held firmly by two guards. The collar of his soiled tan shirt had been turned in at the throat, to accommodate the noose. "I hope they break my neck," he told his guards. "I don't want to choke to death."

Father Shields walked silently behind him, offering no audible prayer. A few minutes earlier, when the priest again visited his cell, Zagar stormed at him, "Don't talk to me about the hereafter. I'll know more about that than you do before long. Go away. Leave me alone."

Sheriff Charles Peters had stationed seven deputies on the gallows, in the event the surly Zagar tried to put up a fight. Instead, the condemned man stared dull-eyed out over the small crowd as guards buckled the straps about his ankles, knees, chest and arms.

Zagar sighed deeply and his body swayed as the white shroud with its black ribbons was draped around him, and a guard took down the noose and looped it about his throat. The prisoner bit his lips and drew in his breath. He was obviously terrified, but doing his best not to show it. The white cap slipped down when it was placed over his face, and had to be adjusted.

Then the two deputies who had been holding Zagar's arms stepped back. The trap was sprung at 8:14, and he shot through the opening. The drop failed to break his neck, and his worst fear was realized. He died of strangulation in fourteen agonizing minutes.

Before Zagar was pronounced dead at 8:28, while his body was still swinging from the rope, Sheriff Peters addressed the witnesses:

"If we had eight hangings a day, gunmen would become indifferent to the punishment. But if we have hangings every once in awhile, each hanging will make them think."

After Zagar's body was cut down it was turned over to the jail janitor. The dying man's last request, to the janitor, had been, "See that my body is cremated."

57

HAENSEL CLAIMS INNOCENCE
AS ROPE SNAPS LIFE

NOVEMBER 19, 1920

Four times Arthur Haensel won reprieves from the death sentence on the day preceding his scheduled execution—two of those times as he sat in the death cell waiting the call of the gallows. When a new date for his hanging was set for November 19, 1920, Acting Governor John Oglesby declined to interfere.

Haensel, a wounded veteran of World War I, had been sentenced to hang for the murder of his 18-year-old wife, Cecelia, on February 4, 1919—a crime he insisted to the very end he did not commit.

The newly-formed American Legion worked to save him, and produced evidence that cast doubt upon his guilt, to no avail. The main witness against him had been his own mother-in-law.

On the night before his death his father, Otto Haensel, and his four brothers gathered in the corridor outside the death cell for a last good-bye.

"So long, dad," the ex-soldier said, running his fingers through his hair, and then digging his fists into eyes.

"Good-bye, Art," the old man said in a trembling voice.

After the family had left, Haensel turned to his jailer,

W.P. Holden, and said, "God, that's hard. That's the worst. The other'll be easy, Mr. Holden, but the old man..." His voice trailed off into a whisper.

"Anything—any last thing I can do for you, Art?" asked the jailer, shuffling a deck of cards.

"No—well, say, Mr. Holden, you might tell Dick Wilson that I'm thankful to him for all he has done for me," Haensel said. "You know, we were together; I was in 501 and Dick was in 503. Tell him I'm going like a man, Mr. Holden. Tell him they'll never get a whimper out of me when I stand up there."

Wilson had also been on death row, but won a reprieve.

A short time later the card game was interrupted by a visit from the Reverend Guido Schuessler, pastor of Redeemer English Lutheran Church, who called to comfort Haensel, a member of his congregation.

After the clergyman left, the game of casino between the jailer and the man about to die continued through the night. "I'm not getting a square deal from Oglesby," Haensel complained. "He would rather take the word of my mother-in-law than that of a man who has served his country and spent weeks in hospitals in foreign lands for Uncle Sam."

Haensel hoped right to the bitter end that another reprieve would save him from the gallows, but when the time arrived—and there was no word from Springfield—he marched gamely to the scaffold, still proclaiming his innocence.

The Reverend Schuessler accompanied him on the last walk. He did not falter, and even smiled as the noose was being adjusted about his neck. Asked if he had any last words, Haensel replied:

"Yes. I thank every one who has treated me kindly, and especially the Reverend Mr. Schuessler, who stands beside me in this, my darkest hour."

With that he took one last look at the rays of light streaming through the long barred windows, and recited the

Twenty-third Psalm along with the pastor as the hood was placed over his face.

When the trap was sprung, his neck was not broken, and a badly tied noose prolonged his suffering for fifteen minutes as he slowly strangled.

58

VIANA HANGED FOR MURDER ON 19TH BIRTHDAY

DECEMBER 10, 1920

Like Frank Campione, who had gone whimpering to the gallows on October 14, Nicholas Viana, a teen-aged choir singer, had been a member of the Sam Cardinella mob. The 18-year-old gunman was sentenced to hang for the murder of Albert Kubalanzo in a $6.50 robbery—the same crime that earned Campione the rope.

Two other gang members won life sentences by cooperating with authorities and testifying against their cohorts. Viana refused to turn state's evidence, however, saying he feared for the lives of his mother and sister.

Women throughout the state, including Jane Addams of Hull House, pleaded that the young choir singer be spared the death penalty because of his age. Governor Frank Lowden refused to interfere, however, asserting, "The law must take its course. Viana's case has been reviewed by the Supreme Court and I have personally investigated it."

On the day before he was scheduled to die, he was taken from the regular cell block and led to the death cell. "Good-bye, boys," he called out to fellow prisoners. "Good-bye to all of you, except Sam Cardinella. May his soul be damned." As he was being led away Viana sang the

"Miserere," as his farewell to the world.

That night, as he waited for members of his family to pay their final visit, he told one of his jailers, "It's the farewell with my mother I look forward to with the most horror. God, how I dread the farewell."

During the visit he told his mother, "I am innocent. If anyone should hang it's Sam Cardinella. He's the guilty one. I entered Cardinella's poolroom in short trousers. In a week I was a criminal."

At his mother's request, Viana sang her favorite song, "Heart O' Mine," one last time while a hush fell over the jail.

After his mother, brother and sister left he sat alone in his cell, mournfully singing "The Long, Long Trail."

Friday, December 10, was Viana's nineteenth birthday. He would not live to see another day.

When his time came, he marched to the scaffold, head erect and shoulders back, as two priests, chanting prayers, walked at his side. He paused for a moment as he reached the trap, then stepped upon it—"a pathetic but apparently fearless figure," one newspaper man wrote.

"My last wish is that Sam Cardinella hang, too. He's responsible for me being here. He headed the gang," Viana said, as jailers adjusted the shroud and the leather straps. "It is sweet to die for a mother, sister and a brother. I forgive all who have done anything against me. I want to thank the sheriff and the jailer and all who have been good..."

His voice cracked and Viana trembled, as he attempted to continue. His knees began to weaken, and a jailer steadied him while others hurried with the final preparations. The white hood was lowered over his head, as he mumbled a final prayer.

The boom of the gallows trap as it dropped open drowned out his voice. Eighteen minutes later he was pronounced dead.

189

59

BRISLANE DIES PROTESTING LAW THAT HANGS HIM

FEBRUARY 11, 1921

Edward Brislane, a natty dresser known as "Immaculate Eddie," did not believe that the death penalty was a deterrent to crime, and proposed that he be publicly hanged in Grant Park to prove his point.

Brislane, an ex-convict whose autobiography ran in a Chicago newspaper under the heading, "Beating Back, from Banditry to a Life of Usefulness and a Respected Place in Society," confessed that he fatally shot William Mills, manager of the Crawford Theater, while attempting to rob the box office.

"I shot Mills. There was no reason for it. I was drunk and a damn fool," he asserted.

After being sentenced to death, Mills wrote the following letter to Sheriff Charles W. Peters, dated February 9, 1921:

> *Dear Sir—Is this a fair proposition?*
>
> *You have been quoted often as saying that public hangings would be a deterrent to crime. I disagree with you.*
>
> *I think the hangings, in public or in the secrecy*

of the county jail, are barbarous and obscene. And yet, for the benefit of the hypocrites who say they believe as I think you really do, what do you say to this?

I am the next on the executioner's list. I go Friday unless the Governor intervenes. I want all the people who are whooping it up for public executions for public example to see me go, if I do go. I don't think 50 per cent of them will have the nerve to stick it out, but there will be less talk and more thinking afterwards.

My suggestion on this is that if you must hang me, do it in Grant Park—and invite the world.

Yours sincerely,

EDWARD BRISLANE

The sheriff rejected the offer. Brislane then put his fate in the hands of the newly elected governor, Len Small. Brislane's would be the first death penalty case to come before the governor, and the public was watching to see how he would react. Small decided to do nothing, and let the execution proceed as scheduled.

Friday, February 11, was a cloudy, somewhat unsettled day, with temperatures ranging in the middle 30s. Brislane, a poster designer for International Harvester, paced his death cell nervously and chain-smoked cigars, waiting for word from Springfield that would never come.

His sweetheart, Bernice Leahy, was allowed to visit him one last time. When she entered his cell he rose to greet her and dried her tears with his handkerchief, assuring her he would be reprieved.

When it appeared the governor would not interfere, Brislane told his jailers, "The system is barbarous. It is wrong to take the life of any human being because he has committed a crime against society. And it is useless. I'd like to show the world how disgusting a hanging can be. It is

wrong to submit any human being to the sordid surroundings of a death chamber such as this."

As he was about to die on the gallows, Brislane offered
one final objection to the state's method of eradicating
convicted killers:

"I am against this horrible form of murder by the state,
but I would rather be standing here for the crime that, so
help me God, I never remember committing, than to be
sitting down there eagerly waiting to see a man die. Let the
state of Illinois take shame upon itself. Good-bye."

There was a loud clang, as the trap fell open, and
Brislane dropped to his death.

Meanwhile, in downstate Marion, Illinois, there was a
troublesome execution.

A man named Settino De Santis was hanged in a
stockade outside the Williamson County Jail for the murder
of two young boys. Before the trap was sprung De Santis
confessed that he had killed a man named Edward
Chapman six years earlier in Johnson City.

What was troublesome about that was that a lynch mob
had already hanged another man, Joseph Bingo, in the
public square for Chapman's murder.

And in Ossining, New York, Jesse Walker, 20, of
Evansville, Ind., a wartime Naval veteran, was put to death
in Sing Sing's electric chair while smoking a cigar, for the
murder of Samuel Walchak, a stationer, during a robbery
attempt.

60

STRAP BANDIT CHIEF
TO GALLOWS CHAIR
AS NERVE FAILS

APRIL 15, 1921

Edward Brislane was only the first to die on the gallows in 1921. It would prove to be a record year for the hangman, with a total of ten condemned killers dropping through the trapdoor in as many months before the year's end.

The strangest execution of all was that of Salvatore "Sam" Cardinella, known as Il Diavolo (the Devil), who had concocted a bizarre scheme to literally return from the dead.

Cardinella, the so-called "Murder King of Little Italy," was the gang leader cursed by young Nicholas Viana just before he was hanged on his nineteenth birthday. Frank Campione, who went whimpering to the gallows on October 14, 1920, was also a member of Cardinella's gang.

A 1920s-era Fagin, Cardinella was ultimately convicted for the murder of Andrew Bowman, a saloonkeeper, during a holdup. He was sentenced to be hanged on April 15, 1921, along with three more members of his gang, Sam Ferrara and Joseph Costanzo, both 21, and 20-year-old Antonio Lopez, known as "the Rooster" because of his practice of breaking into a shrill "cock-a-doodle-doo." Ferrara, Lopez and Costanzo had been sentenced to death for the murder of

Antonio Varchetto, during the holdup of a delicatessen.

As the day of his death approached, Cardinella devised a weird but imaginative plot to cheat the state of its retribution:

He arranged for his body to be claimed immediately after the hanging, and placed upon a hot water mattress in a casket lined with hot water bottles. The casket would be quickly loaded aboard an ambulance equipped with oxygen tanks and other life-saving devices. It would be staffed with doctors and nurses ready to administer hypodermic injections, strap on the oxygen mask, and bring him back to life!

Despite these macabre arrangements, Cardinella appeared uneasy as the clock ticked away the hours and minutes before he would begin his last walk. He went on a hunger strike and lost forty pounds. He also obtained enough nitroglycerine to blow up the entire jail, but his guards discovered the explosive mixture and took it away from him. After that he fought for every hour of life he could wangle.

"When am I going to be hanged?" he finally asked Lorenz Meisterheim, the assistant jailer.

"Friday morning at 8 o'clock."

"Central Standard Time or Chicago Daylight Saving Time?" Cardinella pressed.

"Chicago time, of course," Meisterheim answered. "It's in Chicago where you're going to be hanged, you know."

"It's not fair!" Cardinella screamed. "I was sentenced before the time was changed. That would rob me of an hour of life. It won't mean anything after I'm dead, but it will mean a lot on Friday morning."

Cardinella was so persistent, in fact, that jailers gave in and rescheduled the hanging for 10 o'clock.

On the day before he was to die he was visited by his wife and six children. Cardinella wept copiously, and blubbered in Italian as his youngsters gathered around their father for the last time.

By the time 10 a.m. rolled around the following day he was a mental and physical wreck, pacing his cell and wringing his hands while moaning and sobbing. He refused his last meal, and battled furiously with his guards when Sheriff Charles W. Peters came to get him.

A quivering mass of fear, he finally had to be strapped into a chair and carried to the gallows.

On the scaffold, Cardinella's head bobbed from side to side and he jabbered insanely in Italian as the noose was adjusted and the white cap draped over his head and bright green sweater. The trap dropped at 10:26, and Cardinella plunged through the opening, still seated in the chair.

Cardinella's neck was broken by the drop. He was pronounced dead and cut down at 10:34.

Costanzo and Ferrara walked unsupported to the scaffold six minutes later, while Lopez won a 30-day reprieve, even as a priest was administering final absolution to the prisoner in his cell. When Lopez got the news he gave a rooster crow, jumped up and down flapping his arms, and shouted, "Glory be to God! My prayers have been answered." Lopez was returned to the jail's "murderers' row," while officials proceeded to hang his two companions in crime.

As the two men stood over the same trap through which Cardinella had fallen a few minutes earlier, Ferrara was asked whether he had any last words. "This is a put up job," he asserted. "I am dying an innocent man." He then turned to the Reverend James Shields of Holy Name Cathedral, and spoke to him in Italian as the hood was lowered over his head. Costanzo said nothing, but looked straight ahead.

The trapdoor fell at 10:45, and both men dropped through the opening in unison. At 10:57 they were pronounced dead, and their bodies were cut down.

Meanwhile, no sooner had Cardinella been pronounced dead by the jail physician, than his body—with a scarlet circle around the neck—was placed in a wicker-basket coffin and rushed to an ambulance waiting in the jail yard. Once the casket was loaded aboard, a jail guard saw a woman in nurse's garb and two men who appeared to be doctors spring into action. As the ambulance moved away, the woman began to frantically rub Cardinella's wrists, while the "doctors" began to administer hypodermic injections.

The guard alerted police who overtook the ambulance and brought it back to the jail yard. In it jailers found the casket equipped with a rubber mattress full of hot water, and hot water bottles; an oxygen tank, an electrical battery, hypodermic syringes and other paraphernalia. The ambulance was delayed for an hour, while Cardinella's body grew cold and rigor mortis began to set in. Dr. Francis W. McNamara, the jail physician, reexamined his body and made sure he was dead beyond recall before the ambulance was finally permitted to go on its way.

Still the rumor persisted that Cardinella had outwitted the hangman. To put an end to it, police searched out the body and returned it to the county morgue, where it was placed under close supervision for several days.

Salvatore "Sam" Cardinella was dead. No doubt about it.

The question was then asked: Had Cardinella been the sniveling coward he appeared to be, or was it all part of the grand plan to return from the dead?

Had his jail fast been a deliberate attempt to lose forty pounds to reduce his weight when he dropped through the trapdoor, thus lessening the likelihood of damage to his neck? And had his near collapse at the last minute been another ruse, so he would go to the gallows in a chair, thus reducing the distance of the fall by approximately nineteen inches?

The most bizarre aspect of the case, investigators learned afterward, was that the attempt to revive Cardinella had been done only after a "dry run" with another prisoner.

Authorities discovered that after Nicholas Viana was hanged, his body was whisked away under similar circumstances, in a coffin lined with hot water bottles.

According to information provided by underworld contacts, Viana's body was driven to a room less than two blocks from the jail, where an elaborate resuscitation procedure was administered. And, according to the reports, it worked!

Within an hour, Viana's eyelids fluttered and a faint moan came from his lips. By all appearances, the experiment was a success.

Viana, however, had been a traitor who had condemned Cardinella, his boss. By gangland standards, he was not worthy of the gift of life. The resuscitation was halted and he was permitted to die, once the rescue crew was satisfied that it could be done.

Dr. McNamara agreed that it could have been accomplished, and cited actual instances in which persons who had committed suicide by hanging had been revived immediately afterward.

If Cardinella's accomplices had not been in such a hurry, and had not started working on him before leaving the jail yard under the eyes of the curious guard, he might indeed, like Lazarus, have risen from the dead.

61

TWO PAY ON GALLOWS FOR KILLING SAILOR

JUNE 24, 1921

Grover Cleveland Redding and Oscar McGavick, a pair of self-styled Abyssinians, were convicted and sentenced to die for the murder of Robert L. Rose, a Great Lakes Naval Training Station sailor, during a South Side race riot.

Redding claimed to be a "Prince of Abyssinia," while McGavick was his "chief lieutenant." The two were attempting to burn an American flag during a "Back to Abyssinia (Ethiopia)" demonstration, and the sailor was fatally shot when he tried to rescue the flag. Another spectator, Joseph Hoyt, a clerk, was also slain.

Redding feigned insanity during his trial, but after a jury found him guilty he declared, "Well, I didn't get away with it. I've been acting up, but the jury was wise to me. Guess I'll have to hang."

On the night before they were to die, Jailer Peter Lawrence asked what they would like for their last meals. "Make mine chicken," Redding said. "I'd like a big porterhouse steak," was McGavick's choice. Both men ate with relish, and enjoyed a smoke afterward, seemingly confident that their lawyers would win them an eleventh-hour reprieve.

The double hanging was scheduled for 7 a.m. on June 24. The two prisoners were still asleep at 6 a.m. when the Reverend James Shields of Holy Name Cathedral arrived at their cell. When jailers awakened them, Redding exclaimed, "Time to go? What about my reprieve?"

The two men then stood quietly while their arms were shackled behind their backs in preparation for the march to the gallows. As they stood on the trapdoor, their legs and arms were bound by leather straps, and they were draped in white shrouds.

"Do either of you have anything to say before the sentence of the court is carried out?" asked Lawrence.

"I have something to say, but not at this time," Redding replied. McGavick made no final statement, but was heard repeating the prayers of the priest in a high falsetto voice as the nooses were adjusted and the white caps were placed over the men's heads.

The trapdoor dropped at 7:25 a.m. Redding's neck was broken by the fall, while McGavick strangled. McGavick's body was cut down at 7:39, and Redding's was lowered seven minutes later.

After Dr. Francis McNamera, the jail physician, pronounced both men dead, their bodies were held for one hour before being turned over to relatives. Jail authorities were making sure there would be no repeat of the macabre Sam Cardinella episode two months earlier.

The extraordinary precaution was taken after a Criminal Court judge opined that once a man had been pronounced dead, he was indeed legally dead. If he was revived after being declared dead, the judge suggested, he could go out and commit any crime that struck his fancy, without fear of punishment, because technically a dead man is a non-person—and thus immune from the law.

It was an interesting observation.

62

'LUCKY' LOPEZ HANGED
AFTER TWO REPRIEVES

JULY 8, 1921

On July 8, 1921, when his latest reprieve expired, the hangman finally got around to 20-year-old Antonio Lopez, the last member of the Sam Cardinella mob. The "Rooster" would have nothing to flap his arms and crow about on this day. His last hope faded when Governor Len Small and the State Board of Pardons and Paroles recommended that the governor deny any further stays.

For his last supper, Lopez requested a chicken dinner.

Chicago had been engulfed in a sweltering heat wave, with the temperature rising to 95 degrees on Thursday, as the prisoner languished in his stuffy cell. One of the heaviest thunderstorms in years hit the city that evening, as he munched on his chicken, dropping the temperature fifteen degrees in a few short minutes, knocking out electricity, and flooding thousands of basements, including those under 150 Loop stores.

Lopez could not finish the meal. He pushed it away, saying to his guards, "Dead men should drink, not eat."

He spent most of the night playing cards with his jailers, grabbing only a couple of hours sleep, between 3 and 5 a.m. When he awakened he asked for the final editions of the morning papers, so he could read with his own eyes the fact that his request for another reprieve had been denied.

When he made his final walk to the gallows, Tony Lopez was an all-but-forgotten man. The usual gabby crowd of execution witnesses—silk-shirted physicians, actors, news reporters, town characters, politicians and friends of jail officials—was nowhere to be seen. In fact, the 7 a.m. hanging had to be delayed while jailer George Lee rounded up enough witnesses to make it official.

The cocky young killer had promised to do his cock-a-doodle-doo act one more time on the scaffold, but when the time came he lost his barnyard bravado. In fact, he was on the point of keeling over in a dead faint as the noose was placed around his neck.

"How can they do this to me?" he asked his jailers, in broken English.

One of the guards who stood with him on the scaffold shrugged his shoulders and responded self consciously, "Have you anything to say before sentence is passed on you?"

"How can they hang me for something I didn't do?" the prisoner continued, as his legs were being strapped together. "I didn't kill the man. I didn't even have the gun in my hand."

As the white shroud was draped around his body, his massive chest heaved several times as he drew what he knew would be his last breaths. Then, turning to jailer Peter Lawrence, he made one final plea:

"Can't you shoot me instead of hanging me?"

"It's too late now," the jailer replied.

The white hood was draped over the prisoner's head. The guards stepped back. The trapdoor boomed open at 7:20 a.m., and the "Rooster's" life dropped out from under him— his last wish denied.

63

"LONE WOLF" PAYS LIFE FOR DOUBLE CRIME

JULY 15, 1921

Just one week later the Cook County gallows was ready to accept its next victim, Harry Hollister Ward.

Police in 1920 were looking for two particularly slippery characters, a "Lone Wolf" gunman in bib overalls who had pulled off more than thirty armed robberies, mostly in the Loop, and a "Lovers Lane Bandit" who had fatally shot Howard B. Rhodes while he was enjoying a tryst with a married woman on a lonely road west of Evanston.

It was not until Ward was captured, after he had gunned down Thomas Graney, a street sweeper, and Frank Schwartz, a passerby, during the robbery of Al the Hatter's clothing store on Cicero Avenue, that police discovered the "Lone Wolf" and the "Lovers Lane Bandit" were one in the same.

Ward was shot during his capture, and doctors who dressed his wound at Cook County Hospital discovered he was wearing an impeccable serge suit beneath his blue denim work shirt and overalls.

The 24-year-old Ward, a clean cut blond haired choir singer, had been named after the family minister in his native Iowa. He was sentenced to life in prison for the street sweeper's slaying, and sentenced to death for the murder of Frank Schwartz.

A desperate attempt to free Ward from the gallows was made when a woman smuggled five hacksaw blades into his cell between the pages of a magazine. The saw blades were found after another prisoner finked on Ward, fearing that an escape attempt might jeopardize his own efforts to win a reprieve from the hangman. By the time the saw blades were discovered, Ward had already cut through one of the bars in his cell door.

Rumors persisted, however, that another attempt would be made to spring the condemned man. Several police squads were stationed outside the jail, and on Thursday, the day before the scheduled hanging, deputy sheriffs were posted in the press room of the adjoining Criminal Court Building. This extraordinary measure was taken to prevent Ward's friends from getting into the room and passing a knife or revolver out the window to the death cell, less than fifteen feet away.

Ward maintained a devil-may-care attitude throughout, joking with his wife, mother and sister when they came to say good-bye, and playing cards with his jailers.

A self-styled "tough guy" to the end, he smiled when the death warrant was read to him the next morning, and continued smiling as the noose was tightened around his neck. At 7:29 a.m. the trapdoor dropped and the man who had led two lives paid for his crimes with both of them.

After Ward's body was cut down, the sheriff held it for one hour before turning it over to the family undertaker, to make sure no attempt would be made to revive him, a la Cardinella.

Meanwhile, the Department of Records and Research at Tuskegee Institute released figures showing that there had been thirty-six lynchings in the United States during the first six months of the year, twenty-four more than the number recorded during the same period in 1920.

64

WANDERER DIES SCORNING PLEA FOR CONFESSION

SEPTEMBER 30, 1921

The touching saga of Carl Wanderer and the "ragged stranger" is one of the better known stories ever to come out of Cook County's Death Row.

A World War I soldier, Wanderer had come home with lieutenant bars on his shoulders, and gone to work as a butcher. A quiet church man of the milquetoast variety, he neither smoked, nor drank, nor used foul language.

The city's heart went out to the melancholy butcher in the summer of 1920, when he told how he had won a blazing gun duel with a ragged stranger who had accosted him and his pregnant wife, Ruth, in the lobby of their Northwest Side apartment building.

Carl and Ruth, his childhood sweetheart whom he had married nine months earlier, had just arrived home from a movie when a voice from the darkness ordered, "Don't turn on the light! Throw up your hands!"

The stillness of the night was shattered by a series of gunshots, and when neighbors turned on their lights they saw Wanderer on his knees, raining blows with his army revolver on the head of a shabbily dressed man who already lay dead from three bullet wounds. A second gun, with two shots fired, lay on the ground near Wanderer's 23-year-old wife, who had also been shot. She and her unborn child were dead by the time help arrived.

The slain gunman carried no identification, and his fingerprints were not on file. Police traced the dead man's weapon to a Chicago gun shop, which had sold it to a man named Peter Hoffman, who had subsequently sold it to Wanderer's cousin, Fred. Fred Wanderer told police he had loaned the gun to Carl, the day before the slaying.

Investigators also learned that Carl, the "model husband," had been exchanging love letters with 16-year-old Julia Schmitt, an attractive, though slightly plump, typist.

Confronted with the evidence, the 25-year-old Wanderer admitted that he had masterminded the whole thing. He was tired of marriage. He had hired a skid row bum for one dollar to stage a phony robbery, in which Wanderer would pretend to chase the man away in order to impress his wife.

Instead, Wanderer shot the ragged stranger with his army gun, and then turned the borrowed weapon on his wife, to make it look as though she had been slain by the robber.

Wanderer was sentenced to twenty-five years in prison for the murder of his wife, and got the death sentence for the murder of John Doe. The "ragged stranger" was never identified, and was buried in a pauper's grave.

The condemned killer lost his last appeal on September 20, 1921, and was scheduled to be hanged at 7 o'clock the following morning. Jailer Peter Lawrence took Governor Len Small's final decision to the prisoner in his cell.

"All right, Carl, the governor says you hang tomorrow. Pick up your things and we'll go to the death cell," Lawrence said.

Wanderer quietly took a newspaper picture from under his bed, bearing the inscription, "Carl Wanderer and his wife, Ruth," folded the clipping, and slid it carefully into his inside coat pocket.

"Come on, Carl," the jailer urged. "The governor..."

Wanderer turned and said irritably, "Well, what of it? I've been there before. I ain't afraid to die. I fought in France. I am ready to go."

As he was being led from the cell block, other prisoners called out, "Good-bye, Carl. You'll come back, Carl."

When he reached the second floor death cell, Wanderer was besieged with news reporters, offering him cigarettes, books and matches, and peppering him with questions. Among the newsmen were Ben Hecht of the *Chicago Daily News* and Charles MacArthur of the old *Examiner*.

Hecht and MacArthur, two of the better known rogues of Roaring Twenties journalism, had helped Wanderer pass the hours in his cell by playing rummy with him, and Wanderer was in hock to the pair for ten dollars, with no way to come up with the money.

"We'll call it off, Carl," MacArthur said nobly.

"Thanks, fellows," Wanderer said, knowing that he would not go to the gallows in debt.

"What I'd like to know is, if you have anything in mind for your last words," MacArthur continued.

"Nothing in particular," Wanderer admitted. He hadn't given it any thought.

"Good," said MacArthur earnestly. "Because I've written a speech that I'd like you to recite, ah, before the event. It's only a half page long."

"I'm not good at memorizing, especially now," Wanderer hesitated.

"How about reading it?" MacArthur suggested.

"Let's hear it first," Wanderer demanded. "I don't want to say anything up there that might be against the grain."

"Fair enough," MacArthur agreed. He then read aloud the typewritten speech, which was a blistering attack upon Frank Carson, the *Examiner's* city editor.

"It's just the thing," Wanderer chuckled.

"Say, do you mind if I add a few lines?" Hecht asked.

"No, go ahead," MacArthur said, handing the note to his fellow reporter.

Hecht hastily penned in several sentences denouncing James Gilruth, his city editor at the *Daily News,* and passed the paper to Wanderer.

That night, as Wanderer sat in his cell, chatting with night jailer Frank Kordecki, he was asked whether he believed in life after death.

"I don't know," Wanderer said wistfully. "Maybe I'll see you on the other side. If I do, I'll shake hands with you, anyhow."

His last card game with the jailer was interrupted by a banging noise, as the gallows was tested with heavy sand bags at the end of a rope.

Shortly after 7 o'clock Friday morning Wanderer marched to the scaffold, prepared statement in hand. He was accompanied by a Lutheran minister, droning a prayer. "God have mercy on my soul," Wanderer murmured after him.

As Wanderer stood on the trapdoor he was asked whether he had anything to say. By then, however, his legs had been strapped together and his arms pinioned at his sides, and he realized he would be unable to refer to the typewritten text. As the noose was tightened about his throat, and the white cap lowered over his head, he decided to wing it. In a strident baritone voice that filled the execution chamber, Wanderer began to sing:

> *"Old gal, old pal,*
> *"You left me all alone —*
> *"Old gal, old pal,*
> *"I'm just a rolling stone—*
> *"Old pal, why don't you*
> *"Answer me..."*

At 7:19 the trap dropped with a bang, cutting the singer off in mid-verse.

The *Chicago Tribune* reporter wrote that the body shot into space "to stop with a jerk at the end of the rope."

"Amen," droned the Lutheran minister.

Fifteen minutes later Carl Wanderer was pronounced dead. Sheriff Charles Peters held the body in the jail until 9 a.m. before releasing it, to thwart any possible attempt at resuscitation.

65

LIGREGNI PAYS FOR WIFE MURDER ON THE GALLOWS

NOVEMBER 9, 1921

Frank Ligregni was a jealous husband, who killed his wife over a misunderstanding that would ultimately result in his own death.

On the afternoon of December 21, 1920, Ligregni, a Bible student and chemist, had visited his 23-year-old wife, Genevieve, a country school teacher, in a farmhouse where she was staying near Bartlett.

The purpose of the visit was to try to talk Genevieve into giving up her teaching job, and to come back home and let him support her. During the visit, however, Ligregni noticed some presents that his wife had made for her young pupils. Thinking they were gifts for other men, he flew into a rage and shot her three times through the heart.

Word that the school teacher had been murdered spread like wildfire through the rural community northwest of Chicago, and area farmers quickly organized a posse to hunt down the killer.

Constable Edward Gromer, meanwhile, arrested Ligregni at the interurban station in Elgin, where he had gone to catch a train back to Chicago. As he was taking Ligregni into custody, Gromer was accosted by a crowd of

Bartlett farmers, carrying a rope, who demanded that the prisoner be turned over to them.

Gromer refused, and rushed Ligregni to Chicago, where he was turned over to the sheriff's office.

Ligregni was sentenced to be hanged for his wife's murder. While awaiting the gallows he proved to be anything but a model prisoner. He made four unsuccessful escape attempts. And on the afternoon before he was scheduled to die, he attacked one of his jailers, Charles West, and slashed West's cheek with a shard of glass.

In a break from tradition, Ligregni was scheduled to be hanged in the afternoon, and on a Wednesday rather than a Friday. The date was November 9, 1921. Chief Deputy Sheriff H.C.W. Laubenheimer, who was in charge of the execution, figured that the long wait before the platform fell under the condemned man would be an object lesson to other prisoners.

Snow and rain fell intermittently throughout the Chicago area as the zero hour approached. The hands on the clock pointed to 3:25 p.m. when a deputy on the gallows removed his hat and signalled the crowd of newspaper reporters, grand jurors, actors, doctors, lawmen and other witnesses, to remove their hats. Among those shivering in the cold room were movie actor George Walsh and Diamond Joe Esposito, a mob politician.

Laubenheimer led the march to the scaffold, followed by jailer Peter Lawrence, and two sheriff's deputies, holding Ligregni firmly by the arms as he walked. The Reverend James Shields of Holy Name Cathedral brought up the rear, intoning, "Jesus, Mary and Joseph, I give you my heart and my soul."

"Have you anything to say?" Laubenheimer asked, as the prisoner stood over the trapdoor.

Ligregni offered no response as the shroud was tied about him. As the rope was adjusted about his neck he moved his head, as if to help it fit more snugly. The white cap was then lowered over his head.

At Laubenheimer's signal, an aide concealed from the crowd pulled the bolt and the trap fell, the sound reverberating throughout the building. Ligregni plunged through the opening. As his body swung silently from the end of the rope, the sound of an automobile horn outside the building broke the stillness.

Fourteen minutes later the body was cut down and placed on a table, where Laubenheimer posted a guard for two hours, to prevent any attempt to revive the prisoner.

If nothing else, the late Sam Cardinella had left his mark on the hangman's profession.

66

TOMMY O'CONNOR FLEES JAIL
DECEMBER 11, 1921

Terrible Tommy O'Connor was to have been the eleventh man hanged in Cook County in 1921. As it turned out, that dubious honor went to the aforementioned Frank Ligregni.

No account of this type would be complete without mention of O'Connor, however. Were his name to be omitted, someone would invariably ask, "Where's Tommy O'Connor?"

That, in fact, is a question that lawmen, journalists and historians alike have been asking for more than seventy years.

Born in Ireland ten years before the turn of the century, O'Connor was brought to Chicago by his parents at the age of two. The family settled in "Bloody Maxwell," known as the "wickedest police district in the world."

Tommy made his first known kill on February 1, 1918, when he gunned down Dennis E. Tierney, a retired policeman working as a railroad detective, in the Illinois Central Station at Michigan Avenue and Randolph Street. He was acquitted of that slaying, despite the testimony of eyewitnesses.

His next victim was a boyhood friend, Jimmy Cherin, whose bullet-riddled body was found in an abandoned car in suburban Stickney. Before O'Connor could be tried for

Cherin's death, Louis Miller, a witness to the killing, disappeared.

Without their star witness, prosecutors had to drop the charges, and O'Connor went free.

When the missing witness turned up a year later, murder charges were reinstated against O'Connor. When a squad of five detectives tried to arrest him, O'Connor opened fire, fatally wounding Sergeant Patrick O'Neill.

O'Connor was sentenced to die for the police sergeant's murder. His date with the hangman was scheduled for December 15, 1921.

It was rumored in those days that one could smuggle the world's tallest building into the Cook County Jail. That was hardly necessary. All somebody had to do was slip O'Connor a gun.

On Sunday morning, December 11, he tied up his guards and went over the twenty-foot wall, jumped onto the running board of a passing car, and disappeared forever.

An official investigation into O'Connor's derring-do jailbreak revealed the following:

On the Sunday morning before he was to die, O'Connor was taken from his death row cell for no explained reason, to have breakfast in the bull pen with minor offenders and drunks. This had never happened before.

A guard entering the bull pen with breakfast did so with a loaded revolver in an open holster—contrary to comon sense and the rules of every jailhouse in the world. The bantam-weight O'Connor attacked and overcame the burly guard, decking him with one punch. As the guard lay on the floor, O'Connor grabbed his revolver and keys. Unlocking the bull pen door, O'Connor let himself out and backed into the jail corridor.

It seemed that all the other guards were attending Sunday services in the jail chapel, and the escaping prisoner never encountered a soul while making his way to the freight elevator.

Riding the elevator down to the main floor, he found a ladder conveniently placed against the twenty-foot wall. He climbed the ladder and went over the top.

Obviously, a lot of palms had to have been greased to make this all possible.

Harry J. Busch, a young law student, was driving his father's Mitchell touring car past the jail when O'Connor jumped onto the running board, pointed a gun in the driver's face, and told Busch, "Drive like hell, you son of a bitch. I'm Terrible Tommy O'Connor."

Busch, who recognized the escapee from his photographs, stammered, "I know that," and stepped on the gas. Busch drove north on Clark Street and made a series of turns until he skidded into a factory wall. O'Connor jumped off the running board and ran to a waiting car.

When police arrived to investigate the crash, Busch blurted out, "Tommy O'Connor has escaped!" Police called the jail and were assured that O'Connor was safe in his cell on death row. It was another hour before he was officially reported missing, and with that much lead time, he was long gone.

Tommy O'Connor had beaten the noose.

67

CHURCH HANGED; FAMILY HALTS INQUIRY, SLAYER STILL IN COMA AS HE MEETS DEATH

MARCH 13, 1922

By all accounts, 23-year-old Harvey W. Church went to the gallows without having an inkling as to what he was doing up there, or why. His hanging ranked as one of the more bizarre in the history of executions.

In the fall of 1921 Church, a brakeman for the Chicago & North Western Railway, decided he wanted a new car, but he went about getting it the hard way. When two salesmen delivered the shiny new 1922 Packard to his home on West Fulton Street, he bludgeoned them to death with a baseball bat to get out of paying $5,400 for the auto. He then hacked up Bernard Daugherty's body and threw it into the Des Plaines River near Maywood, and buried Carl Ausmus alive under the dirt floor of his garage.

Church then drove his new car to Adams, Wisconsin, where he was arrested, returned to Chicago, and sentenced to be hanged on March 13, 1922.

A month before his scheduled date with the gallows, Church went into a trance, and spent the next thirty days lying comatose on his cot with his eyelids twitching, while being fed intravenously. Authorities administered every known test to determine whether he was faking it, and were convinced that his coma was real, apparently self-induced through fear of dying.

The condemned man's parents, Elizabeth and Edwin O. Church, decided to forgo the final visit on the night before he was to hang, since he would not know they were there anyhow. They sent his sister, Isabelle, to bid him farewell.

Kneeling at her brother's bedside, she placed her arms about him and kissed him. "Harvey, this is your sister, Belle," she said. "Don't you know me? Can't you understand me? Tomorrow they will take you from us. Mother and father want you to pray for forgiveness."

She then began to sob so hysterically she had to be led from the death chamber.

Church's hanging was scheduled for 4 p.m. the following day. Dr. Francis W. McNamara administered the prisoner's last meal of tubed liquids at noon. Church's last visitor was Brigadier W.G. Anderson, a Salvation Army chaplain and friend of the family.

Kneeling beside the unconscious man's bed, he told him, "Your father wishes me to have you make your peace with God. Please repeat after me the Lord's Prayer: Our Father who art in Heaven. Hallowed be Thy name..." There was no response.

Sheriff's deputies, under the direction of Chief Deputy H.C.W. Laubenheimer, entered the room shortly after 3:30 p.m. to perform functions usually carried out as the condemned man stands on the fatal trapdoor.

They strapped the limp prisoner's legs together, handcuffed his hands behind his back and strapped his arms at his side, and draped the white shroud around his body. They then strapped him into a common kitchen chair, with a back but no arms.

Church's head sagged on his chest as two guards lifted

the chair, tilted it back at an angle of about 30 degrees, and began the unconventional death march to the scaffold.

Approximately 75 witnesses had gathered to watch the hanging, including a dozen physicians, newspaper reporters, other guards, deputy sheriffs, and politicians. The gallows had been erected in the north wing of the jail, which had been emptied of all prisoners.

As the procession entered the room at 3:50 p.m. a deputy sheriff, who had been pacing back and forth on the scaffold, threw away his cigar and announced, "Gents, no smoking. Hats off."

There was a scuffling of shoe leather on concrete as Sheriff Charles W. Peters walked into the chamber, followed by two deputies, walking sideways, as they carried the comatose Church in the kitchen chair between them. The Salvation Army chaplain followed closely behind.

Church's head continued to sag against his chest as the chair was placed over the trapdoor. Only when the noose was adjusted around his neck was the head held erect by the large knot positioned behind his left ear.

"Harvey W. Church, do you have anything to say?" Sheriff Peters felt obligated to ask the question. The limp form in the chair did not respond. A white percale hood was then slipped over Church's head.

At 3:54 p.m. the attendants stepped back. There was a click as the bolt was pulled, and a bang as the floor dropped from beneath the chair. The rope around his neck stopped Church in mid-fall as the kitchen chair clattered to the concrete floor, and bounced against one of the uprights of the scaffold.

A deputy sheriff retrieved the chair and got it out of the way as Church's body spun slowly at the end of the new hemp rope.

Fifteen minutes later he was cut down and declared legally dead. The auto dealer, meanwhile, had repossessed the Packard.

68

SLAYER OF TWO HANGS; FORGIVES EVERYBODY

JUNE 15, 1923

After a record year in 1921, the pace of executions dropped off measurably in Cook County. The comatose Harvey Church was the only person hanged the following year, and Casper Pastoni became the sole recipient of the noose in 1923.

Pastoni, a 32-year-old shoemaker, had been sentenced to hang for the fatal shooting of Elizabeth Witchell and her four-year-old daughter, Elizabeth Ann, after the happily married housewife refused Pastoni's pleas to leave her husband and elope with him.

The chief witness for the prosecution was seven-year-old Agatha Witchell, who was also shot, but had recovered.

"He killed my mamma! He killed my mamma!" she told the jury.

The youngest witness ever to testify in a criminal case in Cook County up to that time, little Agatha clapped her chubby hands with glee when her mother's slayer was sentenced to death. "That's just what he deserves," she chirped. "I'm awfully glad."

Pastoni, deaf in one ear and blind in one eye as a result of turning the gun on himself after slaying the mother and daughter, faced death stoically. His execution was scheduled for June 15, 1923.

The prisoner ate his last meal at 10 o'clock on the night of June 14, and it was a big one. Told he could have anything he wanted, he said, "I'd like two chicken dinners, and put on all the trimmings. Also, a dozen bananas and a dozen oranges, a box of cigars, and a carton of cigarettes. I'm going to eat and smoke, anyway."

Pastoni nibbled at the chicken and fruit, and puffed nervously, first on a cigar, then on a cigarette.

"Say, I'd like to drink," he told his guards. "See if you can't bring me a pint of booze."

"Sorry, booze is out," he was told.

After eating all he could hold, Pastoni chatted with his guards and read from the Bible until dozing off at 1:30 a.m.

After a sound sleep he awoke at 6:12 a.m., and climbed into his baggy, brown trousers, frayed at the cuffs that hung over his worn-at-the-heel shoes. He slipped into a black and white striped shirt, leaving it open at the throat, as he knotted his necktie well down on his chest. Then he walked over to the little window and peered out into the misty courtyard.

"I don't want any breakfast, nothing more to eat until I see the priest," he remarked to his guards. "Crying won't save me from the noose. So what's the use? I might as well smile."

He spent the last hours of his life pacing his cell, lighting one cigar or cigarette after another, taking a puff or two, and throwing it away. By the time the sheriff's men came to get him at 7:04 a.m., the floor of his cell was littered with partly smoked cigars and cigarettes.

Pastoni appeared resigned to his fate as he fell in line between two deputies and began the march to the gallows. He walked with short, tottering steps, his knees crooked in his baggy trousers, his eyes blinking as he tried to take in his surroundings.

"I hope my mother and God will forgive me," he muttered to Franciscan Father Peter Volz, who stood at his side on the scaffold.

"Oh, I have forgotten to give the two Sisters of Mercy $1.50 I have in my pocket," Pastoni recalled at the last minute.

"We'll take care of it for you," a jailer assured him, as the shroud was adjusted and the noose tightened around his neck.

Sheriff Peter Hoffman asked the prisoner, "Do you have anything more to say before the sentence of the court is carried out, Pastoni?"

Pastoni appeared not to have heard him. Perhaps the sheriff was standing on the side of his deaf ear.

Father Volz leaned forward, grasped Pastoni by the shoulders, and repeated loudly, "Have you anything to say, Casper?"

"Nothing, except that I forgive everybody," Pastoni declared. "I forgive everyone in the world for anything they have done to me. God will forgive me. I am willing to die."

At 7:08 a bell clanged to signal a deputy to pull the bolt from the trapdoor. Pastoni sagged. There was a sharp click. The trap was sprung and Pastoni dropped to his death. Thirteen minutes later, at 7:21 a.m., a panel of nine physicians pronounced him dead of strangulation.

69

NEGROES DIE
FOR KILLING OF POLICEMAN

APRIL 17, 1924

The 1924 case of Lucius Dalton and Henry Wilson was a model of expediency. Exactly three months and eleven days after they shot down Policemen Vincent Skiba on a lonely country road on the far South Side they had been arrested, tried, convicted and hanged.

Dalton, Wilson and Edward Duncan had just robbed the Atlantic & Pacific grocery at 8437 South Chicago Avenue, when Officer Skiba and his partner, Joseph Lamb, arrived on the scene. In a gun battle that followed, Skiba was slain and Lamb was wounded.

Feelings ran high in Chicago after the suspects were arrested, and ten armed guards had to be posted in Judge Lawrence F. Jacob's courtroom during their arraignment to prevent a possible lynching. Duncan escaped the death penalty by turning state's evidence, and testifying against his partners.

Both men argued that they were the products of disadvantaged childhoods—Dalton had only an eighth grade education, while Wilson got no farther than the fifth—and should thus be spared the noose. A jury lost no time in disagreeing.

"There is little use of arguing this case to any great length," said Judge John J. Caverly, chief justice of the Criminal Court. "These men went out to commit robberies. When they were stopped by an officer of the law they pulled their revolvers and killed him. I am therefore commanding the sheriff to take the men to a safe and secure spot between the hours of sunrise and sunset on the day of the 18th of April and there hang them by the neck until dead."

Both men refused a last meal on the night before they were to die. "I guess I don't want no chicken. Thanks just the same," Dalton said, shaking his head when a caterer offered to bring in dinner. Wilson agreed, "I guess I don't neither."

Accompanied by the Reverend Peter Volz, a member of the Franciscan Order from St. Peter's Roman Catholic Church, and the Reverend George Knight, an Episcopal priest, the two men spent the evening singing "Rock of Ages" and other familiar hymns in the death cell.

Wilson undressed and turned in at 11:30 p.m., and slept soundly until morning. Dalton stretched out on his cot fully clothed, and slept fitfully. In the morning, Dalton, who had accepted the Catholic faith, received holy communion.

When Sheriff Peter Hoffman's deputies came for the prisoners shortly after 6 a.m., Dalton told his partner, "I'm sorry I got you into this, boy." "That's all right," Wilson replied.

Wilson, a short, stocky, bullet-headed man wearing a green sweater, and Dalton, tall, lanky and well dressed, walked calmly to the gallows, followed by Sheriff Hoffman, Warden Wesley Westbrook, and the two clergymen.

"Have you anything to say before the sentence of the court is executed?" the sheriff asked, as the straps were being tightened about the men's bodies.

"Yes, sir, I have. I want to say something," Dalton replied. The sheriff stepped back, and nodded for him to proceed.

"Dear friends, I don't think that I have received justice. I don't think so. But it's all right. I hope to meet all of you in Paradise," Dalton told the large crowd of witnesses.

The sheriff then turned to Wilson.

"Folks, I don't think I've had justice," the prisoner said. "But that's done and gone. I'm going, now. All right. It's all right. I—I hope I meets you—all of you—in Heaven."

As First Assistant Jailer Hans Thompson stepped forward to lower the noose about Wilson's neck, he added, "I—I'd like to sing a song, folks—if you would let me."

Sheriff Hoffman waved the guard back as Wilson launched into an old Southern plantation song:

> *There is rest for the weary—*
> *There is rest for the weary—*
> *There is rest for the weary—*
> *There is rest for me.*

As Wilson finished his song, guards stepped forward with the ropes and white hoods, fixed them in place, and stepped back. The trap was sprung at 6:35 a.m., and the two white-draped forms dropped through the opening.

Dr. Francis W. McNamara, the jail physician, with a "jury" of twelve doctors, pronounced Wilson dead of strangulation twelve minutes later; and declared Dalton dead of a broken neck one minute after that.

Harry Standige, the jail plumber, who had witnessed some seventy hangings over the past quarter of a century, commented, "I have never seen two men go to their deaths with calmer assurance. They may have been thieves and murderers—but they died like men."

Nearly 200 witnesses had assembled for the execution, one of the largest crowds ever for an indoor hanging. Among them were 23-year-old Alexander Skiba, son of the slain policeman, and Patrolman Lamb. It was the first time a relative of a murder victim had been permitted to witness an execution inside the jail.

"I felt kind of sorry for them, when I saw them mount the scaffold," he said afterward. "But—well, you know, they didn't give my dad a chance. I'm glad it's over."

State's Attorney Robert E. Crowe, on being informed that the sentence of the court had been carried out, declared, "The death penalty is the greatest deterrent in the world for staying the hands of murderers. If there were more hangings at shorter intervals there would be fewer murders and robberies in Chicago."

70

NEGRO HANGED FOR MURDER OF EVANSTON MAN

MAY 15, 1925

Lawrence Washington, 33 years old, divorced, and the father of a six-year-old girl, made his living as a modern-day highwayman. Police were seeking him for two murders and at least fifty armed robberies during a two-month period in the fall of 1924, when he was arrested for the fatal shooting of Nunzio Mascolino, a well-to-do confectioner, in his Evanston candy shop September 14.

In making his getaway after killing Mascolino, he also shot an Evanston policeman.

After being arrested, Washington made a clean breast of things, admitting to every crime in which he was a suspect. Brought before Chief Justice Jacob Hopkins in Criminal Court, he pleaded guilty, thus saving the state the cost of a trial.

Despite the guilty plea, Judge Hopkins sentenced Washington to death.

It was the first death penalty meted out in Cook County since August of 1924, when Judge John R. Caverly spared Nathan Leopold and Richard Loeb, confessed slayers of little Bobby Franks, in the so-called "Crime of the Century."

Judge Caverly's decision was hailed by criminologists

as a giant step in saving slayers from the death penalty, after the defendants' lawyer, Clarence Darrow, argued:

"You may stand them up on the trapdoor of the scaffold, and choke them to death, but that act will be infinitely more cold-blooded, whether justified or not, than any act that these boys have committed or can commit."

Washington, who blamed his misfortune on bad company, spent his last night in the death chamber, reading from the Bible. His sister and a girlfriend visited him for a half hour, and said their good-byes. A clergyman then sat with Washington in his cell until he fell asleep at 10 p.m.

Jailer John Schwantes awakened the prisoner at dawn, and Washington went to the gallows without incident at 6:08 a.m.

71

ACTRESS SEES NEGRO HANGED AS COP SLAYER

JUNE 19, 1925

The fourth black man in a row to go to the gallows was Willie Sams, a "colored bad man," according to the press of the day, who was sentenced to death for the murder of Patrolman Cornelius Broderick.

"I don't ask for mercy; all I want is justice," Sams shouted after Judge Hosea Wells imposed sentence. "In the last year three colored men have been hanged, two for killing cops. But not long ago when two white men killed a policeman, the color of their skin won them life imprisonment."

Prosecutor William McSwiggin (who himself would be murdered) argued, "Sams is a cold blooded murderer. His vocation in life was robbery and if any one interfered with him he would kill. He has taken two lives already. He killed Meyer Oppenheim and he killed Policeman Broderick. He didn't give either a chance for life."

Oppenheim was shot to death when he ran to the aid of his niece, who was being robbed by Sams. Broderick was fatally shot, and his partner, Edward Mulcahy, was wounded, in a gun duel in which Sams took two bullets in the back.

After recovering from his wounds Sams, the 30-year-old father of three small children, got life imprisonment for the Oppenheim slaying, plus death.

Sams spent his last evening with the Reverend H.W. Knight, pastor of Mount Carmel Baptist Church of Oak Park, and the Reverend J.R. Woodson of Progressive Baptist Church. He was also visited in the death cell by his wife, who brought along their three-month-old daughter, and his mother, Pearl Clark.

After they left, Sams sent out for a pint of ice cream, which he ate at midnight under the watchful eyes of two black bailiffs. He then sat up in his cell until 3 a.m., writing letters in which he blamed "women and gambling men" for his woes.

After a breakfast of ham and eggs, toast, potatoes and coffee, the 6-foot 2 1/2 inch, 218-pound prisoner began the march to the gallows at 6:59 a.m.

Sheriff Peter Hoffman, his death watch guards, Axel Frodin and Oscar Andrea, and the two clergymen accompanied him.

"Have you any word to say before this sentence imposed by the courts of the County of Cook is executed?" Sheriff Hoffman asked, as Sams stood on the trapdoor.

"I have," Sams said. Then, in a strong voice, he continued, "My God take me. I ask you, take my soul. Give the man who is guilty of this crime what he deserves, but take me. I ask you, my God, the Father, the Son, and the Holy Ghost. Forgive these men who are about to take my breath, for, my God, they know not what they do."

His message delivered, the noose and white cap were put into place, and a lever releasing the trapdoor was given a yank. Sams dropped through the opening at 7:03 a.m.

The hanging of Willie Sams was the first in the Cook County jail ever witnessed by a woman.

Kathryn De Nauoley, a chorus girl with the Rose Marie company then playing in Chicago, had somehow managed to obtain a reporter's invitation to the execution. "I found it in my hotel room," she would later claim.

The actress, dressed in men's clothing and a slouch hat, was admitted to the death chamber along with the other witnesses. It was not until the last moment, when a sheriff's deputy ordered, "Put out your smokes, gents, and remove your hats," that her identity was discovered.

At that point Sheriff Hoffman saw no useful purpose in delaying the execution, and permitted the hanging to go on as scheduled.

"Never, as long as I live, do I ever want again to see a man face dishonorable death," De Nauoley said afterward. "I thought it would be a thrill. Now I know better."

Of course, all the publicity she got for her show didn't hurt any.

72

WOMAN SLAYER DIES
PRAYING ON GALLOWS
OCTOBER 16, 1925

The next man scheduled to go the way of the rope was Bernard Grant, a 23-year-old cop killer, whose hair had turned white in jail during the five reprieves he had won from the noose. August 14, 1925, was finally set as the date of his execution for shooting Patrolman Ralph Souders during an A & P store robbery. Grant would never know the feel of the rope around his neck, however. On June 22 he was stabbed to death by a fellow inmate.

That put 30-year-old Frank Lanciano next in line for the gallows. Lanciano had fatally shot his 200-pound common law wife, Rose Attillia, 29, during a fit of jealousy.

On the evening before he was scheduled to die, Lanciano paced his cell nervously. After a short nap he awakened at midnight, and began to pray, while fondling his rosary beads. Frequently he was heard to cry out, "I want to live!" At 1 a.m. his jailers brought him coffee, but he refused it. "I'm fasting for the last rites," he explained.

He slept soundly throughout the night, and had to be awakened by his jailers at 5 a.m. when two clergymen came to give him the sacrament. He spurned breakfast, explaining that he wanted to spend the time getting neatly dressed in the new blue suit which had been hanging unused in the cell since his arrest, along with his shiny brown oxfords.

Warden George H. Weideling and Charles Peters, now chief deputy sheriff, called on the prisoner at 7 a.m. "Cheer up, Frank," Peters told him. "We'll do this as quickly as possible."

Wearing his new suit, with his arms handcuffed behind his back, he began the march to the gallows at 7:02 a.m., flanked by jailers Oscar Andrea and Axel Frodin.

"Good-bye, boys. Good-bye, boys. Good-bye, boys," he called out to his fellow death row inmates as he was led into the death chamber, where a deputy called out the now familiar, "Hats off!" as the procession entered the room.

It was 7:06 when he calmly mounted the scaffold and took his place beneath the suspended noose.

Lanciano's lips moved in silent prayer as First Assistant Superintendent George Adams strapped his arms and legs together, adjusted the white cowl and tied it around his neck, then slipped the noose over his head and tightened the big, coiled knot behind his left ear.

A priest from St. Peter's Catholic Church held a crucifix to the prisoner's lips, and he kissed it reverently.

"Have you anything to say before the sentence is carried out?" Peters asked.

"I have nothing to say," Lanciano responded coldly, then continued with his silent prayer.

The white hood was placed over his head, and at 9 minutes after 7 the trap was sprung as Lanciano's voice could be heard murmuring through the cloth, "God's will be done."

The 110-pound prisoner dropped through the opening, and dangled from the end of the rope for twelve minutes, until he was pronounced dead of a broken neck at 7:21. The body was cut down and laid upon a slab, to be claimed by the two clergymen for burial.

Before he died Lanciano telegraphed his legal wife,

Anna, whom he had abandoned in Philadelphia:

"I don't think there is any hope for me now. Please claim my body if it is not too much trouble."

Apparently it was. She did not bother to claim the body, and it was buried in Mount Olivet Cemetery by a local funeral director.

On the same day that Lanciano was hanged in Chicago, John Koval, a Russian immigrant, died in the electric chair in the Indiana State Penitentiary at Michigan City, for the murder of Martha Egelski, his landlady, in Gary.

73

OTHER KILLERS IN JAIL HEAR TRAP AS ONE DIES BY NOOSE

JANUARY 29, 1926

Youth was no exemption from the gallows in Cook County during the Roaring Twenties. Campbell McCarthy, a black teen-ager, was the first of eight convicted killers to die at the end of the rope in 1926. McCarthy, an ex-convict, had been out of Pontiac prison on parole just three months when he shot and killed Christian Gitzen, a watchman for the Lomax Bottling Works on North Paulina Street, on May 4, 1925.

Sentenced to death, he won several reprieves, one of them as his last meal, a chicken dinner, was being delivered by a local restaurant operator. When Captain George Weideling, jail superintendent, notified the 19-year-old prisoner that his execution had been delayed for two weeks, McCarthy begged, "Captain, please let me stay in here until I get that chicken dinner."

His request was granted, after which he was returned from the death cell to his regular cell block.

The *Chicago Herald and Examiner* insensitively reported: COLORED BOY ESCAPES NOOSE.

McCarthy's time ran out on January 29. "I sort of hope we bring you back here, Campbell," one of his guards commented as the youth was escorted from the cell block to the death cell the previous evening.

"I hope that myself," McCarthy said. "I think I'll be back. Something will happen for me before morning."

As he was partaking of his second "last meal" a guard brought him a message from his former cellmate, Samuel Washington, also under sentence of death. "Sam says to tell you good-bye and to save him some chicken."

McCarthy gave the jailer a plate of partly-gnawed chicken bones, and said, "Tell him good-bye, and thank you."

After dinner the prisoner received a final visit from his father, Moses McCarthy. Following a final embrace, the elder McCarthy left the jail in tears. McCarthy then played cards with his guards until falling asleep.

He spent his last hours with two black clergymen, the Reverend T.E. Brown and the Reverend E.C. Williams.

"Somehow it doesn't seem like this is the beginning of my last hour on earth," McCarthy told them. Then, turning to Reverend Brown, he asked, "Would you take down my last statement for me?" The minister took a pencil and pad, and wrote as McCarthy dictated:

"Tell my father and mother not to worry. All is well with my soul. Thank them for their efforts to save me. And see that Sam Washington gets my breakfast."

Sheriff Peter Hoffman appeared at the cell at 7:30 a.m. "We are ready to go."

"I'm ready," said McCarthy, getting up off his bunk.

The sheriff led the procession, followed by McCarthy and Reverend Brown, with two guards bringing up the rear. The three lawmen wore rubber soled shoes. The only sound, as the group approached the scaffold, was the scraping of McCarthy's and Brown's leather-soled shoes on the concrete floor.

McCarthy took his place in the center of the platform, as jailer Joseph Keller adjusted the noose.

"Is there anything you would like to say, Campbell?"

the sheriff asked.

"I have made my peace with God," McCarthy replied.

He stood erect with the noose around his neck, his shoulders back, looking out over the group of witnesses. The only sound in the room was the ticking of a clock, fifty feet down the corridor. Then there was a clatter of benches, as one of the spectators fainted, and lurched forward onto the floor. McCarthy continued to stare straight ahead as the cap was placed over his head.

At 7:37 there was a barely perceptible movement near the wall, as a deputy sheriff released the trap. Then a loud clang as it fell open, the noise echoing throughout the jail.

The white-robed figure shot twelve feet through the opening, until the rope jerked short his momentum. For the next ten minutes he dangled, twitching and convulsing, until all movement stopped. There was another clatter among the spectators, as two more witnesses to a man's death passed out, upending their benches as they slumped to the floor.

The unconscious witnesses were carried out of the room by guards. At 7:48 a.m. several physicians held their stethoscopes against the chest of the man hanging from the rope, and pronounced him dead.

74

TWO DRAKE HOTEL BANDITS
HANGED IN COUNTY JAIL

FEBRUARY 13, 1926

On July 30, 1925, a reckless band of desperados pulled off one of the most spectacular heists in Chicago's history—the armed robbery of the posh Drake Hotel on the city's fabled Gold Coast, while the lobby was crowded with afternoon visitors. A hotel cashier, Frank Blair Rodkey, was killed in the holdup.

After a fierce gun battle with hotel detectives and Lincoln Park police as hotel guests dived for cover, one of the bandits, an Indian known only as Tex Court, staggered out the front door with four bullets in him and dropped dead on the sidewalk under the canopy. The gang's leader, Eric Nelson, commandeered a taxi, but was shot to death when police curbed the cab at Foster Avenue and Clark Street on the North Side.

A third member of the gang, Joseph Holmes, surrendered when he was cornered in the hotel kitchen. A fourth gunman, Jack Wilson, alias Woods, was arrested at Jefferson Park Hospital, where he had gone for treatment of a bullet wound in the hand.

The fifth member of the gang, 20-year-old William Wazel Mulneschuck, got away with $10,000. The loot was never recovered.

Holmes and Wilson were convicted of the hotel clerk's murder and sentenced to be hanged.

Jail superintendent George Weideling ordered special precautions taken, and posted extra guards over the two prisoners, after Woods boasted, "I will never go to the gallows." Weideling also had a five-foot screen of wire mesh erected around the scaffold to prevent Wilson from leaping off the platform to the concrete floor below.

The hanging was scheduled for Friday, February 12, 1926, but was postponed for one day because authorities did not want to stage the double execution on Abraham Lincoln's birthday.

"It's a terrible thing to wait for—to be jerked to death," Wilson complained to his four guards. "And all for what they say I did when I was ginned up and I can't remember."

"Lay off the moonshine that's peddled nowadays," his partner agreed. "We'd never done such a foolish thing if we'd been sober."

"You boys had better get some sleep," Sam Annoreno, one of the death watch guards, suggested.

"What for?" Wilson asked. "Eat, drink and be merry, for tomorrow we die. Let's have some scrambled eggs and toast and coffee. That's the eat and drink part of it, anyway."

"Yeah," agreed Holmes. "And we can do the merry part, too." He then broke into a rendition of "The Prisoner's Song," and was joined by Wilson.

The two condemned men continued singing, "It's A Long Way to Tipperary," "It Ain't Gonna Rain No More," and "Yes, Sir, That's My Baby," throughout the night.

"How about 'When You Come to the End of a Perfect Day'?" Holmes giggled. "I'm getting tired."

"Me too," his partner said. It was 5:30 a.m.

"Let us sleep as long as you can," Holmes told the guards.

Two hours later they were awakened and served the

breakfast they had ordered. Neither man wanted to eat, and passed the trays back to the guards.

"I'd like a cup of coffee, though," Holmes said. Five cups of coffee were brought in, and he and the four death-watch guards sipped the brew together.

Holmes then took communion and received the last rites of the Catholic Church from the Rev. Ernest Kaufholdt, a priest from St. Peter's Church in the Loop. Wilson had spurned religion, but changed his mind as the hour of his death approached. He called Weideling and told him, "I would like to have a minister with me."

The warden called Dr. John Timothy Stone, pastor of the fashionable Fourth Presbyterian Church, in the shadow of the Lake Shore Drive hotel where the shootout occurred. Dr. Stone, who had never witnessed an execution before, agreed to accompany the prisoner to the gallows. He met with Wilson in his cell and gave him a Bible, that had been in his family for years.

Dr. Stone then said the Lord's Prayer with the prisoner. After that Wilson recited a children's prayer:

> *Now I lay me down to sleep,*
> *I pray the Lord my soul to keep.*
> *If I should die before I wake,*
> *Make me a good little boy, for Jesus' sake.*

He said he had learned the verse in the trenches while serving with a Scottish-Canadian regiment in World War I.

Sheriff Peter M. Hoffman had received more than one thousand requests for tickets to the execution from citizens who claimed they wanted to view the hangings "in the name of science" or "to obtain material for a book."

The sheriff finally posted a sign outside his office saying "No tickets for executions Saturday under any circumstances." The sheriff added, "If I admitted all the applicants there would be no room for the executioner."

Ignazio Sylvestri
Agostino Gilardo
Giovanni Azzaro
November 14, 1885

Albert Parsons
November 11, 1887

August Spies
November 11, 1887

George Engel
November 11, 1887

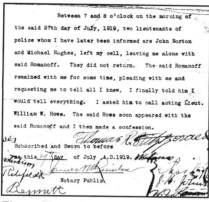

Thomas Fitzgerald signed this affidavit after a reporter, Harry Romanoff of the *Herald and Examiner*, talked—or tricked—him into confessing to the murder of six-year-old Janet Wilkerson, who had disappeared several days earlier. Before he visited the jail, Romanoff bought the biggest doll he could find, and he told Fitzgerald it had belonged to the murdered girl. "Her mother wanted to get it out of the house," he said. "Don't you think it's time you got this off your conscience?" Clutching the doll, Fitzgerald confessed freely.

Adolph Fischer
November 11, 1887

Patrick Prendergast
July 13, 1894

Louis G. Thombs
(Toombs)
August 8, 1902

Johann Hoch
February 23, 1906

Earl Dear
June 27, 1919

John O'Brien
February 20, 1920

Nicholas Viana
December 10, 1920

Salvatore Cardinella, the "Murder King of Little Italy," nearly cheated the state of its retribution. He arranged for his body to be claimed immediately after the hanging on April 15, 1921, and rushed to an ambulance loaded with life-saving paraphernalia, such as a hot water mattress, oxygen tanks, and an electrical battery, and staffed by doctors and nurses ready to revive him. But they sprang into action too fast—even before the ambulance was out of the prison yard—and a guard held up the ambulance until Cardinella was dead beyond recall.

Joseph Costanzo
April 15, 1921

Antonio Lopez
July 8, 1921

Carl Wanderer
September 30, 1921

Casper Pastoni
June 15, 1923

Lucius Dalton
April 17, 1924

**Jack Wilson, alias
Woods**
February 13, 1926

Joseph Holmes
February 13, 1926

Ray Costello
April 16, 1926

Harvey Church lay in a coma, apparently
fear-induced, for thirty days before his
execution on March 13, 1922. On the day of
his death, still senseless, he was carried to
the gallows in a kitchen chair.

Richard Evans
October 29, 1926

**James Gricius
Thomas McWane**
December 31, 1926

John W. Winn
April 15, 1927

Elin Lyons
June 24, 1927

"Terrible Tommy" O'Connor
Escaped, never to be heard from again

Anthony Grecco
Charles Walz
February 20, 1929

August Vogel
May 9, 1930

Leonard Shadlow
October 3, 1930

Canadian financier Russell Scott was sentenced to hang on October 15, 1927, but one week before the execution he carried out the sentence on himself. He was found hanging by his own belt from the top bars of his cell. If he had waited, he would have been the last man to die on the Cook County gallows, before it was replaced by the electric chair.

Lafon Fisher
October 3, 1930

Leon Brown
November 28, 1930

William Lenhardt
December 12, 1930

Frank Jordan
October 16, 1931

Charles Rocco
October 16, 1931

Richard Sullivan
October 16, 1931

Ross King
October 16, 1933

Armando Boulan
December 15, 1934

The Cook County electric chair sent 67 men
to their deaths between 1929 and 1962.
Condemned men took their last steps
through the door on the right.

Chester Novak
March 21, 1935

Andrew Bogaki
October 21, 1936

**"Marble Mildred"
Bolton**
*Death sentence
commuted to 199 years*

Rufo Swain
February 26, 1937

Joseph Schuster
April 16, 1937

Peter Chrisoulas
October 15, 1937

J.C. Scott
April 19, 1938

Robert Nixon
July 16, 1939

Edward Riley and Orville Watson hear themselves sentenced to death for two murders in a tavern shootout. When they went to the chair on June 20, 1941, Riley left a note in the death cell that contained the joker and four aces from a deck of cards. In the note he had written, "Life is like a deck of cards and we are all the jokers. First it's hearts, then it's diamonds. Next it's clubs, and now it's spades."

Steve Cygan
October 13, 1939

Bernard Sawicki
January 17, 1942

John Pantano
September 18, 1942

Paul L. Williams
March 15, 1944

Alvin Krause
September 15, 1944

Julius "Dolly" Weisberg
Died of fright in his cell, May 1947

Charles Crosby
June 20, 1947

Ernest Gaither
October 24, 1947

The morning after James "Mad Dog" Morelli was executed, the *Herald-American* shocked the city with this photograph of Morelli dying in the chair. With help from reporter Basil "Gus" Talbott, photographer Joe Migon hid a tiny Minox camera in the hollowed-out heel of his shoe. As Morelli was fastened into the chair, Migon slipped the camera out of his shoe and Talbott feigned a coughing spell to cover the click of the shutter. The stunt was called "the picture scoop of the decade."

Victor Wnukowski
Frank Michalowski
May 17, 1949

Robert Schroeder
December 13, 1949

Willard Truelove
November 17, 1950

Raymond Jenko
January 25, 1952

Harry Williams
March 14, 1952

LeRoi Lindsey
October 17, 1952

Bernice Davis
October 17, 1952

Before he was electrocuted on March 22, 1962, Vincent Ciucci wrote a letter to Warden Jack Johnson with a new account of the night his family was slain—a bizarre reversal of the story he had told in court. Just hours later, Ed Baumann watched as Ciucci became the last man but one to die in the Cook County chair.

Emanuel Scott
March 19, 1953

Richard Carpenter
December 19, 1958

James Dukes
August 24, 1962

Meanwhile a peculiar group of death penalty opponents went to the house of Judge John P. McGoorty in a last-ditch effort to have the hangings halted, by submitting an affidavit asserting that both men were insane.

The group included three male dancers and a chorus girl from "The Student Prince" theatrical company; Dr. Ben Reitman, president of the Hobo College; a legal stenographer; and Benjamin Salmon, a self-styled humanitarian.

On hearing that the do-gooders were trying to save him and his partner, Holmes sent a message to his sister, Millie Barron, in New York City. "Cheer up. I still have hope of being insane," he said. "But if I must go, I am going with a smile."

The jail was silent as a tomb as the death march to the scaffold commenced at 9:37 a.m. Then the quiet was shattered by a shout from a fellow prisoner, John "Midget" Fernekes. "Good-bye, boys, and good luck!"

"Good-bye," answered Holmes.

Wilson said nothing. Wearing dark trousers and a gray sweater, he walked glumly to the scaffold clutching the Bible Dr. Stone had given him in his hands, manacled behind his back.

As the prisoners stood on the platform, looking out over the crowd of a hundred witnesses while their legs were being strapped together and the shrouds draped around them, Holmes threw back his head to flick a lock of hair out of his eyes. Sheriff Hoffman reached over and took a drooping cigarette out of Wilson's mouth, so the noose could be lowered around his neck.

Among those gathered to watch the execution were Tracy Drake, president of the Drake Hotel; John B. Drake Jr. and William Drake, assistant managers; and J.R. McMurdle, the house detective, who had traded shots with the bandits before police arrived.

Sheriff Hoffman then asked the two prisoners if they

had any last words.

"I plead not guilty—AGAIN," Wilson said.

"Not guilty," repeated Holmes. "And God bless you."

Father Kaufholdt pressed a crucifix to Holmes' lips, and he kissed it as the hood was draped over his head.

"Well, boys, God bless you," the sheriff said.

The next sound anyone heard was the clatter of the trap-door as it slammed open at 9:44 a.m., and the two white-robed figures dropped through the opening.

Wilson's neck was broken by the ten-foot fall. His body trembled, and the well-worn bible the minister had given him dropped from beneath the shroud and fell to the floor. He was pronounced dead at 9:51. Holmes was heard gasping convulsively as he slowly strangled. He was pronounced dead four minutes later.

Both bodies remained hanging until 10:02 a.m., when they were declared too dead to be revived, and cut down.

In downstate Jacksonville, meanwhile, a man named Grimmett was also hanged for murder.

The lone survivor of the dramatic hotel lobby gun battle, William Mulneschuck, remained at large for thirteen years. He was finally captured in San Diego in 1938.

75

COSTELLO BITTER, HOBBS CALM, BOTH PRAY UNDER ROPE

APRIL 16, 1926

The next hanging, just two months later, was also a double header. Falling through the trapdoor together were Raymond Costello, a white man, and Charles Hobbs, who was black.

On July 10, 1925, sixteen-year-old Madeline White was found raped and strangled under a porch at 5931 South LaSalle Street. A polka dot handkerchief, which had been stuffed down her throat, was traced to Costello, a twenty-two-year-old teamster, whose thinning hair had earned him the nickname of Baldy. Despite his pleas of innocence, the polka dot hanky was all a jury needed to consign him to the gallows.

Hobbs, who never denied his guilt, was sentenced to hang for strangling his landlady, Betty Barnett, in a seventy-five cent robbery.

The two men presented a study in contrast as they received visitors in their cell on the night before they were scheduled to die.

Costello was consoled by his white-haired parents, his younger brother, Arthur, and his common-law wife, Mabel Patterson, who brought their three-month-old son, Tommy.

"I didn't do it, mother. I didn't do it," Costello sobbed, as he clung to his mother's neck through the bars.

A few feet away Hobbs laughed uproariously. "Sure, I killed the landlady. Choked her. That's me. Ha-ha-ha!"

His only visitor had been a casual acquaintance, a man he had met in Mississippi.

Shortly before the death march was to begin on the morning of April 16, 1926, Costello was given the last rights by his parish priest, the Reverend Joseph Phelan of St. Anne's Catholic Church. Hobbs was attended by a Presbyterian minister, the Reverend Harry Hooper.

One of the largest crowds ever gathered to witness an indoor hanging, an estimated 400 spectators, were jammed into the death chamber. Those who could not find seats lined the walls, or sat on radiators. Among the witnesses was Gregory White, father of the murdered girl.

Once the condemned men had reached the gallows, the burly Costello had regained his composure, while Hobbs chanted a prayer.

"Raymond Costello, have you anything to say before the judgment of the court is executed upon you?" asked Sheriff Peter Hoffman, as the prisoner's arms were being pinioned.

"Yes, I have," Costello declared in a firm, bitter voice, with a cigarette dangling from his lips. "I am not innocent— I mean, I am innocent. That's all. "

The sheriff then turned to Hobbs and asked the same question.

"I want my Lord, that's all," Hobbs said. As the noose was dropped around his neck he shouted, "Oh, Lord, take me! Oh, Lord, be with me!"

Father Phelan stepped between the two men and began reciting the litany of the dying, as Reverend Hooper positioned himself behind them, and simultaneously recited the Lord's Prayer.

The weird chant echoed through the room as the white

shrouds were adjusted about the condemned men.

"Christ have mercy upon us —"

"Our Father, which art in Heaven —"

"Lord, have mercy upon us —"

"Hallowed be Thy name."

A deputy sheriff reached over and took the cigarette out of Costello's mouth as the white hood was placed over his head.

Though bound hand and foot, Hobbs suddenly broke into what was described as "grotesque shimmy dance," jumping and swaying as if he were at a revival meeting, and repeating the Presbyterian minister's words in a loud but muffled voice through the hood. From time to time he interjected, "Lord, take me! Oh, Lord, save my soul!"

Costello stood firmly on the trap as he repeated the words of the Catholic priest.

"Christ have mercy—"

"And lead us not into temptation—"

At 9:20 a.m., four seemingly endless minutes after the two men had stepped upon the scaffold, the trap was sprung with a resounding clatter.

The two white-robed figures shot downward in unison. There was a snapping sound as the heavy Costello reached the end of his rope. Hobbs, a slightly built man, dangled at the end of his rope, strangling.

Six minutes later, at 9:26 a.m., Costello was declared dead of a broken neck. Hobbs' heart did not stop beating until 9:36.

"Justice is done, but that doesn't bring my girl back," Gregory White remarked, as the two bodies were cut down and wheeled out of the room.

In going through the dead men's pockets, Sheriff Hoffman found that Costello had been carrying a Bible and a match box, containing two razor blades. Apparently he had intended to take his own life, but never got the chance.

The sheriff also found two notes in Costello's pocket,

one to his parents, and the other to Mabel Patterson, the mother of his child. Sheriff Hoffman silently studied the notes:

Dear Mother and Father—I want to tell you that I went loving you two with all my heart. I know you have done everything you could possibly do. You won't approve of the way I went, but I'm really innocent. Tell Art I went thinking of him. Now, please take care of Tommy and Mabel. They got it coming to them. I will say good-by, and God bless you all. Your loving son—Ray.

Dear Mibbs—this is all you will ever hear from me, and I want to tell you that I died loving you and Tommy more than life itself. Just do one thing for me, Mibbs. Stick with mother. She wants you now. Well, good-by, Mibbs, and God bless you. You deserve it. So long. Till the end. Lots of love. — Ray.

76

YOUTH, 19, CONFESSES KILLING BEFORE TRAP CLAIMS JUSTICE TOLL

OCTOBER 29, 1926

At the age of nineteen, Richard Evans fatally shot Policeman Edward Finegan, who had stopped him for a traffic violation in front of St. Anne's Church on the South Side.

A Criminal Court jury took just ten minutes to find him guilty of murder and sentence him to death on the gallows.

Evans blamed the shooting on a companion, but on the night before he was scheduled to be hanged he changed his story and admitted that he was the gunman.

"I'm sorry I lied," he wept. "I realize that I have to go. I believe in a Supreme Being and I want to take this lie off my conscience."

He then wrote a final letter to his mother, Ida:

I just thought I would drop you a line, as it may be my last. I am clean with my God, thanks to your diligent work in bringing me up in the ways of the Lord. I'm sorry if I must go, to die in this way. But I know I have made my peace with God. If I had stayed at home and done what you wanted me to do I would not be here now.

Evans only nibbled at his last meal, a chicken dinner provided by restaurateur Joe Stein, who made it a habit of catering dinners to condemned men on death row.

After a sleepless night, he spent a half hour in prayer with the Reverend Henry Sandvoss, a Lutheran minister, until jailer Edward J. Fogarty came for him at 7 a.m.

Flanked by two guards, the teen-ager walked bravely but slowly down the long corridor to the death chamber, and mounted the stairs to the gallows at 7:08 a.m. Sheriff Peter Hoffman read the death warrant to him as jailers adjusted the sack-like shroud, and placed the rope around his neck. The sheriff then said, "Richard Evans, you are about to die. Is there anything you have to say before the judgment of the court is executed?"

"I want to say that I am ready right now to pay my debt to society and my God," replied Evans, looking more like a young office boy than a convicted killer.

The steel trap dropped with a resounding bang at 7:10, and Evans' body plummeted downward. Sixteen minutes later Dr. William H. McNamara, the coroner's physician, and a jury of twelve other doctors pronounced him dead.

77

GRICIUS AND MC WANE
DENIED LAST WORDS
BY SHERIFF GRAYDON

DECEMBER 31, 1926

The last day of the year was also the last day of their lives for Russian immigrant James Gricius, 22, and his new found friend, Thomas McWane, 20, who had journeyed to Chicago from Muskegon, Michigan.

Shortly after the two strangers had met in the big city they flagged down taxi driver Ludwig Rose, and had him drive them to Cicero, where they tried to rob him. Rose, unfortunately, made a false move, and Gricius shot him dead.

The two men dumped Rose's body out on the street and took off in his cab. A short time later they came upon Frederick Hein, a Sunday school superintendent, who was saying good night to one of his teachers, 23-year-old Marie Blang, after driving her home. After robbing the couple, Gricius shot them dead, too.

McWane was caught first, and he put the finger on Gricius. Both pleaded guilty, hoping to be spared the death penalty. Judge Harry B. Miller would not hear of it. On October 31, 1926, he ordered them to be hanged, and the sentence was carried out two months later.

Several civic and social organizations, meanwhile, tried to save McWane, arguing that Gricius had been the gunman, while McWane was a mere bystander to the murders. The courts would hear none of that, either.

Gricius tried to cheat the executioner by doing the job himself in his cell. He twisted bedsheets about his throat and left a note saying, "Good-bye everybody. I did not kill the girl. So help me God, I didn't kill the girl." Jailer John Langeloh discovered him hanging by his sheets, however, and cut him down before it was too late.

The traditional camaraderie among death row inmates did not exist between Gricius and McWane. They spent their final days sitting in opposite ends of their cell, glaring at one another, barely speaking.

"You got me into this," McWane shouted in one burst of fury. Gricius merely turned his back on his cellmate and shrugged his shoulders.

On their last night on earth Gricius refused to receive the last sacrament from the Reverend H.J. Vaicunias of St. Anthony's Catholic Church in Cicero, and spurned a farewell visit by his parents. He refused to change from the shabby jail clothing he had been wearing to a new suit his parents had brought down, and insisted on pacing the floor of his cell barefoot.

Neither man bothered with a last meal.

McWane tried hard to keep up his spirits by listening to a radio that had been installed in the death cell. He visited as pleasantly as he could, under the circumstances, with his parents, and then wrote two farewell notes, one to his mother, Mrs. M.A. Scharft, and the other to his sweetheart, Katherine Lulofs, in Muskegon. After a late night visit from the Reverend Eric Borlund of the Swedish Covenant Church of America, he appeared on the verge of collapse, and told his guards, "I'm afraid I will have to be carried if I have to go to the gallows in the morning."

He then played a half-hearted game of rummy with his

guards, until 4 a.m. when he fell into a fitful sleep on his cot.

By morning he had regained his composure, however. He arose early, combed his hair, and stood smiling in a neat blue suit, clean white shirt, and patent leather oxfords when guards came to the cell at 7:17 a.m. to begin the death march.

Gricius, on the other hand, refused to change out of his dirty undershirt and baggy trousers, or to put on his shoes. "I came into the world barefooted, and I'll go out of it the same way," he asserted.

Both men looked curiously up at the nooses dangling above them as they took their places on the scaffold.

As the ropes were being adjusted about their necks, McWane was consoled by Reverend Borlund, but Gricius turned his head away from Father Vaicunias, saying, "I will go on my own."

Just before the white hoods were lowered over their heads, McWane turned to the newly elected Sheriff Charles E. Graydon and whispered, "I want to say something."

Graydon, possibly nervous at officiating at his first execution, ignored the prisoner, and signalled that all was in readiness. The trap dropped at 7:20, just three minutes after the march to the gallows had begun.

Gricius and McWane fell together, and their bodies were whipped upward simultaneously as they reached the ends of the ropes. Guards rushed forward and held the bodies to keep them from spinning and swaying. The white robe enveloping Gricius fluttered momentarily, as he made one last gasp for life. McWane's robe fell and rose for several minutes, while he strangled, until he, too, went limp.

Twenty minutes later the two slayers were pronounced dead, and their bodies were cut down. It was the third double-hanging of 1926.

For the record, the executions were listed as the ninety-ninth and one hundredth in Cook County since it was incorporated.

78

OSCAR QUARLES DIES AS SAM WASHINGTON IS GIVEN REPRIEVE

FEBRUARY 17, 1927

The next double hanging was scheduled for February 17, 1927. Oscar Quarles, a 21-year-old black man, had been sentenced to death for the fatal shooting of Morris Dushoff, a sales clerk, during the robbery of an Atlantic & Pacific food store on East 50th Street. Sam Washington, also black, got the death penalty for shooting his common-law wife, Minnie Moore, to death during a quarrel over insurance papers.

The condemned men were moved into the death cell at 6 o'clock the night before the scheduled hanging, after giving up all hope. Both men were baptized by the prison chaplain, and spent the rest of the night preparing for the ordeal that faced them, playing cards, talking, praying, and occasionally trying to grab some fitful sleep.

At 5 a.m., as Quarles lay dozing, two deputies tiptoed into the cell and quietly removed Washington, cautioning him not to awaken his partner.

Less than two hours before Washington was to hang, Sheriff Charles E. Graydon had convinced Judge Henry B. Miller to issue a sixth stay of execution. The sheriff had taken the unusual action after examining court records, which convinced him that Washington had been given "a raw deal."

"He had no friends, no money, and no competent legal assistance," the sheriff said. "All he's entitled to is life imprisonment.'

Meanwhile, as an icy north wind rattled the dingy windows of the county jail, Quarles awoke to discover that he was alone in his cell. He was still wondering what happened to Washington when guards unlocked the cell door at 7:02 a.m. and marched him to the gallows.

"I am an innocent man," Quarles protested. "It is a known fact that I have to die some day, and if I said I had killed, I would die with a lie on my lips."

His lips were moving in prayer as his limbs were bound. Then, quickly, before the white hood was slipped over his head, he glanced from side to side, in apparent wonderment as to why he was suddenly standing on the platform alone.

Spectators who knew Quarles' reputation as a wise-cracker, half expected him to offer a clever pronouncement when asked if he had any last words. Sheriff Graydon didn't ask, however. He merely gave one of his deputies a nod, the trap clanged open, and Quarles plunged downward. Eighteen minutes later, at 7:25, he was pronounced dead.

The execution was witnessed by one of the smallest crowds in years—twenty-six people. Because of complaints about mob scenes at previous hangings, Sheriff Graydon followed the strict letter of the law in limiting the number of witnesses to less than thirty.

Among would-be witnesses who were turned away was an unidentified woman, who tried to slip into the jail wearing men's clothes. "You'd better go home and wash your dishes," Warden Edward J. Fogarty told her, as he showed her to the gate.

As for Sam Washington, his case was reviewed during the week-long reprieve, and his sentence was commuted to life in prison.

79

ROPE KILLS WINN; SCIENCE FINDS HIS BRAIN SMALL

APRIL 15, 1927

John Walton Winn, age 40, a dim-witted clod with Boris Karloffian features, beat a South Chicago contractor named Albert Nusbaum to death as a favor to Nusbaum's 59-year-old wife, Eliza. "Grandma Nusbaum," as she was widely known, wanted Albert out of the way so she could collect on his $50,000 life insurance policy.

Winn obliged Grandma Nusbaum because, he said. "I love her like a mother." His adoration earned him a date with the rope, while she got life in prison in lieu of an insurance settlement.

Warden Edward J. Fogarty described the mild-mannered Winn as "the calmest man ever to enter the death cell." Although he did not request spiritual comfort, Winn, who had no relatives in Chicago, agreed to permit Norman H. Camp of the Moody Bible Institute and two Salvation Army workers to visit him in his cell on his last night.

"I have made my peace with the Supreme Being and am ready to go in the morning," Winn told them. "I do not believe in some of those old fashioned ideas about religion, but I do believe in a Supreme Being. After I am hanged my spirit will return to help mother (Mrs. Nusbaum)."

One more thing: Winn agreed that his body would be turned over to Dr. Harold S. Hulbert, an alienist, for study after the hanging.

Dr. Hulbert had earlier thwarted efforts by social workers to halt the execution on grounds that Winn was a small boy in a man's body. The doctor advised Chief Justice William J. Lindsay of Criminal Court, "Winn is abnormal, feeble-minded and has the mentality of nine years. But there is no psychiatric reason to interfere with his execution."

Shortly before going to the gallows, Winn wrote a note to Mrs. Nusbaum, which he asked Warden Fogarty to deliver after he was gone:

> *Dear Mother: Jest a few words before I leave this Earth to go to Heven I want to leave this little message for you. I have gave my hart to God. I pray you still trust in God mother. God is my reffige and my stringth. I hope to meate you in heven. I remane as ever these last few owers I have to live your foster son John Winn.*

Winn, who stayed up throughout the night, was comforted by Salvation Army Major J.C. Habkirk, a jail chaplain. Two Sisters of Mercy from Columbus Hospital also visited him briefly as the hour of his death approached.

"Do you suppose God thinks it is a sin to smoke cigarettes?" he asked, taking a long draw on one held between trembling fingers. "I have confessed all my sins to God. I know He has forgiven me for the crap games I played when I was a boy."

In the days before his death, Winn had all of his clothing brought down to the jail, so he could distribute it among fellow inmates. He set aside one suit to die in, along with a white shirt with a stiff collar, and a checked four-in-hand tie.

The day of Winn's execution, April 15, 1927, was Good

Friday. While officials had postponed the hanging of the Drake Hotel bandits a year earlier out of respect for Abraham Lincoln's birthday, they did not let a religious holiday stand in the way of the gibbet.

Winn, his hair slicked back and dressed in his best suit, began his last walk shortly after 7 a.m., accompanied by Major Habkirk. As they passed a group of reporters, Winn smiled and told them, "You boys are still young. Within the span of your lives you will learn some day that I am not guilty of the murder for which I am to die. I'll meet you all in Heaven."

The party reached the trap at 7:06 a.m., and Winn stood staring straight out over the small group of twenty-eight witnesses as he was quickly trussed up, robed and hooded. Not a word was spoken by anyone on the platform. At 7:08 the floor dropped out from under Winn's feet, and he was left dangling in mid air at the end of the rope. Twenty minutes later he was pronounced dead.

One reporter wrote:

"John Walton Winn collected 'the wages of sin' today at the end of ten feet of new hempen rope. The paymasters, the sheriff and jail superintendent, made the transaction most business-like and efficient."

After Winn's body was cut down it was placed on a rubber-wheeled cart and rolled into an autopsy room, where Dr. Hulbert and Dr. Jacob Goodman opened his skull.

"Our examination showed that the brain in Winn was smaller than usual, especially the frontal region, which is the seat of intelligence," Dr. Hulbert wrote in his report. "We found that physically he was an old man for his years. He had hardening of the arteries and a wasting of the left side."

In the state capitol in Springfield, on the same day that Winn was hanged, Senator Charles Thompson of downstate Harrisburg introduced legislation to do away with the gallows and bring the highly successful electric chair to Illinois.

80

LYONS, POLICE SLAYER, IS HANGED SMILING

JUNE 24, 1927

Elin Lyons, a dark-skinned bandit who claimed to have been a Colombian soldier of fortune, got his fifteen minutes of fame on June 24, 1927, when he became the last person to die on the gallows in Cook County.

The 48-year-old Lyons was given the death penalty for the fatal shooting of Policeman Julian Bonfield, who had burst upon the scene as Lyons and a companion were robbing thirty-two female employees of a Southeast Side mail-order firm of their fur coats, jewelry and Christmas savings on December 15.

He offered a unique defense: the policeman had shot himself. A jury gave his story short shrift, and deliberated less than thirty minutes before finding him guilty of murder.

Lyons had won several earlier reprieves, and was hopeful for another miracle to the very end.

"But if I have to die I'm ready," he said. "The last time I had a delay it was Friday the Thirteenth. I ought to be able to beat an ordinary Friday."

As the condemned man sat in his cell a guard passed by whistling, "Oh, How I Hate to Get Up in the Morning."

Lyons grinned sardonically and said, "Me, too—

especially today."

When a guard brought him the three pork chops he had requested for his last breakfast he commented, "I'd share this with you, old fellow, except that you'll get another. I won't."

In an eleventh-hour effort to save Lyons's life Albert G. Benavides, Colombian consul in Chicago, personally appealed to Governor Len Small for clemency, but the governor refused to intervene. At 5 a.m. Benavides rushed to the home of Supreme Court Justice Frederic De Young to plead for a stay of execution, but De Young, too, declined to interfere with the legal process.

Two hours later, Lyons was standing on the trapdoor. He smiled grimly as the hood was adjusted over his head, and stood erect as the final seconds of his life ticked away. Suddenly the trap was sprung. His body shot through the opening at the end of the rope, and Cook County had hanged its last man.

Officer Bonfield's widow, on being told that the sentence had been carried out, said bitterly, "If more men like Lyons were hanged, there would be fewer policemen's stars in a case in the chief's office."

The era of the noose and the cross-beam had come to an end.

81

SENTENCED TO DEATH, SLAYER ENDS OWN LIFE

OCTOBER 8, 1927

Actually, there was to have been one more hanging before the gallows was retired from service—that of 29-year-old Russell T. Scott, a millionaire Canadian financier turned holdup man.

In 1923 Scott, married and the father of three children, was the head of a $30 million financial sales corporation bearing his name in Toronto, with a dozen branch offices and 800 employees.

He was also, it would appear, somewhat of a ladies man. Two women sued him for breach of promise, and one received a $10,000 judgment against him: Scott, then 25, was forced out of his own company, which went into receivership. He fled to the United States, where he worked variously as a salesman, vaudeville performer, bootlegger, dope peddler and finally a common stick-up man.

On the evening of April 2, 1924, just two weeks after arriving in Chicago from New York, he fatally shot Joseph Maurer, a 19-year-old soda jerk, during a holdup of the City Hall Pharmacy, in the heart of the La Salle Street financial district. Scott was arrested, confessed to the slaying, and was sentenced to hang. Because of a surly attitude and inability to get along with fellow inmates, he was eventually placed in solitary confinement.

For the next three years Scott and his wife, Catherine, devoted all their efforts to saving his life. He won several reprieves, one on July 17, 1925, just hours before he was to have begun the march to the scaffold. Finally, after every legal remedy had been exhausted, his next date with the gallows was set for October 15, 1927.

On October 8 Scott's wife, wearing a bright red dress, visited him in his cell. She brought him a basket of food, but he didn't touch any of it. "My bronchitis is bothering me," he complained. "I don't think I could keep it down." After his wife had been there a half hour, he told her, "You'd better go home. I'm not feeling well and I want to lie down and rest."

At 10:45 p.m. F.G. Harkins, a jailer, made a routine check on Scott and found him lying on his cot. Twenty minutes later, however, Deputy Warden Otto Schuler found him hanging from the top bars of his cell by his own belt.

A physician was called, but it was too late. Scott had carried out his own death sentence, and cheated the hangman out of his fee. State's Attorney Robert Crowe, on learning of the suicide, declared, "Scott did what the law should have done years ago."

There was still one bit of unfinished business, however. Terrible Tommy O'Connor, who had gone over the wall six and a half years earlier, was still under sentence to be hanged by the neck until dead.

After Scott's suicide the gallows was dismantled and stored away in the event that O'Connor might one day be apprehended. When the old jail on Illinois Street was torn down, the scaffold was stashed away in the basement of the new Cook County Jail, behind the Criminal Courts Building at 26th Street and California Avenue.

Fifty years later, when a custodian discovered the musty rope and lumber still gathering dust in the boiler room, Chief Judge Richard J. Fitzgerald ordered it thrown out.

"Heck, under present laws we couldn't execute the guy even if he surrendered tomorrow," Fitzgerald stated. Then the judge added, "But just out of curiosity, I'd like to see what the old gallows looks like. I think in view of the fact that it's a somewhat historic piece of the past, we should reconstruct it one more time before we destroy it."

And so the old six-man gallows, which had claimed the lives of 96 convicted murderers since it was built in the 1870s, was erected, noose and all, one more time. A painter lettered a sign: "Tired of Waiting, Tommy," and tacked it to one of the timbers.

After Judge Fitzgerald got his look at the hoary death machine, it was disassembled to be carted off to the junk heap. That's not what happened to it, however.

Larry Donley, owner of the Seven Acres Museum in Union, Illinois, about 50 miles northwest of Chicago, drove into the city and saved the gallows from destruction.

"As a boy I had heard about the gallows waiting for Tommy," he explained. "They did away with the wall from the St. Valentine's Day Massacre, and I just couldn't let that happen to this piece of Chicago history."

Donley and his son, Michael, spent hours laboriously hauling the old timbers out and loading them aboard a truck. The pieces were then carted out to Union, where the gallows was reassembled. It stands there today, just the way it stood on that wintry Sunday in December of 1921, when Terrible Tommy broke his date with the hangman.

BOOK III

ILLINOIS MAKES
THE SWITCH

1

THREE MEN DIE IN FIRST STATE ELECTROCUTION INDIAN AND 2 NEGROES GO TO CHAIR AT JOLIET

DECEMBER 15, 1928

Hangings were slowly going out of style in America, in part because they could be so grotesque if they were not properly carried out.

There were repeated examples of the fall failing to snap the recipient's neck, leaving the condemned man or woman to dangle from the rope, wheezing and kicking for as much as a quarter of an hour, while slowly strangling to death.

A classic example was that of Alexander Jefferson, hanged in Brooklyn, New York, on August 1, 1884. He was yanked five feet into the air when the weights were dropped, flailing the air with his feet. Kicking and writhing, he somehow managed to free his hands, pulled off the black hood, and feverishly tried to untie the noose.

Failing to loosen the knot, he pathetically reached his arms out pleadingly to the stunned witnesses as he moaned, his face hideously distorted, for eight minutes until gasping his last breath.

There were other gory instances in which the

executioner miscalculated the victim's weight in relation to the length of the fall and snapped the head clean off.

One such instance involved train robber Jack Ketchum, who told the hangman as he tightened the noose around his neck in New Mexico on April 26, 1901, "I'll be in hell before you start breakfast."

What happened next was reported in the *New Mexican:*

"Sheriff Garcia, at 12:17 p.m., cut the rope and the body shot down. The fall severed his head from his body. He alighted on his feet and his headless trunk stood for an instant upright, then swayed, then fell and giant streams of blood spurted from the severed neck. The head, remaining in the black cap, rolled to one side and the rope, released, flew high in the air."

An almost identical incident had occurred at the hanging of Josiah Potts and his wife, Elizabeth, in Elko, Nevada, for the murder of Miles Faucett.

The two fell through the trap in unison, but Mrs. Potts was the heavier of the two, and when she reached the end of her rope the carotid arteries were severed, causing blood to spurt from her neck. An examination of the bloody corpse afterward revealed that the drop had all but severed her head from her body, with the rear neck muscles alone remaining intact.

As late as the 1960s, at the Washington State Prison in Walla Walla, a condemned man's head was nearly ripped off, spraying spectators nearest the gallows with his warm blood.

Instances like these caused legislators throughout the country to look for a better way of disposing of people convicted of taking another person's life.

New York was the first state to do away with the gallows, in favor of the electric chair. William Kemmler, who had murdered his paramour, Tillie Ziegler, was electrocuted in Auburn State Prison on August 6, 1890. It was, for all intents and purposes, an experimental execution.

A post mortem examination revealed that blood vessels directly under where the electrode had set on Kemmler's head had carbonized, and the outer part of his brain had hardened. On his back, where the other electrode had been placed, his body was burned clear through to his spine, with the flesh resembling overdone beef.

Electrocuting a prisoner could be tricky business. If the electrode on the head was not pressed down firmly enough, the electricity could arc and burn the convict's head off.

When a man named Martin D. Loppy was electrocuted, his left eyeball popped, causing the aqueous humor to run down his cheek. And when William G. Taylor was electrocuted in Auburn on July 27, 1893, the jolt caused his legs to shoot straight out with such force that they ripped the front legs loose from the electric chair. A wooden box had to be shoved under the front of the chair before the execution could continue.

Gradually, as the kinks were worked out, additional states switched over to the electric chair as a more efficient means of dispatching the criminal element—Ohio in 1896, Massachusetts in 1898, and New Jersey in 1906.

Other states were slower to fall into line. In some cases, it was argued that a convicted killer should be made to suffer for his crime, and electrocution was too quick. Proponents of the chair suggested that the agony of waiting could be as torturous as the final moment itself, and just thinking about that massive jolt would be a part of the punishment.

On July 13, 1928, the State of Kentucky electrocuted seven convicted killers in one day at the state penitentiary at Eddyville.

The death march began at 12:15 a.m. with Hascue Dockery, 21, of Harlan, Kentucky. In rapid succession Milford "Red" Lawson, 35, of Corbin, Kentucky; Charles Paul Mitra, 23, of St. Louis, Missouri; and Orlando "Red" Seymour, 21, of Louisville—all white men—were led to the fatal chair.

The executions of the four white men were followed quickly by those of three black men, William Moore and James Howard, both of Louisville, and Clarence McQueen, of Cynthiana, Kentucky.

The State of Illinois also made the switch in 1928, and the first electrocution proved to be a triple-header. Two black men and an American Indian died in the newly-installed electric chair in the state prison at Joliet on December 15, for the murder of William Beck, a 34-year-old farmer from Milburn, just outside of Waukegan.

The slayers, who had robbed the farmer of $2,500 in treasury notes, were nabbed after one of them, Dominic Bresette, a 20-year-old Chippewa Indian from Wisconsin, complained to Lake County Sheriff Lawrence Doolittle that his two partners, Claude Clark, 41, and John Brown, 32, both of Chicago, had cheated him out of his share of the loot.

Clark became the first person to be executed by electrocution in Illinois. He was led into the chair at 7:12 a.m., and lifted out dead by a guard six minutes later. Brown was led in at 7:21, and his body was carried out at 7:28. Bresette was seated in the chair at 7:35 a.m. and carried out dead at 7:41.

A total of thirty-five men witnessed the electrocutions, including the twelve Waukegan jurors who had imposed the death penalty. Also among the spectators were Sheriff Doolittle, three newspaper reporters, four physicians, Catholic and Protestant chaplains from the prison, five prison guards, Warden Elmer J. Green and other prison officials.

Bresette's last act before "riding the thunderbolt" was to give Sheriff Doolittle a letter, asking Anna Beck, the widow of the murdered farmer, for forgiveness.

BOOK IV

THE THUNDERBOLT

As in Book II, each of the succeeding chapters
carries the headline that appeared in a newspaper
of the day.

1

FIRST ELECTRIC EXECUTIONS IN COOK COUNTY

FEBRUARY 20, 1929

While most of the state's executions would be carried out at the old prison in Joliet, since it was hardly economical for every county to maintain its own electric chair, Cook County had enough criminals and a large enough budget to construct a chair of its own. The imposing, black-painted wooden device was installed on a gray rubber mat in the old 1852 wing of the county jail at Dearborn and Illinois Streets.

The first electrocution took place the following year, and it was a doubleheader. Anthony Grecco became the first man to die in Cook County's new chair, quickly followed by Charles Walz, who would be the last to die in the old jail building.

Walz, 17, and Grecco, 19, were arrested for fatally shooting plainclothes policeman Arthur Esau, 37, on a spring day in 1928, when he walked in on an armed robbery of the Community Drug Store on North Clark Street. The two youths had embarked on a holdup spree to get money to buy clothes and jewelry for their girlfriends, Dolly Kazor and Gertrude Piatkowski, who called herself Trudy Ryan.

Esau was the fourth police officer slain by robbers in the month of April, and the eighth since the beginning of the year. The public was in an uproar, and police lost no time in arresting the suspects after one of them left his cap and jacket at the scene.

The youthful bandits were brought in chains to a courtroom in the Desplaines Street police station, where Deputy Police Commander William E. O'Connor and Detective Chief Michael Grady had gathered 250 robbery victims, to see whether any could identify the suspects.

As Walz and Grecco stood facing the crowd in a lineup with three other men, O'Connor announced, "One of these men shot and killed a policeman. They went into a drug store..."

"Just a minute, commissioner," interrupted Walz, cockily rattling his chains. "You'd better let the man that knows this story tell it."

O'Connor, somewhat taken aback, nodded for the prisoner to go ahead.

"Gimme a cigarette," the bushy-haired Walz demanded, smiling at the crowd. Walz was given a cigarette, took a long draw on it, and continued with his story:

"All right. Me and Tony Grecco—this fellow here on my left—went into a drug store at 3404 North Clark Street on April 27. It was a stick-up. We took a clerk and a customer back to the rear and tied 'em up.

"Tony watched them two and I went out front. In come a fellow. It was Esau, I found out later. 'How do you get these boxes of pens open?' I said. This Esau says he'll show me. He steps behind the counter and opens a box. I pull my gun and tell him to put 'em up. He jumps back and I plug him.

"The police have been telling that I shot him twice. That's bunk. I shot him three times—once in the head, once in the heart and once in the shoulder. Sure, I killed him, and I ain't scared to say so."

Walz interrupted his narrative to giggle, took a few puffs on the cigarette, and continued:

"I hollered to Tony to bring my coat and hat. I'd laid them down on a chair. But he came out in too big a hurry and we left them. We took a taxicab, changed once and went to my mother's home on South La Salle Street. I laid low and sent Tony to get Trudy Ryan and Dolly Kazor, the girls that had been staying with us at the Wacker Hotel. Later we moved to Catalpa Avenue, where Dolly's sister lives.

"Ladies and gentlemen, I am telling you a true story!" he said, pausing for effect. Then, nodding toward the two girlfriends, who were in the audience, he added, "If it hadn't been for them we wouldn't have killed anyone."

At this point the commissioner asked whether any of the victims of other robberies could identify either of the two youths.

"That won't be necessary," Walz grinned. Looking out over the crowd, he pointed out a dozen people whom he had robbed.

Walz and Grecco were subsequently tried and convicted of Officer Esau's murder, and sentenced to death.

The first electrocution in Cook County was originally scheduled to have been that of David Shanks, convicted murderer of Jennie Constance, a Northwestern University student, on January 30.

Shanks shared the death cell with Walz and Grecco. When it appeared that his time had finally come, he willed his entire estate, consisting of $1.01, to his two cellmates. Then he won an eleventh-hour stay of execution, and hotly demanded his money back.

Shanks' death penalty was ultimately commuted, leaving Grecco and Walz to test the new form of execution on their own. After several stays their time ran out.

On the last afternoon of their lives, February 19, 1929, Grecco's parents and sister called to talk with him through the thick wire mesh of his cell, while Walz was visited by his father and 15-year-old brother. Grecco, a fair-haired youth with flattened features and pale blue eyes, was dressed in his Sunday best, a brown suit and clean white shirt. The tousle-haired Walz slouched comfortably in an old striped sweater that buttoned down the front.

At six o'clock restaurateur Joseph Stein sent over two fried chicken dinners, with green peas, mashed turnips, hashed brown potatoes and currant cake. It was the same "last meal" the two condemned prisoners had wolfed down the previous Thursday night, before winning a stay of execution.

After dinner the two were handcuffed and taken down the main stairway, to be marched across the jail courtyard under the murky winter sky, to the old jail wing where the grim death chair waited. It was their last bit of fresh air, such as it was. They were lodged in a cell on the second tier, where the tops of their heads were shaved, and their right trouser legs were slit to the knee.

At two minutes before midnight the door to their cell was thrown open, and three guards entered to tell Grecco that his time had come. He had removed his coat, shirt and tie, and wore a scapular over his bare chest as he walked from the cell, followed by the Reverend Ernest Kaufholdt, the jail's Catholic chaplain. A black hood had been placed over his head, and two of the guards guided him so he would not stumble.

Walz, left behind in the cell, was heard whistling gamely as his partner was taken away.

The blindfolded Grecco was marched down a short flight of iron stairs, through a crowd of eighty spectators sitting on wooden benches, and positioned in front of the chair.

At the stroke of midnight he was pressed firmly into the seat, as six guards sprang forward to fix the leather straps around his chest and abdomen, clamp his arms to the arms of the chair, and to apply the copper electrodes to his shaven head and right leg. An elastic cord was passed under his chin to hold the headpiece in place.

At 12:01 a.m. Warden Edward J. Fogarty motioned everyone away, and turned to give the signal for the switch to be thrown. Suddenly the crowd gasped. Father Ernest had stepped forward with a crucifix in one hand, and laid his other hand on the condemned man's shoulder as he murmured words of prayer.

"Do you want to be killed?" Fogarty exclaimed gruffly.

The priest backed quickly away. A faint whining, like a vacuum cleaner, was heard from the control room. There was a sharp crack, like that of a mallet striking wood, as Grecco's head snapped back, his spine arched and his body jerked, as the 2,300 volts hit him. He remained in that strained position for two minutes. A thin spiral of smoke wisped upward from the electrode on his leg.

At 12:03 the electricity was turned off and the body sagged. Dr. Francis McNamara, the jail physician, Dr. Konstantine Theodore and Dr. Victor Likenhauz stepped forward and pressed their stethoscopes to the prisoner's crimson chest. "That's all," Dr. McNamara said, as the other two physicians nodded in agreement.

Grecco's body was quickly unstrapped, placed in a wicker casket, and carried from the room. The body had scarcely been removed when Walz was marched in still whistling under the black cap. As the guards positioned him in front of the chair he was heard to say, "I'm all right. Leave me alone."

He then sat down in the warm chair, and as the straps were being tightened, called out, "Well, good-bye, folks. Good-bye. Good...." Suddenly his throat muscles bulged and his body jerked taut as the switch was thrown and the 2,300 volt charge coursed through his system.

At 12:13 he, too, was pronounced dead. Walz, who had celebrated his eighteenth birthday while in jail, had just become the youngest person ever executed in Cook County.

As his body was placed in a wicker casket to be carried out, Chief Deputy Sheriff Charles W. Peters, who had officiated at more than forty hangings, declared, "This was far more humane than the gallows."

In cleaning out the men's cell after the execution, a deputy found a poem entitled "The End of My Earthly Trial," which Grecco had written in pencil on a sheet of lined tablet paper:

> 'Tis hard to leave this world behind,
> And yet if I must go
> I take it all for granted that
> Fate has willed it so.
>
> I have no fear of dying,
> But the one thing I regret
> Is the grief I've caused my loved ones,
> That they will never forget.
>
> If on earth there would be justice,
> As I'm sure there is above,
> In each heart would be no hatred,
> Only everlasting love.
>
> And there would be no electric chair
> That I would have to face,
> For they would know I'm innocent
> And save me from disgrace.
>
> My hopes on earth are shattered,
> I know that I must try
> To forgive the ones who wronged me
> As I prepare to die.
>
> And when I meet my Maker,
> On my face will be a smile;
> I bid farewell to everyone
> At the end of my earthly trial.

2

2 NEGROES DIE IN CHAIR FOR HOLDUP KILLING

JUNE 20, 1921

Exactly four months to the day after Anthony Grecco and Charles Walz were executed, the electric chair was called upon for the second "double header" in a row. This time the occupants of the seat would be Napoleon Glover and Morgan Swan.

What was new, however, was the setting. An improved chair had been constructed and set up in the basement of the new county jail, just west of the new Criminal Courts Building at Twenty Sixth Street and California Avenue. No longer would it be necessary to risk an escape attempt while marching a condemned man across the courtyard. He would simply be transferred to one of three downstairs death cells adjoining the room containing the chair.

And, since the new jail was situated far from generous Joe Stein's downtown restaurant, the traditional "last meal" for a condemned man would have to be prepared in the jail kitchen.

Glover, 19, and Swan, 23, had been sentenced to death by Judge Marcus Kavanagh, after pleading guilty to the murder of Charles Metlock during a South Side drug store robbery on November 11, 1928. In fact, the two men had insisted on pleading guilty, even after Kavanagh warned them that he felt it was his duty to impose the death penalty.

Judge Kavanagh granted two stays of execution, while the condemned men appealed his sentence.

At one hearing the judge himself appeared before the pardon and parole board to oppose clemency for the confessed killers. "There are no fewer than 500 young Negroes on the South Side whose business is robbery and whose instrument is the gun," he argued. "I have been told and have good reason to believe, that these men will murder anyone for the princely sum of $10."

The judge added that he strongly advocated the whipping post as a deterrent to robbers and rapists.

A week before the two were scheduled to die on June 20, 1919, the judge did an about-face, and went before the state pardon board to recommend that the two death sentences he meted out be commuted to life imprisonment. Citing the two last-minute reprieves the prisoners had won, he told the board, "Inasmuch as they have already twice suffered the punishment of anticipation of death, I believe they will be sufficiently punished by a life sentence."

The board declined to interfere with the scheduled electrocutions.

On the night before Glover and Swan were to die, Assistant Jailer Frank Dahlke and jail chef Walter Freeman provided them a chicken dinner with all the trimmings. Glover calmly devoured the meal but Swan, clearly frightened at the prospect of what lay ahead, refused food and nervously paced the floor of his cell.

As the midnight hour drew near the condemned men's lawyer, Roland Libonati, made a telephone appeal directly to Governor Louis Emmerson. The governor told Libonati, "I granted a stay two weeks ago, and I do not feel justified in interfering again."

Precisely at 1 a.m. Warden David Moneypenny opened

the door to the death chamber and entered the room, where the electric chair sat facing several wooden benches occupied by forty news reporters and official witnesses.

Swan, his face covered by a black mask, was marched in, flanked by two guards, and with a priest holding a crucifix leading the grim procession. Five guards, who had spent the previous day rehearsing, quickly strapped him into the chair and applied the electrodes to his shaven scalp and right leg.

"Father!" Swan called out from under the mask.

"I am here," replied the Reverend Ernest Kaufholdt, the jail chaplain.

A moment later, at 1:04 a.m., Swan's body stiffened as the first jolt of 1,800 volts was applied at a signal from the warden.

After six seconds the current was turned off, and the body relaxed. Doctors Konstantine Theodore and J.C. Byer put their stethoscopes to Swan's chest. His heart was still beating.

The two physicians said, "He's still alive," and stepped away from the chair. The figure in the chair stiffened again as the current was turned back on, this time increased to 2,300 volts. A few moments later the doctors stepped forward. "He is still alive!"

For the third time Swan's body snapped rigid as another 2,300 bolts was shot through his system. At 1:10 a.m. he was finally pronounced dead. His body was unstrapped, placed on a stretcher, and wheeled out of the room.

Six minutes later the tall, gangly teen-aged Glover was led the fifty paces down the hall to the death chamber and strapped into the lethal chair. "Say a prayer for me," were his last words.

"May God have mercy on your soul," Father Kaufholdt replied.

The current was turned on at 1:17, and one minute

later, after the application of three shocks, Glover, too, was declared dead.

The first electrocutions in the new jail had gone off without a hitch. There would be plenty more to come.

3

NEGRO SLAYER OF POLICEMAN DIES IN CHAIR

APRIL 11, 1930

Aaron Woodward, a 35-year-old black man, was caught in the act of robbing a clergyman, the Reverend W.D. Pertiolay, on a South Side street on the night of July 29, 1928. Woodward tried to shoot his way out, using Reverend Pertiolay as a shield. The minister and a police officer, Jerry O'Connell, were slain in an exchange of gunfire, in which Woodward was wounded and captured.

Woodward was convicted of the policeman's murder, and sentenced to die in July of 1929. Six times, however, after final preparations had been made, he was spared. Finally, on April 11, 1930, the appeals well ran dry, although Woodward refused to give up hope. As he paced the floor of his cell, puffing on a large cigar, on the night before he was scheduled to die, he joked with Warden David Moneypenny:

"I'm that great big man from the South—didn't know that, did you? No, I'm not nervous—don't expect to be. You see, I've made this trip six times before but always got a reprieve."

There would be no more reprieves, however. As the death hour approached, Moneypenny ordered extra guards stationed throughout the jail after hearing rumors of an attempted jailbreak while authorities were busy with the execution.

Woodward's last request was for a steak dinner. "A man can take it easier with a full stomach," he told the warden.

Witnesses began to file into the execution chamber shortly after 11 p.m., taking their seats before a glassed-in stage on which the electric chair sat, like an exhibit in a giant display case.

After-effects of previous electrocutions—the smell of burning hair or singed flesh, and the aroma of human feces—had resulted in the chair being installed in a room sealed off from the witnesses. The anal sphincter relaxes upon death, causing the bowel to release its contents. The results were not always pleasing to the senses, even when nothing else went wrong during an execution.

The condemned man's entrance to the chamber was announced by the flapping of a canvas drape over the doorway. Blindfolded, Woodward was ushered into the room by three beefy guards, followed by the Reverend Joseph Higgins, repeating the litany for the dying.

As he was being strapped into the chair, Woodward attempted to remove the mask over his eyes. "A man's got the right to face death with open, seeing eyes," he argued.

"I'm sorry, Aaron, but that's against regulations," Warden Moneypenny told him.

The prisoner then interrupted Reverend Higgins, saying, "I have great confidence in the mercy of God. I am not afraid to face my maker. Father, I want to say only one prayer."

Then, repeating after the clergyman, he began: "Oh, Lord, before whom I am about to appear...

Abruptly his body stiffened as Moneypenny threw the switch at 12:08 a.m.

After the current was turned off, a guard stepped forward and briefly studied the lifeless form in the chair. He then unbuttoned Woodward's shirt and laid it open for medical examination. A panel of thirteen doctors applied stethoscopes to the ruddy chest and pronounced him dead at 12:11 a.m.

Two minutes later Woodward's limp figure was unbuckled, lifted out of the chair, and carried off the brightly-lighted stage, as the reporters ran to the phones to call in their stories.

4

AUGUST VOGEL, WHIM SLAYER, DIES IN CHAIR

MAY 9, 1930

On the night of October 15, 1929, a group of waitresses and soda fountain employees from the Walgreen's drug store at 41 South State Street got together for a late-night house party. When the gin ran out, they all piled into a borrowed car and went out to look for more.

At 75th Street and Stony Island Avenue their car brushed another, driven by Lyle Perrenoud, a 27-year-old salesman, who was driving his wife and another couple home.

The driver of the other car, 22-year-old August Vogel, got out and calmly shot Perrenoud through the heart. Vogel, a former Walgreen's soda jerk, fled town after the shooting, and was arrested in Wooster, Ohio, the following evening.

The handsome, friendly-looking Vogel was brought back to Chicago, convicted of murder, and sentenced to death. Judge Otto Kerner scheduled his execution for May 9, 1930—Good Friday.

Nervously cracking his knuckles while chewing gum, the blond-haired prisoner sat in his cell in the Cook County jail and talked about his chances of escaping the electric chair.

"I still have hope that something will happen to save me. Did anybody ever die on Good Friday? I guess they want to make an example of me. But I don't want to die, not when the spring is just breaking.

"My mother doesn't know anything about this. She thinks I'm out on parole, and that they are just trying to convict me as a suspect. Mother can't read the papers and they have kept the radio tuned away from the news flashes. My wife, Katherine, and my sisters, Annabelle and Bertie, tell me that she will die if she hears about this....

"Dick Loeb only got life for what he did. I was his cell mate in 1924. I was in for a robbery. They called him the 'thrill slayer' and now they call me the 'whim slayer.' Ain't that kinda funny?"

Vogel's brother, George, who was along on the fatal night, and was sentenced to prison for his part in the salesman's murder, confessed to Warden Henry C. Hill that he was the actual slayer, in an effort to save his brother.

Before going to the chair, however, August wrote a note exonerating him:

"I, August Vogel, being of sound mind, do hereby swear the shooting of Lyle Perrenoud was by my hand, and no one else's. I make this statement, knowing that I am about to die."

That afternoon his mother, Goldie Vogel Mitchell, and Vogel's two sisters were permitted one last visit with him in the jail. Mrs. Mitchell still did not know that her son had been sentenced to death. She was told that he was in jail for a parole violation.

"Promise you'll be good when you get out," she begged her son.

"I promise, mother," he said. "And I'll send you a telegram on Mother's Day."

Two hours before he was scheduled to die, Vogel sent for Warden David Moneypenny, and told him:

"I don't want to die with a lie on my lips. I lied when I

said this killing was a result of gin and anger. I deliberately planned a robbery. I was watching for anybody worth robbing. I had a revolver and an automobile. I know how to handle revolvers, but this was the first time I had ever handled an automatic. As I pressed it against the man and told him to put his hands up, the gun went off, although, so help me God, I didn't mean to shoot."

Shortly before 1 a.m. on May 9, Warden Moneypenny returned to the cell and told Vogel it was time. The man who was about to die walked with seeming calm to the electric chair, accompanied by Father Otto Ernst, the Catholic chaplain.

The electrodes were quickly applied, and a jolt of 1,900 volts was sent crashing through his body for two minutes. After a brief pause, a second charge of 900 volts was administered for one minute.

Vogel was pronounced dead at 1:06 a.m.

He was to have died at one minute past midnight. Warden Moneypenny took Daylight Saving Time into consideration, however, and performed the execution under Central Standard Time, giving Vogel one extra hour of life, in the event of an eleventh-hour reprieve. It never came.

In handing down the death penalty against Vogel, Judge Kerner had issued the following statement:

"The purpose of punishment is that it shall be a lesson to the offender and a deterrent to others. The court is unable to imagine any form of punishment which might be a lesson to the defendant, in view of the fact that he has heretofore served time for robbery, and notwithstanding that fact again engaged in a robbery while armed with a deadly weapon. To impose a life sentence would not be a deterrent. What must be made evident is that a murderer, such as this defendant, shall never again be at liberty to walk among his fellow men."

5

BANK GUARD'S
KILLERS DIE IN
ELECTRIC CHAIR

OCTOBER 3, 1930

The noontime holdup of the Franklin Trust & Savings Bank on January 18, 1929, sent shock waves throughout the entire city. Five men with pistols drawn swarmed into the crowded bank at the busy intersection of 35th Street and Michigan Boulevard and started shooting.

Martin French, a 75-year-old bank guard, was mortally wounded. Leo Poquette, the assistant cashier, was hit by a bullet in the thigh as he dropped to the floor to reach for an alarm. Edgar F. Olson, another assistant cashier, lunged toward a drawer containing a pistol, grabbed it, and had it shot away with part of his hand.

After terrorizing the lunch-hour crowd of nearly a hundred patrons, the bandits fled with only $1,000. All of the robbers were black, as was the slain bank guard, a former Chicago policeman.

Rewards totaling $8,000 were posted for the killers of the bank guard, as one of the biggest manhunts in the city's history was mounted. By dawn of the following day eighteen notorious gunmen had been taken into custody and scores of unsolved crimes were cleared up.

Four of those arrested were identified as the bank robbers—Leonard Shadlow, Lafon Fisher, Leon Brown and Melvin Jenkins.

The four not only confessed, under police beatings, but agreed to re-enact the deadly event. Bruised, black-eyed, manacled, and under heavy guard, they were taken back to the bank, where unloaded revolvers were placed in their hands. Various employees assumed the duties they were occupied with at the moment the robbers burst in.

Jenkins, taking a position near the front door, raised his empty .45 caliber pistol toward the interior of the bank and told police, "I was like this."

"I was here," explained Shadlow, weapon in hand. The other two bandits likewise showed where they were at the time.

Their subsequent trial became the first in Illinois history in which the newly-developed science of ballistics was put into play.

Major Calvin H. Goddard, a New York firearms expert, testified that the bullet that killed French had come from Leon Brown's gun. Shadlow's weapon was the one that wounded Poquette, and Fisher's gun had shot Olson.

The three gunmen were sentenced to death. Jenkins, who turned state's evidence and testified against his partners, was sentenced to life in prison.

For the next eighteen months lawyers for the trio engaged in a desperate battle to save them from the electric chair. During that time they twice carried the case to the State Supreme Court, were granted seven stays of execution by Governor Louis L. Emmerson, and allowed two sanity trials. The Chicago and Cook County Bankers Associations vigorously opposed the stays, terming them "a woeful delay of justice."

By the time every avenue of escape had been exhausted, young Fisher had become a hopeless cripple, paralyzed from the waist down because of a tubercular spine, and had to be carried to the execution chamber. Some argued his paralysis was the result of police beatings, but police scoffed at the charge.

Fisher and Shadlow were scheduled to be electrocuted on October 3, 1930. Brown had won yet another stay, while his lawyers appealed a court ruling in which he had been declared sane.

As the hour of their impending deaths drew near, Shadlow and Fisher prayed and sang religious songs. Walter Freeman, the county jail chef, prepared a last meal of duck, with all the trimmings.

Shadlow would be the first to die. Sheriff's deputies came by the cell for him at the stroke of midnight, and he walked calmly to his doom. He was strapped into the chair and the switch was thrown at 12:08 a.m. One minute and forty-two seconds later he was pronounced dead by a jury of eight physicians.

The helpless Fisher was then carried into the death chamber by four deputies. He was strapped into the chair at 12:14. His body resisted the initial surge of electricity, and a second charge had to be applied before the doctors pronounced him dead at 12:20.

The bank murders for which they were executed had indeed stunned Chicago—but not for long.

Less than a month later, on February 14, 1929, seven men were lined up against the wall of a garage on North Clark Street and machine-gunned and shotgunned to death in what will forever be known as the infamous St. Valentine's Day Massacre.

No one was ever brought to justice for Chicago's most violent valentine.

6

BROWN DIES IN CHAIR FOR BANK HOLDUP SLAYING

NOVEMBER 28, 1930

It was Thanksgiving Day when Leon Brown was called upon to pay the supreme price for the wanton shooting of bank guard Martin French, the former Chicago police officer.

Brown's life had been spared earlier by Criminal Court Judge Charles A. Williams, who was under the misapprehension that the prisoner's lawyers needed time to appeal the death sentence. When he learned that the Supreme Court had already refused to hear an appeal, he set the electrocution for November 28.

November 27 was Thanksgiving Day, and Brown made the very most of his last hours before meeting his maker.

At noon he feasted on cooked goose, the county jail's traditional Thanksgiving fare. Then, when asked what he wanted for his last meal, he ordered a turkey, all for himself. A twelve-pound turkey was procured and cooked to his specifications for his evening meal.

After dinner the prisoner's head was shaved, his trousers were cut off at the knees, and his shirt was opened at the throat. At the stroke of midnight Brown was taken from his cell and dragged unwillingly by two burly guards to the death chamber. The Reverend John Higgins walked closely behind, chanting a prayer.

Sheriff John A. Traeger and his team of deputies were waiting when the death party entered the room. Brown, whose knees were beginning to sag, was quickly seated into the chair, the hood was lowered and the leather straps were tightened. The sheriff raised his hand, and an unidentified executioner, unseen by the witnesses, pulled the switch at 12:03 a.m.

Warden David Moneypenny had been studying electrocutions throughout America, and had developed a "new method" of execution, which he felt would dispatch the victim of the chair as rapidly as possible while at the same time doing the least possible damage to his corpse.

Two thousand volts of electricity shot into his body and coursed through him for seven seconds. Then the switch was pushed back until a meter registered 500 volts. It remained in that position for another minute and a half.

Brown was in the death chair just a little more than three minutes. Two minutes and fifteen seconds after he was given the initial jolt, six physicians, headed by Dr. Konstantine Theodore and Dr. Francis McNamara, the jail physician, pronounced him dead.

Two professors from Notre Dame University, who said they were conducting a "scientific investigation," were also permitted to apply their stethoscopes to Brown's unbeating heart.

He was then unstrapped from the chair and his body carried to a slab in the county morgue.

7

LENHARDT DIES IN CHAIR; GLAD OF GOOD DEED

DECEMBER 12, 1930

On October 4, 1930, convicted killer William Lenhardt—the "Lone Wolf Of Cleveland"—almost duplicated Terrible Tommy O'Connor's disappearing act. But while O'Connor cheated the hangman by going over the wall, Lenhardt was prepared to shoot his way to freedom. He might have made it, too, had not one of his fellow death row inmates let the cat out of the bag.

The talkative inmate, Frank H. Bell, awaiting death in the electric chair for the murder of a restaurant owner, was talking to Sergeant Frank Donohue, an investigator for Coroner Herman Bundesen, when Donohue wondered aloud, "What makes you so nervous, Bell?"

The prisoner swallowed several times and blurted out, "There's a gun on this floor. "

"Where?"

"In Lenhardt's cell."

"What's the idea, Bell?" Donohue pressed.

"Donohue, there's going to be a jail break at 3:30," Bell whispered. "Lenhardt's going to bolt for it."

The time of day mentioned was significant. That was the hour when visiting time expired, and scores of visitors would be streaming out through the jail gate.

Lenhardt's cell was searched. A fully loaded .38 caliber automatic pistol was found stashed under his pillow, along with several steel saw blades, fifteen extra bullets, and a coil of rope with which he had intended to tie up the lone guard on duty in the tier.

An examination of the cell itself revealed that Lenhardt had sawed away a section of his cell door and was ready to go.

In the street outside the jail, Assistant Warden George Gibson and jail clerk Hugo Pfeuffer recognized a former inmate, Howard Soske, waiting for Lenhardt in a taxicab. Soske admitted his role in the escape plot, and said the gun had been obtained from Lenhardt's mother, Julia Glovka, who lived in Cleveland, Ohio. Soske said he slipped the weapon, ammunition, rope and saw blades to Joseph Connior, a jail guard, who smuggled them to the prisoner.

Connior, the 62-year-old father of seven children, admitted smuggling packages to Lenhardt's cell for a payoff of $19. "But I didn't know what was in them," he insisted.

The shifty-eyed Lenhardt had every reason to want to escape from jail. The only future he had on the inside was the electric chair. An Army pensioner with a police record for armed robbery, he had been sentenced to die for the fatal shooting of Milton Valasopulos, a South Side restaurant owner, during a holdup.

Two days before his scheduled execution, his mother, the jail guard and a trusty who was in on the plot went on trial for their roles in the abortive escape attempt. All were freed by a Criminal Court jury after Lenhardt testified in their behalf.

Lenhardt considered his mother's acquittal his last good deed. "'I am glad that I could do one decent thing at the end," he said. "But it hurts to think of her left all alone to make her way through life."

At an impromptu interview as the hour of his death

approached, Lenhardt told reporters, "I am not afraid to die. Watch me in the chair. I will smile then, as I smile now."

"Have you got anything to smile about?" one reporter asked.

"Yes—I saved my mother from the penitentiary," he said.

The prisoner's last request was that Miss Charlotte Siavitt, the attorney who had successfully defended his mother, be permitted to see him die. The request was denied, on the ground that no woman had ever been permitted to witness an execution since the end of public hangings—with the exception of Kathryn De Nauoley, the chorus girl who had slipped into the gallows room disguised as a man in 1925.

Charlotte Siavitt accompanied Julia Glovka, a tired old woman in frayed clothes, on her last visit to her son, on the night of December 11, 1930, just hours before he was scheduled to die. Lenhardt, freshly shaven and immaculately dressed, told the elderly woman, "Good-bye, sweetheart, good-bye. You are the only sweetheart I ever had." Then, sobbing himself, he added, "Don't cry, mother. Everything will be all right. Thank you for everything you did for me. Maybe your life will be pleasanter after a while."

At 6 p.m., after his mother had left, Lenhardt turned to one of his guards and remarked, "Six hours and five minutes more. Then...what?"

Two hours later Lenhardt's young wife, Agnes, tried to get in to see him, but was told it was too late. Preparations for the execution were already underway. The prisoner's head was being shaved, his suit jacket was laid aside while his white silk shirt was unbuttoned at the throat, and his trousers were cut off at the knees, like English shorts. He was then given the last rites of the Catholic Church.

Newly elected Sheriff William D. Meyering, who would be officiating at his first execution, called for the prisoner at midnight. He was accompanied by former Sheriff John E.

Traeger. The "Lone Wolf of Cleveland," displaying the same careless bravado he had maintained throughout his seven and a half months in jail, walked steadily to the ominous black chair, flanked by six armed jail officers.

Warden David Moneypenny was waiting in the execution chamber when the death party arrived. Lenhardt, wearing a black silk mask over his face, looked like a boy in short pants as he was guided into the only unoccupied seat in the room, and strapped in by five deputies at 12:01 a.m. A group of fifty witnesses watched the drama intently from the other side of a large glass panel.

One minute later the current was turned on, and his body stiffened at the shock of 1,900 bone-cracking volts. Four jolts were administered in all, before he was pronounced dead at 12:14 a.m.

The official pronouncement was made by Dr. W.E. Buehler, a member of Governor Louis Emmerson's Board of Pardons.

At the same moment Lenhardt died, John E. Preston, 34, was being readied for the electric chair in the old Joliet Penitentiary for the murder of Agnes Johnston, a 26-year-old stenographer, near West Chicago. He won a last-minute stay of execution, however, on a plea by his lawyers that he was insane.

After three trials, Preston was finally declared sane, and the death penalty was carried out at 5:18 in the morning of October 9, 1931.

8

FOUR DIE IN CHAIR;
200 WATCH

OCTOBER 16, 1931

The electric chair was dusted off only once in the entire year of 1931, but in the pre-dawn hours of October 16 it received a workout that would never be matched. Before the sun rose that morning, four men were marched to the chair, strapped in, and carried away dead. The quadruple electrocution was a record that would stand until the grim piece of jailhouse furniture was "retired" more than thirty years later.

The men who "went to the chair" that autumn morning were:

• Frank Jordan, 20 years old, a two-gun bandit who fatally shot Policemen Anthony Ruthy and Patrick Durkin at the downtown corner of Michigan Avenue and Randolph Street.

• Charles Rocco, 24 years old, who stabbed Courtney Merrill, a South Side banker, to death in a robbery.

• John Popescue, age 21, who was Rocco's partner in the Merrill murder.

• Richard Sullivan, age 35, the killer of Christ Patras, a restaurant manager.

A fifth man was also to have been executed that night.

He was Frank H. Bell, 31, known as "The Squealer," because he had tipped off authorities on William Lenhardt's intended jailbreak.

Bell, who had been Sullivan's partner in the Patras murder, and was also involved with Sullivan in the slaying of *Chicago Tribune* reporter Jake Lingle, won a reprieve just 35 minutes before he was to have been strapped into the chair.

Among those who had gone to bat for Bell was Warden David Moneypenny, who said Bell probably saved his life and that of other jailers by betraying his friends.

Meanwhile, a tragic vignette was unfolding as the prisoners awaited their fate.

James Rocco, a construction laborer in Suffern, New York, and his wife had not heard from their son, Charles, since he ran away from home some years earlier. Then, on a Friday afternoon in 1931, a neighbor brought them a New York newspaper which carried a picture of a man who resembled their missing son. The Roccos studied the news photo. They were sure it was their boy. An accompanying article stated that he and a companion, John Popescue, were scheduled to be executed for the murder of the Chicago banker.

The stunned parents went to Police Chief C.L. Lunney of Suffern and pleaded for his help. "Can that boy on death row be our son?" they asked. "We don't know what to do."

Lunney sent the newspaper clipping to Sergeant Joseph Starshak, of the Chicago police department's missing persons bureau. Starshak assigned Detective Petrie Mitchell to check it out. Mitchell went to the county jail to talk to the prisoner.

On seeing the clipping Rocco, a "tough guy" who had refused to discuss his past, broke down and admitted he was the long missing son.

"I didn't want my folks to know that I was going to die in the chair," he said. "I hoped that my family would never find out. Now that they know about me, I'm going to write home. I know it will be harder to go, now that they know."

On the evening of their deaths, Rocco, Popescue, Jordan and Sullivan were placed in one cell, so they could spend their final hours together. Trying to blot out what lay ahead for them, they played cards and listened to phonograph records. Given their choice of a last meal, all had ordered chicken.

"I really don't mind dying, as long as Bell goes first," Sullivan bitterly told his cell mates as he picked at a chicken bone. "I can't forgive a stool pigeon. I'll get a big laugh when they turn the juice on that double-crosser."

The hated Bell, in an isolation cell nearby, paced the floor nervously. When authorities came for him, he did not know until he'd been removed from death row that he had won a last-minute reprieve. The other four prisoners also believed he was being taken to the electric chair.

With Bell out of the picture, the handsome Jordan became the first to go. Leaving his last poker hand behind, he walked firmly to the death chamber at 12:11 a.m., led by Warden Moneypenny and flanked by several deputies. His eyes were blindfolded, and he wore an undershirt, house slippers, and trousers rolled up at the knees. Some 200 spectators watched as he was quickly strapped into the chair. One minute later the switch was thrown, and 1,900 volts shot into his body. After four minutes the electricity was turned off. Jordan was pronounced dead at 12:17 by a jury of fourteen physicians.

Jail guards hurriedly removed his limp body while Moneypenny and the deputies went back for the next victim, as a Catholic priest stood against the rear wall, intoning the prayer for the dead.

Then it was discovered that the electrode that fit over the prisoner's head had been damaged, and frantic repairs were made.

Rocco, his thick, bushy hair shaved off, was brought

into the room at 12:21, and he was inmediately strapped into the warm chair. The current was applied a moment later. At 12:24 the juice was turned off, and five minutes later the jury of physicians agreed that Rocco, like his predecessor, was dead.

Rocco's partner in crime, Popescue, was brought in next, and the procedure was repeated. As the current was turned on at 12:32, the initial jolt hit him with such force that the black mask fell off, giving horrified spectators a grim look at his contorted face. The juice was shut off at 12:35, and he was pronounced dead at 12:38.

Sullivan was the last to die. There was a triumphant smile on his face as he was marched to the chair, secure in the belief that the hated Bell had finally gotten what was coming to him. He died without ever knowing that Bell had been spared.

"I didn't have the heart to tell him," Sheriff William Meyering said. "I didn't want to make Sullivan's unhappy last hour any unhappier."

There is one postscript to the story:

Several hours before Sullivan went to the chair, Meyering received a dispatch from Manchester, New Hampshire, indicating that the prisoner had lived and died under an alias. His real name was Mark J. Davis, and he was the "black sheep" of a respected New England family.

9

BELL, WAITING FOR DEATH TONIGHT, PENS NOTES

JANUARY 8, 1932

If Frank Bell thought he was going to escape the chair by squealing on his pals, he was fatally mistaken. The coveted stay of execution he had won proved to be only temporary. The hated convict, a boyish-faced man with rat-like eyes, followed his cellmates to the death chamber on January 8, 1932.

Specifically, Bell had been sentenced to death, along with Richard Sullivan, for the fatal shooting of Christ Patras, manager of the Villa Rica Cafe at 2572 North Clark Street.

While on death row he also implicated himself and several others in the murder of *Chicago Tribune* reporter Alfred "Jake" Lingle, in the Randolph Street underpass to the Illinois Central station two years earlier. Bell claimed that he drove the get-away car for Patras and Joseph Traum, an Indiana gangster, after they crept up behind Lingle and shot him in the back of the head. He claimed that Patras was killed because he reneged on his promise to pay for Lingle's murder.

A massive investigation, spurred on by the *Tribune,* determined that Bell's story was a hoax. A man named Leo V. Brothers was subsequently convicted of Lingle's murder, and sentenced to fourteen years in prison.

Bell's only motive in telling the lie was an apparently frenzied attempt to stay out of the chair. It didn't work, however.

A born Baptist, he converted to Catholicism the day before he was scheduled to die, and was baptized by the Reverend Ernest Kaufholdt of St. Peter's Church.

The prisoner spent his last hours in a private room on the main floor of the county jail, writing letters, insisting to the bitter end that Leo Brothers was innocent of Jake Lingle's murder.

Sheriff William Meyering and Warden David Moneypenny had invited 500 people to witness the electrocution of the highly-publicized prisoner. The blindfolded Bell walked unassisted as he was led from his cell and through the small green door to the death chamber promptly at midnight, and was seated into the chair at 12: 01 a.m.

Seconds later, as the throng of witnesses watched through the large glass panel, his back arched and his body stiffened as 1,900 volts of electricity blasted into his system. The juice hit him with such force that one of the leather straps broke and his left leg shot straight out, causing the slipper to fly off.

The electricity had to be turned off and the straps readjusted before the electrocution could continue. The switch was then turned on again, and charges five seconds, one minute, and one minute and twenty-five seconds long were passed through his body before he was pronounced dead.

10

2 KILLERS DIE IN CHAIR

JANUARY 15, 1932

Ben Norsingle, just 19 years old, and his partner, John Reed, age 26, were a couple of small-time holdup men who never lived long enough to make the big time.

They were arrested for the fatal shooting of John Martin, the 45-year-old manager of a Southeast Side meat market, during a $59 robbery on August 3, 1931. A Criminal Court jury took just forty-five minutes to find the two black men guilty of murder and sentenced them to death in the electric chair.

The senseless slaying had aroused the neighborhood since Martin, known as a "friend of the colored," regularly spent half his weekly paycheck to provide food during those depression days for area residents.

Neighbors aided police in identifying Reed, who was arrested in his Prairie Avenue home, and Norsingle, who was picked up in Dallas, Texas, and returned to Chicago for trial.

The condemned men were sentenced to die on December 18, but won a one month reprieve. There was no second delay, however, as the day of their deaths was set for January 15, 1932—just one week after Frank Bell's execution.

Both men went to their deaths calmly, after being

escorted into the execution chamber at midnight.

Reed was placed in the lethal chair at 12:01 a.m., and electrocuted before a small gathering of reporters and witnesses. He was pronounced dead four minutes later. Young Norsingle went to the chair at 12:08, and was pronounced dead at 12:15.

For the would-be holdup men, it was all over in less than fifteen minutes.

11

POLICE KILLER DIES;
WIDE-EYED AS
HE'S PUT IN CHAIR

OCTOBER 13, 1933

Chicago boldly thumbed its nose at the great depression that
was sinking the nation into despair by bringing a world's
fair—A Century of Progress Exposition—to its fabled
lakefront in 1933.

In that same year, a casual conversation between two
men waiting for haircuts in a Southwest Side barber shop
led to murder. It also presented the city with its greatest
unsolved mystery since Tommy O'Connor gave the hangman the slip back in 1921.

Morris Cohen, a 38-year-old barber, was snipping away
at a customer's hair while listening idly to two men seated
along the wall. They were talking about payday for people
on emergency relief rolls who had been assigned to work at
Navy Pier. They mentioned how convenient it was that an
enterprising currency exchange operator always set up a
table nearby, so the workers could cash their checks on the
spot. And he always seemed to have enough money to go
around.

Cohen, suffering from the same financial woes that
troubled so many in that era, listened intently. The next

payday would be August 14, one of the customers mentioned.

Cohen thought about the money table for several days, and shared the information with a friend, 23-year-old Hyman Sinnenberg. They decided to take advantage of the opportunity.

On the appointed day George Turner, paymaster for the Relief Commission, appeared at Navy Pier to distribute checks to relief workers during the lunch hour. Thomas B. Rawls, operator of a South Side currency exchange, was on hand with more than $1,000 in a money box to cash checks for a fee of fifteen cents each.

Half a dozen Bureau of Streets clerks were seated at desks in the second floor office as some sixty relief workers lined up to receive their checks. Suddenly Cohen and Sinnenberg barged in with revolvers drawn and shouted, "Everybody lie down on the floor!" Jerome Hartnett, a clerk, reached for a telephone, but changed his mind when one of the robbers fired a shot that zinged past his head.

The only police officer on duty at Navy Pier, 36-year-old newlywed Joseph P. Hastings, heard the shot and came running. Sinnenberg was rifling the cash box as the policeman entered the room and drew a bead on him with his service revolver. He did not see Cohen, who was standing against the wall.

Cohen opened fire on Hastings, who got off two shots before he fell with a bullet wound through the heart.

Then, as the two robbers were about to flee with the cash box, Cohen did a curious thing. He hurled his own weapon at George Stumpf, a janitor, and picked the dead policeman's pistol up off the floor. Stumpf picked up Cohen's gun and fired several shots at the robbers as they fled down a ramp.

Next the bandits hijacked a car in which two steeplejacks, John Boros and Jack Banz, were leaving the pier after a morning of fishing. The gunmen ordered the fishermen to drive them to the fashionable Ambassador East Hotel, where they jumped out of the car and fled on foot in opposite directions.

Cohen ducked into the Ambassador garage, where a suspicious employee spotted blood on his white shirt and called police. Policeman Harry Lyons found Cohen crouched in the back seat of an automobile, using his shirt to try to staunch the flow of blood from a chest wound. He surrendered without resistance.

Stuffed behind the seat of the car, police recovered Officer Hastings' service revolver—a damning piece of evidence that would put Cohen in the electric chair.

In an example of speedy justice at its fastest, Cohen was captured less than two hours after the policeman's murder, and indicted by the grand jury the following day. He went to court just nine days after the murder, and was convicted and sentenced to death in a trial that took only six hours and forty-five minutes. Judge Kickham Scanlan sentenced him to die in the electric chair on Friday, October 13, 1933—the earliest possible date which could be set under the law.

While awaiting his date with the chair, Cohen was something of an oddity at the county jail—a member of the Jewish faith on death row. Whereas the death cells had become familiar prayer grounds for an unending parade of Catholic priests and Protestant clergymen over the years, they proved strange surroundings for Rabbi Meyer Lipman, when he called to comfort Cohen.

Three men were to have been executed on October 13, but George Dale and John Scheck won reprieves, leaving Cohen to make the last walk alone.

"This was the time of year I liked best of all, and I would give anything for one last trip into the country with my wife," he told his wife, Sarah, when she visited him for the last time.

Dr. Clarence A. Neymann, a Northwestern University

psychiatrist retained by death penalty foes to examine the prisoner, pronounced Cohen legally sane.

"He is dull and backward mentally, a borderline case, perhaps, but he is not feeble minded," the alienist reported. "It is my personal belief that Cohen got a raw deal and that the confession which the police got from him was the result of physical punishment."

The shrink's opinion did nothing to delay Cohen's execution. His last hope faded when Governor Henry Horner declared at 11 p.m. that he would not intervene in the proceedings.

"It looks pretty dark, but if I have to, I guess I can take my medicine," Cohen said upon learning that his final appeal had been turned down.

Blindfold, but walking with a firm step, he was led to the death chamber at 12:05 a.m. As he was seated in the chair, and the death cap containing the electrodes was being lowered over the top of his head, Cohen asked curiously in a muffled voice, "What is it? What are you doing?" The guards offered no reply as they tightened the straps that fixed his arms and legs into place.

At 12:07 Cohen's body stiffened as he was given a one-minute jolt of 1,900 volts; then three lesser charges of 900 volts for two more minutes.

A team of twelve physicians pronounced Cohen dead at 12:10 a.m., and the 175 witnesses who held tickets to his electrocution filed silently out of the room. Among them was James Hastings, brother of the police officer for whose life Cohen paid with his own.

Total time elapsed from the afternoon Policeman Joseph Hastings was gunned down until Cohen died in the electric chair—sixty-one days.

And what of Cohen's partner, Hyman Sinnenberg? He escaped with the loot and was never heard from again.

Fingerprint checks have indicated no subsequent arrests. His prints were also run through the Federal Bureau of Investigation and compared with those of World War II and Korean War veterans, and came up negative, indicating he never served in the armed forces. If alive today, he would be in his mid-eighties.

12

ROSS KING GOES
TO HIS DEATH WHIMPERING

OCTOBER 16, 1933

Down through the years executions were traditionally scheduled for a Friday, the day Christ died on the cross. Whether someone misread the calendar or what is not known, but the electrocution of Ross King was marked down for a Monday, just three days after Morris Cohen went to the chair.

There was no rhythm to the macabre procedure. Cohen had been the first person executed in Cook County after a hiatus of twenty-one months, and now the chair would be put to work for the second time in three short days.

Like Cohen, King, 34, was a convicted cop killer. A parolee from the Michigan State Prison, he shot and killed Policeman Harry Redlich during the armed robbery of an advertising agency at 9 South Kedzie Avenue on July 8.

As the clock wound down on his life, King abandoned all hope of cheating the executioner, and steeled himself for his impending fate. His wife, Helen, battled to the bitter end to save him while he passed the time playing cards with his jailers, Stewart Jamieson and Peter Ringold.

"Nah, I won't get a break," he remarked, when the guards spoke of his wife's last-minute efforts.

King, who also used the alias of Kenneth Smith, had been considered one of the toughest prisoners ever held in the jail, and Warden David Moneypenny ordered extra guards placed on duty outside his cell.

In discussing his limited future, King had crowed, "Swift death in the 'hot seat' is better than life in prison. I know; I've been to prison. To go there for life would be a lifetime of hell."

The prisoner lost much of his bravado, however, when Morris Cohen was executed, putting him next in line for the chair. "If you can pull anything to get me out of this, I'd appreciate it," he told his lawyer, William Scott Stewart, as the zero hour approached.

After his head had been shaved, and his trouser legs cut off, King decided to make his final peace with God, and asked his guards to find a clergyman. When a Franciscan friar arrived, King refused to see him, and demanded, "I want a Methodist." Jailers quickly brought in John Fenn, a prison evangelist with a Methodist background. He remained with King until a jailer rapped on the cell door at midnight.

"What—time is it—getting—to be?" King stammered nervously.

"It's time to go, Ross," he was told.

King appeared ready to swoon as the black hood was placed over his shaven head, and deputies locked their arms firmly about his. Quickly, he was half walked, half dragged the twenty paces from the death cell to the electric chair, trembling and blubbering, "God have mercy on my soul! God have mercy on my soul! God have mercy on my soul."

He was still mumbling the phrase when he was strapped limply into the black armchair, and the electrodes were attached to his skin.

The initial jolt of 1,900 volts at 12:03 a.m. caused his fingers to clench and his back to arch stiffly for one minute. The body relaxed as the current was momentarily turned off, then stiffened again as a second and third shock of 900 volts coursed through his body over the next 120 seconds.

At 12:06 a.m. a jury of physicians placed their instruments to King's chest and pronounced him dead. Seventy-five witnesses, mostly newspaper reporters and physicians, got up from their wooden benches and filed silently out of the room.

Elgar Brown, who covered the execution for the *Chicago Evening American,* began his front page story with a verse by Friedrich Von Logau:

> *Though the mills of God grind slowly,*
> *Yet they grind exceeding small;*
> *Though with patience He stands waiting,*
> *With exactness grinds He all.*

Morris Cohen and Ross King were the only prisoners executed in Cook County that year.

13

3 DIE IN CHAIR,
SHECK IN HYSTERICS

APRIL 20, 1934

There is another mystery in Chicago, every bit as baffling as "Where's Tommy O'Connor?" and "Whatever became of Hyman Sinnenberg and the loot from the Navy Pier heist?" It centers around a diminutive blonde 29-year-old gun moll by the name of Eleanor Jarman.

The story begins at 2:39 in the afternoon of August 4, 1933, outside Gustav Hoeh's haberdashery at 5948 West Division Street. While thousands of visitors were enjoying the refreshing breezes that wafted over the Century of Progress Exposition on the city's lakefront, the siesta-like atmosphere of Hoeh's West Side neighborhood was shattered by a crash as the door of the men's clothing store burst open, and two men and a woman spilled out onto the sidewalk.

The 71-year-old Hoeh was struggling desperately with a dark-haired man much younger than himself, and a blonde woman, barely five feet, three inches tall. The woman was throwing her entire 110 pounds into the battle, clawing, scratching and hammering her fists on the elderly shopkeeper until he collapsed to the pavement. Then shots rang out. The dark-haired man and the blonde woman jumped into a waiting car and sped off, leaving Hoeh lying dead in front of his shop.

Five days later Eleanor Jarman and her boyfriend, George Dale, 29, were arrested for Hoeh's murder.

They were also implicated in forty-eight other holdups in which the "Blonde Tigress," as police dubbed Jarman, used a blackjack on uncooperative victims while her partner held a gun on them. Witnesses to Hoeh's slaying said she struck him on the head before Dale pumped the fallen shopkeeper full of bullets.

After a speedy trial, just three weeks after their arrest, Dale was sentenced to death and Jarman to 199 years in prison. Dale's execution was scheduled for April 20, 1934. He was consigned to death row, while Jarman was shipped off to the women's prison at Dwight, where she would not become eligible for parole until 1999 at the age of 95.

Two other prisoners were also sentenced to die with Dale, in what would become the county's first triple-electrocution. They were John Scheck and Joseph Francis.

Using a gun his mother had slipped to him during his trial for the murder of a Niles Center (now Skokie) cashier in a bank robbery, the 21-year-old Scheck shot and killed Policeman John G. Sevick while trying to flee the courtroom of Judge Charles P. Molthrop in the Criminal Courts Building. A jury set a new speed record in finding Scheck guilty of the policeman's murder—twenty-two minutes— and a judge promptly sentenced him to death.

Francis, a 35-year-old black man, had been given the death penalty for the slaying of Joseph Hartell, a milk wagon driver, during a holdup.

On the last day of their lives, Scheck and Dale occupied themselves putting together jig-saw puzzles, while Francis sat reading the Bible. He had been baptized into the Catholic faith after his arrest.

"I'm not afraid to die," Scheck said as he slipped pieces into the puzzle. "My life is ruined anyhow. I might as well get it over with."

"You know, kid, I'm not sure we're in favor of capital punishment," Dale replied, trying to inject some humor into the situation.

Scheck had sixteen visitors that afternoon and evening, including his mother and sister, whose loud wailing filled the jail corridors as they left at 6:30 p.m.

Dale was visited by his sister, Margaret Hull, of St. Louis. He made her promise never to tell the rest of the family of his fate. As Margaret was leaving, Dale tbrew her a salute and called out, "I'll see you later."

He then sat down and wrote a letter to Eleanor Jarman:

"Dear Eleanor—I just thought I would write you a few lines, maybe for the last time. I don't know. But don't ever think I have forgotten you..."

Francis, whose only relative was an 83-year-old grandmother in Birmingham, Alabama, had no visitors.

That evening Dale and Francis shared their last meal of tenderloin steak, fried chicken, French fries, lettuce, corn, peaches, toast and coffee. Scheck, his bravado all run out, was too terrified to eat.

Back in the days of public hangings, executions were generally held in the early afternoon to accommodate the large crowds drawn to them. After the gallows was moved indoors, executions were performed in the morning hours, usually between 7 and 9 a.m. With the introduction of the electric chair, however, jail officials decided to get the distasteful job out of the way the sooner the better, and carried out their assignments shortly after midnight on the appointed day.

All this changed on April 20, 1934, when Sheriff William D. Meyering and Acting Warden George Gibson decided that Scheck, Dale and Francis should die at dawn. They hoped this would discourage demands for tickets from morbid curiosity seekers.

But it presented a logistics problem for the city's six

downtown newspapers. The two morning dailies would be cranking out their final editions just about that time, and 5 a.m. was very nearly the copy deadline for the first editions of the four afternoon papers. Coming out on time was imperative to the newspapers, since their circulation departments had to meet train schedules or the papers would be left on the platforms.

To help solve the problem the City News Bureau, which serviced the media, ran a telephone line into the death chamber, and installed a phone on a table in the back of the room behind the witness benches. The line was connected directly to the City News switchboard at 155 North Clark Street, with trunk lines running to the city desks of the two morning papers, the four afternoon dailies, the Associated Press and the United Press.

Dick Henry, the regular City News reporter at the Criminal Courts Building, was assigned to cover the triple electrocution, backed up by police reporter Walter Spirko.

As the gruesome drama was about to unfold, Spirko took a seat on the front row of benches facing the chair, notebook in hand, while Henry stood on the table in the back of the room with an open phone line to his downtown office.

As the first prisoner was marched into the room at 5:01 a.m., followed by the Reverend Ernest Kaufholdt, wearing a brown robe and carrying a crucifix, Henry began rough-dictating his story into the phone to a rewrite man. "John Scheck was led into the execution room at dawn, in his stocking feet, with his trousers grotesquely snipped off at the knees. He wore a clean white undershirt, and the top of his head was shaved clean..."

Was it a murderer's ego or his flare for the dramatic that led to what happened next? The blindfolded Scheck startled the crowd by crying out, "Good-bye, everybody!" Perhaps it was false bravado.

As he was pressed into the chair and the straps were

being tightened, he cried, "Don't smother me, boys. You're smothering me. Thanks, fellows, and good-bye, everybody... Oh, you're smothering me..."

Those were his last words as the current hit at 5:02 and his body stiffened.

"Take it, you son-of-a-bitch, and like it!" a voice thundered from among the spectators. It was Policeman Thomas Leddy, John Sevick's former partner, who attended the execution with the slain policeman's two brothers, Joseph and Michael Sevick.

The brothers smiled grimly. At 5:07 a.m. Scheck was pronounced dead, and his body was quickly removed from the chair to make room for the next occupant.

Leddy remarked, "Boy, am I glad he's gone!"

Father Kaufholdt abandoned his chanted prayer and turned to go, shaking his head sadly.

George Dale, displaying a rotund stomach he had acquired during his incarceration, was guided into the room at 5:11, followed by the Reverend Henry J. Sandvoss, a Lutheran minister. Raising one hand as a farewell gesture Dale shouted, "So long, folks! So long!"

As one electrode was clamped on his shaven head, and the other affixed to his right leg, he began to pray in a monotone:

"Lord, have mercy on my soul—amen. Lord, have mercy on my soul—amen. Lord, have mercy on my soul—amen. Lord, have mercy on my soul—amen." On the fifth time he got no farther than "Lord have mercy..." when the jolt hit at 5:13 and his body strained at the straps.

"The flesh on his shoulders and arms is turning red as rare beef, and saliva is running down from under the mask," the City News reporter dictated into the phone from atop the table in the back of the room.

"Water from his bladder is pouring from his trouser legs, and forming a pool beneath the chair. A wisp of smoke is curling up from the right leg. George Dale is burning,

burning..."

Several onlookers turned away, but two of the spectators, Earl and Norman Hoeh, sons of the murdered Gustav Hoeh, kept their eyes riveted on the man in the chair.

"Give it to him. Give it to him," Earl Hoeh mumbled under his breath. "Daddy, that's all square now. Norman, we can tell mother it's all square."

"It isn't enough," Norman grumbled aloud. "They ought to make him suffer more. It's too easy."

At 5:18 Dr. Francis W. McNamara and a panel of six physicians stepped forward and pressed their stethoscopes to Dale's reddened chest and nodded. The dead body was quickly removed from the chair and wheeled out, to make room for the next contender.

Joseph Francis entered the chamber at 5:21. He appeared calm, and was praying as he was strapped into the chair. The initial jolt of electricity was applied at 5:22. At 5:29 he was pronounced dead, and his body was taken away at 5:30.

"That's it," Henry said, hanging up the City News phone. The entire program had lasted exactly thirty minutes.

As the nearly 200 witnesses arose from the benches and filed out of the room, Spirko ran to the warden's office with his penciled notes to fill in details and round out Henry's story, while other reporters called their offices to do the same.

Before he retired Spirko, who later became a police reporter for the *Chicago Sun-Times,* would witness sixteen executions—more than any other newsman.

But the story of George Dale and his pint-sized gun moll was not over. Shortly before noon on August 8, 1940, on the eve of the seventh anniversary of her arrest, Eleanor Jarman scaled a 10-foot fence topped with barbed wire, discarded her prison frock and pulled on a polka-dot dress she had stolen from Dwight staff headquarters while mopping floors, and disappeared.

The FBI and Illinois State Police launched one of the biggest woman-hunts in the nation's history, but the "Blonde Tigress" was never heard from again. All authorities know for sure is that she never got into serious trouble from that day on, because if she had, her fingerprints would have given her away.

14

JUDGMENT DAY AT JAIL: 2 DIE SINGING 'GOIN' TO HEAVEN ON A MULE'

OCTOBER 12, 1934

The Century of Progress world's fair on Chicago's lakefront was winding down, after being held over for one year, as jailers on the West Side dusted off the electric chair for another multiple execution on October 12, 1934.

Warden David Moneypenny had observed that, no matter what time of day or night an execution was held, the morbidly curious would gather, so he returned to the midnight schedule.

The next two subjects of the Grim Reaper's list were George Walker, age 20, and Alonzo McNeil, 29, a pair of armed robbers who had shot a policeman to death. In a style quite different from today's journalism, the *Evening American,* in referring to their execution as atonement for their sins, reported:

> *These sins included the quite inexcusable slaying of Policeman John Officer of the Wabash av. station, who, in addition to being a colored man, like his killers, was also a good citizen and a hero of the first water.*

The incident occurred on April 13, when Officer Officer came upon Walker and McNeil while they were industriously frisking eight patrons of a bootery on East Forty-third Street. In a brief exchange of gunfire, the policeman took two bullets in the chest.

As they waited in the death cell on the night they were scheduled to die, McNeil and Walker sang lustily, as though they hadn't a care in the world:

When I pass away, on that Judgment day,
I'm goin' to Heaven on a mule!
By and by, I'll be ridin' high,
Across that rainbow in the sky—
To Heaven on a mule!

Seated among the 150 witnesses waiting to watch the execution were two of the slain policeman's brothers, George and Patrolman Elmer Officer, who had served with him at the Wabash Avenue Station.

"It seems like it's right. They shot my brother and they ought to be done away with," Elmer said as the clock ticked away the final minutes of the two prisoners' lives. "John's widow, Erie, tried like everything to come down here and see it, but we withstrained her. Still, it seems like it's right."

Also among the front row spectators was lightweight boxing champion Barney Ross, who had obtained a celebrity pass to the event.

"I want to see a killer die," Ross explained vindictively. "Eleven years ago a robber shot my father to death—almost in the same circumstances that these boys shot a policeman to death. He was a merchant, and he died trying..."

The boxer's voice trailed off emotionally. He did not finish his sentence. There were three sharp raps on the iron door leading to the death chamber. A guard opened it, and the shadow of Alonzo McNeil played across the brick wall as he was half led, half carried, to the electric chair.

"The Lord have mercy," he exclaimed as he was strapped into the lethal device. His voice was cut short as the electric charge coursed through his body at 12:02 a.m. Three minutes later he was pronounced dead, and his body was removed as the Reverend William Lysles, who had accompanied him to the execution room, looked on.

Again, three knocks at the metal door. Young Walker, guided by a guard on either side, strode purposefully into the room and took the seat. As sheriff's deputies fastened the straps he urged them to "Hurry it up."

In the background the Reverend Robert Kees, a clergyman from suburban Wheaton, began reciting the Twenty-third Psalm, "The Lord is my shepherd..."

The jolt struck Walker at 12:13 and his body strained against the restraints, as a wisp of smoke rose from his thigh.

Barney Ross, the world boxing champ who wasn't afraid to face any living man, abandoned the witness bench and bolted out of the room. Holding a white handkerchief to his face he muttered, "I've had enough."

Three minutes later Walker, too, was pronounced dead and the doctors solemnly withdrew their stethoscopes.

If, indeed, the two cop killers had gone to Heaven, their mode of transportation had not been a mule, but a thunderbolt.

Their bodies were claimed by James Hall, an enterprising South Side funeral director. He laid the two corpses out on slabs in his undertaking parlor where, for the next ten days, thousands of curiosity seekers filed past, paying ten cents a look.

Over the cadavers Hall had hung a card: "Please Help Bury the Boys."

15

POLICE SLAYERS PAY FOR CRIME IN DEATH CHAIR

DECEMBER 15, 1934

By December 1 a new sheriff, John Toman, had taken office, and he appointed a new warden to the Cook County Jail, the affable Frank Sain. They had just two weeks to prepare for the county's next execution—another double-header. The condemned men were Armando Boulan, 28, and Walter Dittman, 29, convicted cop killers.

On the evening of September 1, Officer Earle M. Jensen, a motorcycle policeman in suburban Oak Park, had pulled a suspicious car over to the curb. When he attempted to question its occupants, he was shot dead. Other police arrested Boulan and Dittman a short time later. Each blamed the other for the shooting.

Boulan, a Puerto Rican who ran away from home when he was twelve, was a soldier of fortune who had served in both the British and American armies in World War I, and was wounded in battle. Dittman was a hard-working truck driver from Aurora. Both turned to banditry to help put food on the table for their families in the depth of the Depression.

Although each man insisted the other had pulled the trigger, a jury convicted both prisoners of Jensen's slaying and sentenced them to death.

As Dittman, a giant of a man, waited on death row, he declared, "When they pull that switch on me they will snuff out three lives. My old father and mother will die as well as me."

To wile away the time as the end of his life approached, he composed a grim poem.

The Chair of Death

I see it grimly waiting patiently for me,
To send me as its victim into eternity.
Not a whit or bit of mercy does it show
for man or beast.
Its only song is, "Die, you dog, for your slide
to hell is greased."

It's not the thought that I'm to die that makes
me want to pray.
It's because I'll not be there, my own, to wipe
your tears away.
God knows, and so do you, that I never
slew nor stole,
And though the whole world's turned against me,
He'll have mercy on my soul.

A willing crowd turned out to witness the execution on December 15, but many, including some of the city's top politicians, went away disappointed when Sheriff Toman refused to admit anybody without a legitimate invitation.

At three minutes past the midnight hour a group of seventy-six spectators watched apprehensively through the glass partition as Sheriff Toman stepped into the death chamber and whipped off a large white dust cover that had been draped over the grim black chair.

Sitting in the front row were Roy T. Jensen, the slain policeman's brother, and Officer Ellsworth Mitchell of the

East Chicago Avenue station, his brother-in-law, along with Oak Park Police Chief Benjamin Barsema, Captain Thomas Kern, Lieutenant William Koerber, and Patrolmen George Oliver and Loyal Wilcox, who arrested the slayers.

Boulan, the swarthy soldier of fortune, was brought in first—but not willingly. Two sheriff's deputies, each with one hand under an armpit and the other grasping a wrist steered the prisoner into the room and quickly seated him in the chair.

A mask covered the top half of Boulan's face and shaven head. He was clad in the now traditional meet-your-maker costume—trousers cut off above the knees and an armless blue undershirt. The lower half of his face was grim, and his mouth twitched slightly as the headpiece was lowered and the straps were tightened so he could not move.

The assistants stepped away from the chair, and Sheriff Toman gave a signal to an unseen aide in the control room. Boulan's body stiffened as 2,000 volts of electricity hit him at 2:04 a.m. A minute later the body relaxed as the current was turned off, then came the lesser jolt for a minute and a half; off again; and then one more 90-second shot.

At 12:10 a.m. six doctors pressed their stethoscopes to Boulan's still chest and declared what every member of the audience already knew. He was dead.

Quickly and efficiently the headpiece was removed and the straps were undone, as the body sagged in the chair. One deputy took the corpse by the arms, another grabbed his legs, and he was carried out of the chamber.

Moments later the blindfolded Dittman, an enormous, paunchy man, was all but carried in by four strong deputies, and the procedure was repeated. At 12:13 the sheriff nodded, and Dittman's skin flushed as the 2,000 volts coursed through his body. As his limp body was being carried out at 12:22 a.m., a tattoo, "Death Before Dishonor," was visible on his right arm.

"I'm satisfied. So is my staff," Police Chief Barsema said as the ruddy corpse was carried out. "We had to talk mighty hard to Betty Jensen, Earle's widow, to make her stay at home. But now we can call her and tell her that the slate is clean."

Dittman's body was turned over to his family, but nobody claimed Boulan's remains. The St. Vincent de Paul Society gave him a burial in Mount Carmel Cemetery.

16

"TOUGH" NOVAK DIES IN CHAIR, TOUGH TO END
MARCH 21, 1935

"I'll be the toughest guy that ever took the hot seat," 30-year-old Chester Novak boasted self-assuredly as he played solitaire in the death cell and scanned the newspapers telling of his impending electrocution.

Earlier the balding, baby-faced bandit, during an all-encompassing press conference in a jail office, matter-of-factly told reporters, "I don't believe in God or the hereafter. I think the Russian Communists have the right idea, but I'm not a Communist. I think President Roosevelt and the governor are doing a good job. I'm a victim of circumstances—but I wouldn't advise anyone to follow in my footsteps."

The "circumstances" he referred to were the parents he had never known, who died when he was an infant. He got in with a bad crowd, and was sent to prison for nine years for armed robbery.

"I couldn't get a job after that, so I went back to robbery. A fellow has to live, you know."

On July 1, 1934, he and a pal, George Gross, held up Henry Mendelbaum, a 49-year-old delicatessen owner, who was walking with his wife, Belle, near his shop at Damen and Pierce Avenues. Mendelbaum's arms were full of packages, and when he delayed reaching for the sky, Novak shot him dead.

Novak was sentenced to die in the electric chair, and Gross got 199 years in prison.

"I win," Novak chortled. "You'll die by inches in stir. I'll go to hell in a hurry."

The time to make the trip came at one minute after midnight on March 21, 1935.

Warden Frank Sain, knowing that even the toughest of cons softened as they were about to meet their maker, asked Novak, "Would you like to talk to a priest?"

"When I do, I'll let you know," the short, stocky prisoner sneered.

Novak sat calmly as he was strapped into the chair, and the electrodes were attached. Then his body stiffened as 1,900 volts of electricity shot through him, followed by doses of 900 volts for 55 seconds, and again for 60 seconds.

It was then that Novak proved just how tough he really was.

Deputies loosened the leather straps and pulled aside Novak's undershirt as five physicians stepped forward and placed their stethoscopes to his reddened chest.

"This man is alive!" one of them said in horror. "His heart is still fluttering!"

The doctors nervously left the room while the straps were tightened for a second time, and two more lethal charges of electricity were sent through his body.

It was 12:12 a.m. before the panel of physicians agreed that tough guy Novak was finally dead. Two uniformed deputies in natty tan jackets removed him from the chair and placed his body on a gurney.

Novak's body was removed to the Cook County Morgue, where it lay unclaimed for two weeks. Then, as was customary, the corpse was wrapped in a white sheet, placed in a three-dollar pine coffin, and buried in Potter's

Field, the last resting place of the poor and the friendless.

More than 25 years later, after he'd been elected sheriff of Cook County, Sain was asked to name the toughest person he had ever known. "That's easy," he remarked. "Chester Novak."

A month after Novak went to the chair, two men were similarly executed in state prisons. Thomas J. Lehne, 43, a former police officer from Venice, Illinois, was electrocuted at Menard for murdering his girlfriend's husband, Charles Puhse, in Granite City. And Fred Blink, 42, a Whiteside County farmer, who murdered five people, went to the chair at Stateville prison.

Blink, who had quarreled with a neighbor, John Hamilton, over a $35 debt, settled the argument by shooting Hamilton, two women and two other men. During his trial, in which he was prosecuted by L.L. Wynn, he blamed the massacre on "poisoned whisky" given to him by Tim Corrick, husband of one of the slain women.

As Blink was being strapped into the chair he announced loudly, "I wish I had Corrick and Wynn on my lap."

One month after that, three men convicted of the murder of a bank cashier, a township supervisor, and Sheriff Glen Axline of Marshall County during a holdup in Lenore, Illinois, died in the electric chair in the first triple execution ever held at Joliet. They were Fred Gerner, 27, and Arthur Thielen, 42, both of Rockford, and John Hauff, 32, of Chicago.

On October 15, 1935, Gerald Thompson, 26, was executed at Joliet for the rape murder of 19-year-old Mildred Hallmark in Peoria. Among the 100 witnesses was John Hallmark, the slain girl's father, who said afterward, "We are satisfied. No other punishment would have fitted the crime."

17

TWO YOUTHFUL GUNMEN DIE IN ELECTRIC CHAIR

OCTOBER 21, 1936

In October of 1936, Mrs. Pearl Puutio escaped going to jail for bigamy in a most unusual way. One of her husbands died in the electric chair, leaving her with the legal limit.

The husband who departed was Frank "Bones" Korczykowski, 27, who, along with Andrew Bogacki, 26, a fellow ex-convict, had been convicted of the fatal shooting of Policeman Jerome McCauley on May 29, 1935.

Midway through their trial, Korczykowski, Bogacki and a third man, Paul Jenkot, 24, made a sensational break for freedom from the Criminal Courts building after over-powering their guards and forcing them to remove their handcuffs. Judges, bailiffs, lawyers, defendants and court employees fled in terror as the three desperate men battled their way through the corridors.

Before being recaptured after a running fight over five floors of the building, the trio slashed two deputy sheriffs with makeshift daggers and beat two others with fists and blackjacks.

Two days later Korczykowski and Bogacki were sentenced to death for Policeman McCauley's murder and Jenkot, who had driven the getaway car, got 199 years in prison.

"I'm happy about it," Korczykowski said as he was being led back to the county jail. "I didn't want to go to prison."

Bogacki and Korczykowski would be the first prisoners to try out the electric chair since it was renovated in April. At that time the troublesome leather straps were removed and replaced with U-shaped metal clamps that could be snapped into place over a condemned man's arms and legs the instant he was placed into the chair.

After a hearty last meal, the two men spent their last evening playing cards with their jailers and writing letters to friends.

Earlier in the day Korczykowski was visited by his bigamous wife, Pearl, while Bogacki received a visit from Rita Raciborski, whose husband, Dennis, was serving time for robbery in the Joliet penitentiary. She identified herself to jailers as Mrs. Bogacki.

The executions were scheduled for October 21, 1936, at a few minutes after 1 a.m., to conform to the Central Standard Time of midnight at Springfield, the state capital. Daylight Saving Time was not uniform, but a matter of local option in those days.

Korczykowski, his face hidden by a black mask, was half-led, half dragged into the brightly lit death chamber by two jail guards, and quickly clamped into the chair by three sheriff's deputies. Warden Frank Sain, Sheriff John Toman, and a Franciscan chaplain stood nearby. Six physicians, including Dr. Meyer Levy, the jail physician, were seated on a bench in the room.

As the guards stepped away from the lethal chair, Toman gave a signal, and the switch was thrown at 1:03 a.m. The prisoner stiffened in the chair. A slight wisp of smoke was visible from the electrode on his shaven head, and another wisp rose from his bare leg where the other electrode was attached.

He was pronounced dead at 1:09 a.m.

After a short pause, during which Korczykowski's body

was removed from the chair and new electrodes were attached, Bogacki was led into the room and the procedure was repeated. He was clamped into the chair at 1:14 a.m., and pronounced dead at 1:20.

Both men's bodies were placed in wicker caskets in an anteroom, where they would be held until claimed by relatives for burial.

Among the 200 spectators in the witness room were Officer McCauley's four brothers, Patrick, Joseph, David and Robert, along with his partner, Edward Brieske, and the six policemen who had served as his pallbearers.

Shortly thereafter, Pearl Puutio was hauled into Felony Court on a charge of bigamy, for having married Korczykowski while still wedded to Arthur Puutio. When he was informed that Korczykowski was no longer around, Judge Harold O'Connell raised his eyebrows and dismissed the charges.

18

STILL PREFERRING DEATH, MILDRED GOES TO DWIGHT

FEBRUARY 26, 1937

Hollywood, in all its imagination, could not have devised a stranger scene than the one that unfolded in the basement of the Cook County Jail on the night of February 25, 1937: A middle-aged white woman, the son of a prominent rabbi, and a black former college athlete sat huddled in the stark, green death cell, waiting to be summoned to the electric chair.

Some 330 miles across the state in the penitentiary at Menard, a black husband and wife shared Illinois' other death cell, awaiting a similar fate.

Mildred Mary Bolton, a 46-year-old Chicago housewife, was the only woman ever sentenced to death in Cook County. Her unlikely companions on that cold February night were Joseph Rappaport, age 30, and Rufo Swain, 27. The occupants of the death cell at Menard were Mrs. Minnie Mitchell, 34, and her husband, Allen, 32.

Rufo Swain and Allen Mitchell would never see the sunrise.

"Marble Mildred," as Mrs. Bolton was known, had become a self-made widow by shooting her husband, Joseph, to death in a jealous rage in his insurance brokerage office at 166 West Jackson Boulevard.

Rappaport, the rabbi's son, became a member of the grim trio after being convicted of slaying Max Dent, a government informer, who was to have testified against him in a narcotics case.

Swain, a college athlete from Arkansas, was in the death cell for the rape and murder of Mary Louise Trammel, 24, the wife of a dining car steward, who was beaten to death in her downtown hotel room.

There was only one death cell in the county jail, and the fact that Mrs. Bolton had to be confined with the two men greatly troubled Warden Frank Sain. He resolved to do something about it.

Mrs. Bolton did her best to keep up the spirits of her two fellow prisoners during the long evening. As Rappaport paced the cell nervously, she told him, "Don't lose your courage, Joe. Keep your head in the air. Everybody believes you're innocent, and that ought to be of some comfort to you."

"I am innocent. I pray God will not allow my life to be taken for a crime He knows I did not commit," he replied. "But, if I got to go, I'm going with a smile."

Rappaport still clung to hopes that pleas by the noted criminal lawyer, Clarence Darrow, and Rabbi H. Olschwang, president of the Orthodox Rabbinate of Chicago, might save him from the chair.

All three prisoners were served elaborate dinners, and ate heartily. It was the fifth "last meal" for Rappaport, who had sat in the death cell four times before.

While the prisoners were dining for what might be the last time, Governor Henry Horner, a foe of the death penalty, spent an hour in solitude in the executive mansion in Springfield, wrestling with the dilemma that faced him. Shortly after 9 p.m. he issued a statement regarding Rappaport's plea for clemency:

"Notwithstanding my own views as to the death

penalty as the punishment for murder, it is the law of this state and a law which we are bound to obey. Upon the recommendation of the pardon board I have declined to grant a pardon or commutation of sentence in the case of Joseph Rappaport."

It was not the end of the line for Rappaport, however. A short time later, Sheriff John Toman personally led him from the death cell for the fifth time.

"Has the governor come through and commuted my sentence?" the prisoner asked apprehensively.

"No, I'm afraid not, Joe," the sheriff told him. "But he did give you a five day reprieve because of the holiday."

The date for Rappaport's execution had fallen on the Feast of Purim, an occasion of holy observance among Orthodox Jews. Governor Horner feared criticism if he permitted a member of the Jewish faith to be executed during the three-day feast period, so he gave Rappaport a new date.

"By the way, sheriff, that was a fine steak dinner I had tonight," Rappaport laughed nervously, as he was returned to his old cell block.

Then, shortly before she was to have gone to the chair Mrs. Bolton was told that she, too, was being spared. The politically conscious Horner, who did not want to go down in history as the first governor to permit a woman to be executed, had commuted her sentence to 199 years in prison.

Mrs. Bolton accepted the news with the same outward calm as she had exhibited during what would have been her final hours. In fact, she seemed disappointed that her life had been spared. "I would have preferred it the other way," she told Sheriff Toman. "It's not going to be easy for me to leave here. You've all been so good to me."

She chatted amiably with reporters, who crowded around her after receiving the news. But she refused to be photographed. "I don't have my good clothes on, and I wouldn't want anybody to see me looking like this," she apologized.

What Horner did for Mrs. Bolton he also did for Minnie Mitchell, who, with her husband, Allen, had been sentenced to death for the murder of Sam Simpson in an insurance collection scheme in East St. Louis.

A week earlier the governor had granted them a reprieve so he could study their cases. He now commuted Mrs. Mitchell's sentence to 199 years in prison, rather than become the first governor to let a women go to her death—but denied clemency for her husband. "There is nothing to justify it," he declared.

Shortly after midnight Rufo Swain and Allen Mitchell were executed simultaneously, Swain in the electric chair in the Cook County Jail and Mitchell in the penitentiary at Menard.

After Swain's execution, Warden Sain used Works Progress Administration (WPA) funds to remodel the jail to provide three identical death cells, so male and female prisoners would never again have to sit and await the executioner in one cell.

19

DRAMA OF LIFE AND DEATH ENDS FOR RAPPAPORT

MARCH 2, 1937

Construction work on the new death cells was already underway five days later when, after five reprieves, time finally ran out for Joseph Rappaport.

The son of the highly respected Rabbi Israel Rappaport, he had been sentenced to death for the murder of Max Dent, who was scheduled to testify against him in a narcotics case. Dent, a poorly educated man of 34, who eked out a depression era living as a federal informant, was shot to death outside his home on Chicago's West Side on the evening of October 8, 1935.

In his pocket, police found a crudely scrawled note:

> *Notice if any thing happens to me it would be caused from Joe Rapport (sic) he has tried to put me out of the way several times on account of the case I have against him. Max Dent.*

Furthermore, Dent's mother, Anna, told police she recognized Rappaport as her son's slayer.

Rappaport insisted on his innocence, however, and the battle to save the condemned man from the electric chair was one of the most spectacular in the city's history.

Clarence Darrow, the most famous criminal lawyer of his time, threw himself into the battle as did clergymen of all faiths, scores of politicians, and hundreds of private citizens. A petition signed by twenty rabbis representing the Orthodox Rabbinate of Chicago was presented to the State Board of Pardons and Paroles asking that Rappaport's sentence be commuted.

Governor Horner arrived in Chicago from New York on March 1, 1937, the day before Rappaport's sixth date with the electric chair. As the governor got off the train the condemned man's sister, Rose Rappaport, broke loose from the welcoming crowd and grabbed him by the arm. "Please, governor, please listen to me," she pleaded.

The flustered governor walked straight ahead, without responding. Later in the day, however, he met with the woman and Rappaport's lawyer in a downtown hotel to hear her plea, but offered no encouragement.

The historic battle reached a dramatic climax on the night of March 1, just three hours before Rappaport was scheduled to be executed. In a highly unusual move, a lie detector was set up in the death cell in a final effort to determine once and for all whether the prisoner had taken Dent's life. Never before had such a move been made in an effort to save a condemned killer.

The test was administered by the master, Leonarde Keeler, one of the nation's top lie detector experts, who had played a major role in the development of the polygraph.

Governor Horner, the only person who could save Rappaport, sat by the telephone in the executive mansion in Springfield, awaiting the outcome of the examination.

Outside Rappaport's cell, a group of interested lawyers and public officials watched through the bars as Keeler administered the life-and-death test. They included Sheriff John Toman, Warden Frank Sain, Assistant State's Attorneys Marshall Kearney and John Boyle, who had prosecuted

Rappaport, defense attorney William W. Smith, and Konstantine Theodore, the jail physician.

The needles on the lie detector graphs followed a fairly even course as Keeler asked routine questions to set the stage for the examination. Then he asked Rappaport a series of pointed questions:

"Do you know who shot Max Dent?"

"Did you shoot Dent?"

"Did you have anything to do with Dent's death?'

Twice Keeler went through the series of questions, slightly rewording them each time, and each time Rappaport answered "No," the needles danced all over the chart.

When the tests were completed at 10 p.m. Keeler shook his head and told the group outside the cell, "He lies."

Smith sighed glumly, "It's the end."

Keeler then went to the warden's office and telephoned Governor Horner. "Rappaport lied when he denied killing Dent," he said.

As the governor was receiving the news, Rappaport sat down in his cell and wrote a bitter farewell letter to his mother: "I hope the federal men are satisfied now."

Rappaport's head was then shaved and the legs of his trousers were cut off at the knees in preparation for his execution. Shortly after midnight he walked calmly to the electric chair, and was strapped in at 12:04 a.m.

After the three electric charges were administered, the thick black belt across his chest was unbuckled and three physicians stepped forward to examine the body. Two of the doctors pressed their stethoscopes to Rappaport's chest and pronounced him dead. The third shook his head. He did not agree. So the belt was tightened across Rappaport's chest and another jolt of electricity was sent through his body. After the power was turned off, the third doctor agreed with the others—he was gone.

An hour after Rappaport's body was removed from the chair, a man identified as Anton Zeman was arrested by police on a charge of making a phone call, in which he threatened to kill Sheriff Toman for electrocuting the prisoner.

Investigators determined that Zeman had bet a friend $50 that Rappaport would win another reprieve, and he was disgruntled over having to pay up.

20

CRIME CAREER OF PAROLEES ENDS IN CHAIR

APRIL 16, 1937

By April 16, 1937, the three death cells ordered by Sheriff Frank Sain had been completed, and the eight-year-old electric chair was "improved." The electrodes were shifted, a headpiece was devised that covered the prisoner's entire face, and a floor lever was installed to automatically clamp down the prisoner's arms and hold his legs firm the instant he was seated.

This would cut the time from the placing of the prisoner in the chair to the administering of the fatal jolt to just six seconds.

Sain also added three dummy switches to the circuit connected to the chair, so none of the four guards who would push the buttons would know who really performed the execution.

The first clients of the new procedure were Francis "Doc" Whyte, Stanley Murawski and Joseph Schuster, all paroled ex-convicts turned cop killers.

Schuster, 30, and handsome enough to have been a matinee idol, had turned to armed robbery because he couldn't hold a steady job. On the night of January 14, 1937, shortly after being released from prison on parole, he shot and killed Policeman Arthur Sullivan on a West Side elevated platform when the police officer tried to bring him in for questioning.

When he appeared in court before Judge John J. Lupe, Schuster insisted on pleading guilty, even though the judge tried to talk him out of it. Judge Lupe had never sentenced a man to death, and didn't want to do so now.

"I'm guilty. I never pleaded anything but guilty," Schuster argued. "I committed the crime and I've always said so."

"Do you realize that I could sentence you to death?" asked Lupe.

"Yes, I do, and I still plead guilty."

He left the judge no choice.

"There is only one penalty to fit the crime you committed," said the judge, obviously under a tremendous strain. "I have searched the records in this case for something on which to pin a bit of hope. You robbed while on parole, and then callously killed this policeman, while he was doing his duty—never giving him a chance.

"This is not an easy duty for me to perform. But the court owes to society the stern performance of its duty. I must sentence you to death."

"Thank you, your honor," Schuster replied.

Murawski, 37, and Whyte, 47, both ex-convicts with long criminal records, shot and killed Policeman Michael Toth in a South Side pool hall, when the officer responded to a report of a man with a gun.

Each man implicated the other when they went to trial, and both were sentenced to death.

More than 5,000 people, including several hundred police officers, applied to Sheriff John Toman for tickets to the execution of the three cop killers. A total of 147 invitations were issued to the "triple-header," scheduled for April 16, 1937.

Among the spectators were three brothers and four

brothers-in-law of Policeman Toth.

Schuster's last request was to visit with his fiancee, 22-year-old Gertrude Ondra, but she refused to see him.

"I'd sooner die than have to serve life or 199 years in prison, except that it's a terrible blot on my family to go as I'm going," Schuster said as the hour of his death drew near. "I'm bothered about my old girl, too. I haven't seen her for six weeks, and I don't know what to make of her."

Whyte shared some of the concern over how the execution would affect his family.

"I'm worried only that this will reflect on my wife and five children. To give way to despair won't help. The whole thing is a mystery. We can't all be prosecutors. Somebody has to be the sacrifice on the altar," he said. "Some fellows get the breaks. Some don't. But I hate to think of gossips pointing out the poor kids and saying, 'Their father was executed.'"

Murawski was resigned to his fate.

"I blame myself for this. Every man leads his own life and he can't be jerked into nothing if he doesn't want to go. But the death sentence never scared nobody. Nobody ever thinks it will happen to him," he mused. "No man has a chance after he has served a term in prison. An ex-con never gets a break."

Earlier in the evening, Whyte asked for a priest, and was visited by Father Eliguis Weir, Catholic chaplain from the Joliet penitentiary.

Schuster was visited by his parents, including his invalid mother, who was carried into the jail in a chair for the last reunion.

Whyte spent his last hours reading newspaper accounts of the impending execution. "Well, I guess that's the way things stand," he sighed. "I might as well be getting ready for the worst."

As the death hour approached, Schuster's lawyer, William Scott Stewart, made two futile attempts to win a stay of execution. Both were denied by the Illinois Supreme Court, and Governor Henry Horner refused clemency.

At one minute after midnight four uniformed deputies stood facing the row of four red buttons on the control panel on a wall alongside the execution chamber—one of them "live" and three not wired to anything. Through a window they could see the chair, and Sheriff Toman, who would give them the signal.

Schuster was the first of the trio to make the final march to the death chamber. He was taken from his cell and led to the electric chair at 12:05 a.m. Six minutes later he was pronounced dead.

His body was placed on a gurney and quickly wheeled out as Murawski was brought in at 12:17. He was pronounced dead five minutes later.

Whyte was marched in and clamped into the chair as soon as his partner's body was removed. By 12:34 a.m. he, too, was dead.

In cleaning out the death cell, jailers found a note left behind by Whyte, thanking Warden Sain and his assistants for their kindness.

21

MOVIE MORON HEARS
SENTENCE TO DIE IN CHAIR

OCTOBER 15, 1937

In 1936 kids attending a Sunday matinee paid ten cents, and adults a quarter, to take in a Shirley Temple movie at the neighborhood theater. On March 14 of that year a 12-year-old girl named Shirley Tupler complained to an usher in the Midwest Theatre on Archer Avenue that a man was pestering her during the show.

The usher, John McConaghy, tapped the man on the shoulder, beckoned him out of the aisle, and escorted him to the office of the theater manager, Irving Fehlberg.

"What's this all about? The little girl says you were trying to mess around with her or something," Fehlberg said. "Were you bothering her in there?"

The customer, a beefy, dark-haired Greek immigrant named Peter Chrisoulas, responded by drawing a revolver and shooting Fehlberg dead.

Chrisoulas, 40, who had never been arrested before, was convicted of murder, and sentenced to death.

"I'm not afraid to die. I'm afraid of what comes after," he said. "I hope this never gets back to my brothers and sisters in Greece. The disgrace would kill them. I'm afraid they might even think of suicide."

He explained that his father died when he was six, and his mother died of a broken heart two years later. He couldn't let his sisters support him, so he came to the United States at the age of twenty-one, got a job as a mechanic, and sent money home to them.

A bewildered man, whose hair turned from jet black to gray during the year he was in jail while his lawyers fought to save his life, Chrisoulas soon became the butt of fellow prisoners' jokes.

"Don't shake and shiver so much," they kidded. "You're gonna burn. You'll never be cold again."

Chrisoulas didn't understand what they meant by "burn." All he knew was that he couldn't seem to get warm. Although warmly clad in a shirt, trousers, shoes and sweater tucked into his pants, he demanded that his overcoat be brought to his cell. From that moment until he died he wore his coat at all times. He asked for additional blankets, and huddled under them at night, still wearing his overcoat, to keep warm.

He won three stays of execution during this period, but Governor Henry Horner refused a fourth delay, and Chrisoulas was scheduled to be electrocuted on October 15, 1937.

"I no mean to kill," he said, when Warden Frank Sain brought him the news that his final appeal had been turned down.

Just an hour before midnight Chrisoulas, who earlier in the evening had turned up his nose at a steak dinner, decided he wanted to eat after all and jailers stood by in amazement as he polished off his last meal with gusto.

Then Chrisoulas, who had let his personal appearance go to seed during his imprisonment, asked for a shave.

All cleaned up to meet his maker, he stepped along briskly with his overcoat draped around his shoulders as Assistant Warden John Dohmann led him down the corridor to the electric chair. Accompanying him were the Reverend

Albert E. Selcer, jail chaplain, and the Reverend Gabriel Matholoulos of the Greek Orthodox Catholic Church.

An audience of 100 men looked on as he was guided into the room and clamped into the chair. At 12:04 a.m. his back arched and his fingers snapped into fists as the four deputies leaned into the red buttons and the electric current one of them released hit him. Six minutes later he was pronounced dead.

Warden Sain had considered taking motion pictures of the execution to be shown later to jail inmates, as an example that crime did not pay, but he wasn't able to do so.

"While I think the idea is a splendid one, I really have no authority to do such a thing. I would first have to receive authorization from the sheriff and the courts," he explained.

After Chrisoulas' body was removed from the chair it was claimed by priests of the Greek Orthodox Church of Assumption, who officiated at his burial in Elmwood Cemetery.

22

SLAYER BATTLES GUARDS, DIES IN ELECTRIC CHAIR

APRIL 19, 1938

Probably no man feared the electric chair more than J.C. Scott, a powerfully-built 22-year-old black man, convicted of murdering a gypsy fortune teller who predicted he would die a violent death.

His victims were Mary Eli, 52, the fortune teller, and her daughter, Catherine, 26, who were beaten to death just before Christmas in their Maxwell Street apartment in the course of a robbery that netted Scott $368.

Scott fled to his native South Carolina, where he was arrested two weeks later. Within twelve hours after being returned to Chicago he was tried, convicted, and sentenced to death.

On hearing the sentence Scott, who stood six feet two inches tall, went berserk in the courtroom of Judge Fred Rush, screaming, "Shoot me now! I'd rather be shot than die in the electric chair."

It took seven deputy sheriffs to subdue the prisoner in front of the bench, and he was carried out of court in handcuffs and leg irons.

A heavy guard was placed over the prisoner after he boasted to fellow county jail inmates, "They'll never get me in that chair. I'll get away or get shot in the attempt."

His execution was scheduled for April 15, 1938. Good Friday fell on that date, however, so he was given a four-day delay until Tuesday, April 19.

Up until 7 p.m. on the evening before his death he continued to threaten, "They'll never get me in that chair." After that he appeared to calm down, however, and spent his last hours playing rummy with his guards, George Longway, Alfred Stewart and William Schultze.

At 9:45 p.m. Sheriff John Toman entered the death cell with several men, including the Reverend Albert Selcer, the jail chaplain. "Is it time?" Scott asked the chaplain, looking up from his card game. "Call me when you want me."

The rummy game continued until 11:40 when a barber was brought in to shave his head and leg so the electrodes would fit snugly.

Minutes later, when it became time for the death march, every bit of calmness left Scott and he battled furiously as jailers tried to get him out of the cell. He was dragged, kicking and screaming, all the way to the chair as 100 spectators looked on.

At one point he succeeded in tearing off the black hood that had been placed over his head, and moaned, "Please, let me see it all."

As he tried to break away again at the last moment, two more guards rushed forward and helped the others to virtually throw the giant prisoner into the chair and affix the clamps.

A second later he was rendered unconscious by a 1,900-volt jolt, followed by two shocks of lesser voltage, until he was pronounced dead at 12:07 a.m.

It was four months to the day after he had fatally beaten the gypsy fortune teller and her daughter.

23

KIDNAP-KILLER OF ROSS PUT TO DEATH IN CHAIR

JULY 14, 1938

A six-room brick bungalow in the suburbs cost $5,500 new in 1937—but few people had the $500 down payment that would enable them to move into one. There were exceptions, of course, even during those lean times. One of them was Charles S. Ross, a wealthy, 72-year-old retired greeting card manufacturer.

On September 25, 1937, he left his North Side luxury apartment to get a shave and a haircut. Then he picked up Florence Freihage, his former secretary, and took her to dinner. On the way home their car was forced off the road on North Avenue, and Ross was abducted at gunpoint.

After Ross's wife paid a $50,000 ransom demand, FBI agents arrested a 28-year-old lumberjack from Ironton, Minnesota, John Henry Seadlund, when he placed a bet with some of the ransom money at a Chicago race track.

Seadlund led federal agents to Spooner, Wisconsin, where Ross had been kept chained in an abandoned well in sub-zero temperatures before being savagely beaten and shot in the head. Seadlund had also shot his accomplice, James Atwood Gray, to death.

Seadlund was tried in U.S. District Court in Chicago,

where he pleaded guilty to kidnapping, and was sentenced to death. "Don't bother to appeal," he told his lawyer. "I'd rather get the chair than rot in jail the rest of my life." He was transferred to the Cook County Jail, where he would become the first federal prisoner to die in the county's electric chair.

For a time it appeared that Sheriff John Toman would deny the government the use of his jail because of an order from the attorney general in Washington barring Chicago newspapermen from the execution. He later gave in, after being advised by Attorney General Homer S. Cummings that the regulation applied to all federal executions.

The execution was scheduled for one minute after midnight on July 14, 1938. Cummings ruled that this meant Central Standard Time, not Daylight Saving Time, so the death penalty would be carried out at 1 a.m. Chicago time.

Seadlund spent his last days reading adventure stories and writing letters to his mother, Delia, in Minnesota, and to his sister and brother-in-law. In them he said he was reconciled to his impending death, and looked forward to seeing his dead father and his dog, Bo.

Federal Marshal William H. McDonnell was in charge of the electrocution, at which only twenty-two men could be present, by government order. These included U.S. officials, physicians, guards and Severin E. Koop, a Minnesota undertaker, who had been sent to claim the body and bring it back to Ironton for burial. The ruling was so strict that Sheriff Toman had to obtain special permission from Washington to attend the event in his own jail.

Warden Frank Sain's jailers, who would perform the actual execution, brought Seadlund from his cell shortly after 1 a.m., and strapped him into the chair at 1:08. Less than five minutes later he was pronounced dead.

FBI Director J. Edgar Hoover, who had followed the case with interest, declared, "John Henry Seadlund was the meanest man who ever lived."

24

VICTIM'S MATE
SEES KILLER DIE

JUNE 16, 1939

The forerunner of today's television evangelists was Father Devine, a Harlem cult leader, who toured the country in 1939, preaching the word of the Lord, and stuffing his pockets with donations from followers hoping to be saved.

One such believer was 19-year-old Robert "The Kid" Nixon, a black youth from Louisiana, who was sentenced to die for the murder of Florence Johnson. The wife of Chicago fireman Elmer Johnson, she was beaten to death with a brick in her apartment on Lake Park Avenue.

After Nixon's arrest he also confessed to the murders of Mrs. Florence Thompson Castle in the Devonshire Hotel, Anne Kuchta, a student nurse at Chicago Hospital, and a woman and her twelve-year-old daughter in Los Angeles.

Nixon, who believed that his faith in Father Devine would somehow save him, won seven stays of execution— enough to convince almost anyone of the power of prayer.

"He ain't the Lord, but he's powerful close to him. He just about holds the keys to Heaven, that man does. He's going to bring me peace. What have I got to worry about?" Nixon said. Between Father Devine and God, he said, "Them two are going to see me through. They know I ain't bad, and they ain't gonna see me come to no harm."

Despite his faith in the Lord and Father Devine, all appeals ran out, and Nixon's final date with the electric chair was set for June 16.

While Nixon was awaiting his turn at the chair, Elwin Wood, a Grundy County farmer, was electrocuted in the Joliet penitentiary on April 14 for the murder of his lifelong friend, Abner Nelson, a wealthy farmer from Morris.

Wood had shot Nelson to death February 19 in a ransom kidnapping plot, and thrown his body into the Illinois River near Seneca. On March 6 he was sentenced to death on his plea of guilty. The sentence was carried out on the earliest possible date, with no delays. The total time elapsed from the commission of the murder to the confessed slayer's execution—54 days.

Two months later Robert Nixon also ran out of time. His mother, Anna, came up from Monroe, Louisiana, to be what comfort she could during her son's last night on earth. His girlfriend, Estelle Brown, also sat with him until she and his mother were asked to leave at 9:30 p.m.

Nixon was then transferred to the basement death cell, where his morale went to pieces and he babbled incoherently to the Reverend Albert C. Selcer, the jail's Episcopal chaplain.

For his last meal Nixon ordered a sirloin steak and french fries. He took two nibbles and pushed the rest away.

His head shaved, and wearing black trousers cut off at the knees and a white undershirt, Nixon was in a state of near collapse as he was half carried to the chair shortly after 1 a.m.—taking Daylight Saving Time into consideration.

His muscular body tensed as the first wave of 1,900 volts shot through him at 1:02 a.m., causing wisps of smoke to rise from his head. Then the body relaxed as the current was momentarily turned off, only to stiffen again with the application of 900 volts, until smoke poured so thickly from his right leg that it appeared he would catch afire.

"I could have pulled that switch," muttered one of the fifty spectators. It was Elmer Johnson, husband of the murdered woman. As he watched a team of physicians pronounce Nixon dead at 1:11 a.m. he commented, "This won't help my wife any. But I don't mind telling you that I feel swell."

Warden Frank Sain was asked afterward what it cost the taxpayers to execute a prisoner. Sain got out his records and did a little figuring. Based on the Nixon case, he said, the total cost came to $6,281.

Here's how he arrived at that figure:

The police investigation cost $983, three inquest sessions cost $120, and grand jury fees amounted to $142.50. To that you must add $4,393 for thirty-three days Nixon spent in court, and 386 days in jail at $1 a day. Of that amount, fifteen cents a day went for food. Arrangements for Nixon to travel the "last mile" came to $277.10. That included $185 in guards' salaries; $55 for bailiff's wages; $7 for electrician fees; $12 for engineers' services; $1 for Nixon's last meal; $17 for the doctors to pronounce him dead—and ten cents worth of electricity.*

*Editor's note: While Sain ran a tight jail, he apparently was not a whiz at arithmetic. The figures he listed came to a total of $6,301.60.

25

50 SEE SLAYER
GO TO HIS DOOM

OCTOBER 13, 1939

Europe was again embroiled in a bloody war in 1939, and in the Far East the Chinese were fighting the Japanese. In Chicago, the eleven year old case of a murdered police officer was finally marked closed.

Sergeant John Chiska was shot to death on April 5, 1928, when he interrupted the robbery of a candy store at 2218 North Lorel Avenue. The gunman was identified as 25-year-old Steve "Red" Cygan, a neighborhood hoodlum.

Cygan seemed to have disappeared from the face of the earth, however, and for nine years police were unable to find any trace of him. Then, in October of 1937, a fingerprint check by the FBI revealed that a prisoner known as Ray Smith, who was serving time in the Michigan State Prison at Jackson for a Detroit robbery, was none other than Steve Cygan.

He had picked the most unlikely hiding place—behind prison bars—where no one ever thought to look.

When Cygan was released on parole on June 20, 1939, Chicago Detective Ben Bazarek was waiting for him at the prison gate with an extradition warrant. He was returned to Illinois, convicted of murder, and sentenced to death in the electric chair on October 13.

On his last night Cygan was visited by several brothers and sisters, and a Roman Catholic priest. His last act was to write a farewell letter to his parents, denying that he had killed Officer Chiska.

A group of twenty-two inmates in Cygan's cell block had gone on a hunger strike to protest the impending execution. Cygan reciprocated by refusing the traditional last meal.

As a somber group of fifty witnesses gathered in the basement of the jail for the Friday the Thirteenth execution, Cygan's terrified cries could be heard from the death cell in the adjoining room. "I didn't do it! I'm innocent!" he screamed, while beating his fists against the brick walls. "I never killed that policeman."

While the witnesses waited on the wooden benches facing the ominous chair on the other side of a large panel of glass, a man in overalls walked in, examined the chair's fittings, and then left. He returned with a shallow pan of salt water, in which he carefully dipped the two sponge electrodes, one for the prisoner's head and one for the right leg.

Back in the death cell Cygan was all shouted out as the midnight hour approached, and he struggled only weakly as blue-shirted jail guards shaved his head, put the black mask over his face, and led him by his trembling arms to the electric chair.

With swift, rehearsed precision he was swung around with his back to the chair and pushed into a seated position. In an instant the clamps locked his arms and legs to the chair as a leather strap was tightened across his chest. Then the metal cap containing the electrode was pressed firmly down on his head, causing the saline solution to run down the side of his face as the wet sponge was flattened against his shaved skull.

The lanky, six-footer looked almost like a boy as he sat

in the chair, his white, bony knees protruding from the cut-off pants, as he clenched and unclenched his fists nervously.

At 12:02 the new sheriff, Thomas J. O'Brien, gave a signal that all was in readiness, and the mammoth electrical charge hit. The prisoner's body stiffened and strained against the restraints. Five minutes later Father Ernest Kaufholdt made the sign of absolution on the dead man's brow.

A deputy pulled aside the limp figure's undershirt as five doctors stepped forward to make it official. Each one left a small white circle on Cygan's reddened chest as he withdrew his stethoscope and nodded that the man in the chair was dead.

When Rose Chiska, widow of the slain policemen, received word that the execution had been carried out she said, "Now I can forget how my husband died. I have been nervous about it, but now I can rest."

26

NEGRO HOLDUP KILLER PUT TO DEATH IN CHAIR

OCTOBER 27, 1939

Two weeks after Steve Cygan was executed, the electric chair was ready to dispatch its next victim, the long-awaited Charles Price.

Price, now 28, had shot and killed Nicholas Miller, an insurance collector, during a robbery on March 30, 1936. After his arrest he also admitted killing Harry Rubin, a poultry merchant, four months earlier.

While some convicted killers had been put to death within two months after the initial crime, Price had managed to skirt the chair for more than three and a half years while winning eleven stays of execution.

His lawyers were among the first to base their appeals on the famous Scottsboro case, arguing that Price's constitutional rights had been violated because there were no blacks on the grand jury that indicted him. When that failed, Price's lawyers brought his wife, Matilda, to court on October 26 to testify that her husband was insane. That didn't work, either.

Price was executed the following day.

There was one final delay after he was fastened into the chair just after midnight. The chin strap that held the electrode tightly to the top of his head broke, and guards hastily substituted another one. The red button was pushed at 12:03 a.m., and Price was pronounced dead seven minutes later.

Among the fifty witnesses who viewed the electrocution was Arthur Miller, brother of the slain insurance collector. "I've waited three and a half years for this," he said.

Across the state line in Milwaukee, meanwhile, the Wisconsin Humane Society was vigorously opposing a proposal to get rid of undesirable starlings by baiting them with oats soaked in alcohol. The humane society argued that there was nothing to prevent songbirds from nipping at the laced oats, and falling prey to cats "or other foes" while intoxicated.

27

COLORED BANDIT GETS CHAIR FOR POLICE SLAYING

APRIL 19, 1940

It was 1940, time for the annual census, and the census taker did not overlook the sprawling Cook County Jail, which housed more prisoners than San Quentin.

Every inmate's presence was duly recorded by Tony Moravick, the jail storekeeper assigned to the task. Among those he interviewed on April 18 was 25-year-old Howard Poe.

"I'll be glad to cooperate, but I don't see the point," Poe shrugged. "I'm going to die one minute after midnight."

"Well, you're here now, and I have to count everyone living on the premise as of April 1," Moravick explained. He also listed the seven other prisoners currently on "death row"—a record number.

Poe had been one of five bandits who shot and killed Policeman Patrick O'Malley in a gun battle following the attempted robbery of a North Clark Street saloon on August 21, 1938. Two of the five were shot to death by police, and another was captured and sentenced to 199 years in prison. Poe and the fifth man got away. Poe was captured a year later in Cleveland. His partner was never apprehended.

Poe was returned to Chicago, tried for the policeman's

murder, and sentenced to death. He lived less than ten hours after being recorded in the 1940 census.

A powerfully-built man, he did not go to the chair willingly. When Warden Frank Sain and his deputies came to the death cell to get him he put up such a battle that jailers had to literally carry him into the execution chamber.

Even after being strapped into the chair he continued to struggle until 1,900 volts of electricity knocked his brain out of commission at 12:03 a.m. Seven minutes later the panel of physicians pronounced him dead.

Seated among the spectators was Policeman Walter O'Malley, brother of the police officer Poe had slain. "That man got what he deserved," O'Malley said softly, after the current was turned off.

The population of the United States had just been reduced by one.

28

VICTIM'S SONS
SEE SLAYERS DIE

MAY 17, 1940

Victor Wnukowski and Frank Michalowski were also among death row inmates counted in the 1940 census, and remained part of the population for one month afterward—until May 17.

Nig Wnukowski and Freako Michalowski, as they were known, along with Henry Drewek, had been convicted for the fatal shooting of Viggo Peterson, 64, in a North Side tavern holdup seven months earlier.

Up to that time juries in Chicago had consisted of the traditional "twelve good men and true." In 1939, however, women were permitted to serve on juries for the first time in Cook County.

The first "mixed jury" to hear a murder trial in Criminal Court found Wnukowski, Michalowski and Drewek guilty as charged on December 9, and the eight women on the panel showed no reluctance in consigning all three defendants to the electric chair.

Wnukowski, 24, Michalowski, 25, and Drewek, 22, were scheduled to die on May 17. For their last meal they gorged themselves on lemon and banana cream pie, and then posed one last time for photographers.

"How about taking a picture of me reading my Bible? My mother is coming to visit me, and I'd like to have a picture to give her—one that would help ease the suffering I've caused her," Wnukowski said. "I know I'm going to die tonight. I'm sure the pardon board won't act. I wish it was over with now."

Less than an hour before the switch was to be thrown Drewek won a reprieve, leaving his two partners to go it alone. Drewek's death sentence was later commuted to sixty years in prison, and he was ultimately released on parole.

For Michalowski and Wnukowski, however, it was the end of the line.

The viewing room, where about fifty witnesses sat on wooden benches facing the empty chair under a bright spotlight, reeked of booze. A number of reporters assigned to the story had obviously stopped along the way to steel their nerves.

The youngest member of the group was 20-year-old Don Agrella, chief copy boy at the *Times*. He had come to town from Ishpeming, Michigan, with ideas of becoming a big city reporter, and when no one else from his paper wanted to cover the multiple execution, he jumped at the chance.

Ray Brennan, the rewrite man to whom Agrella would phone in his story, took him to the Pall Mall lounge next door and poured three straight shots into the cub reporter before sending him out to Twenty-Sixth and California. "You might need these when you watch those sons-a-bitches burn," Brennan growled.

Also seated on the witness benches were the murder victim's three sons, Viggo Jr., George and Albert Peterson. Their mother and sister had applied for tickets to the execution as well, but were turned down.

Wnukowski, wearing a white undershirt and blue pants cut off at the knees, was led blindfolded to the chair first, at 1:06 a.m. His last words to Deputy Sheriff Edwin Olson as he was being strapped down, were, "I am innocent." Six minutes later he was pronounced dead.

As young Agrella scribbled the time of death on his note pad, he was almost overcome by the smell of burning flesh that permeated the crowded room.

Fighting back nausea, he held his breath and told himself, "Don't heave. Don't heave. If you do you'll never live it down."

As soon as Wnukowski's limp body could be removed, Michalowski was marched into the death chamber at 1:16 a.m. "I am sorry. Please be sure to tell Mrs. Peterson," he said as his arms and legs were being clamped in place. The manmade thunderbolt struck seconds later, and he was pronounced dead at 1:23 a.m.

"I've been waiting for this for seven months," Albert Peterson muttered through clenched teeth. "I'm glad it's a tooth for a tooth and a life for a life. Now I feel happy."

As the three Peterson brothers left the building they were confronted by Leonard Wnukowski, the brother of one of the men just executed. "I came to see if the Petersons' lips are full of blood they sucked from my brother's body," he shouted bitterly. The Petersons hurried to their car without commenting.

The early edition of the *Herald-American* reported:

> *Two young men who might have made mothers and sweethearts proud became gawkish puppets this morning as they were half carried into a shining chair that jolted death into them.*

The next evening on the city's Northwest Side, in Faikel's Hall where a dance was in progress, Michalowski's friends were hawking raffle tickets: "Buy a chance to help bury Frank Michalowski. Buy a chance for only five cents."

It was from this social club on North Leavitt Street, where the aroma of leather factories hung in the air, that the three men started off on their killing spree on an October evening just seven months earlier.

29

BITTER FATHER SEES GIRL'S SLAYER DIE

DECEMBER 13, 1940

In the summer of 1940 the Democrats held their national convention in Chicago to nominate President Franklin Delano Roosevelt for an unprecedented third term. As his renomination was made unanimous by acclamation at 1:37 a.m. on July 18, he turned to a friend and sighed, "That's that."

Not everyone in the city was glued to the radio during those early morning hours for the historic announcement, however.

Residents of the area around Diversey and Central Avenues, on the Northwest Side, were combing the neighborhood for eight-year-old Mazie Smith, who had failed to come home for supper.

She was last seen playing with friends near her house at 2913 North Parkside Avenue around 5 o'clock. When she hadn't came home by dark her father, Harold, a milkman, inaugurated a neighborhood search.

A friend of the family, Deputy Sheriff Edgar Ward, found the little girl's body shortly after midnight, under a coal pile in the basement furnace room of a tavern at 2850 North Central Avenue, two blocks away. Her head had been crushed and her clothing was in disarray. Dr. Paul Schmitt, the coroner's physician, said she had been raped.

Police found a disconnected water faucet which appeared to have been one of the murder weapons. They also found a blood-stained furnace shaker, which had been put back into place.

And despite the fact that it was the middle of July, a roaring fire blazed in the furnace, indicating the child's slayer had been preparing to dispose of her body.

Suspicion quickly focused on a member of the search party, Robert Schroeder, a 26-year-old porter who occupied sleeping quarters in the rear of the tavern, when police noticed blood on his trousers.

Questioned by Sergeants Francis Donohue and Oliver Karwoski of the coroner's staff, Schroeder admitted having struck the child with the furnace shaker. After beating her to death, he said, he had dinner, and then pitched a game of horseshoes behind the tavern.

The bushy-haired Schroeder was tried and convicted of murder. A Criminal Court jury of six men and six women deliberated five hours and took six ballots before agreeing that he should be sentenced to death.

The date for his execution was set for Friday, December 13.

As the hour of his death approached, Schroeder, shorn of his thick head of dark hair, nervously paced his cell and wept while lawyers made a last-ditch effort to save him.

"There's just one thing I want to hear—that they've granted my request for a commutation of my sentence," he told his father, Lewis, wiping tears from his face.

Mazie's father had traveled to Springfield to personally oppose clemency for the man who had murdered his child. "I want justice done here! I want fair play!" he told the State Board of Pardons and Paroles.

Clemency denied.

Smith, his eyes bloodshot from lack of sleep, then rushed back to Chicago where he took a front row seat to witness Schroeder's execution.

As Schroeder, supported by two guards, was led into the execution chamber at 12:02 a.m., Smith put his arms around the shoulders of a deputy sheriff who sat next to him. But his eyes never left the prisoner, who faltered as he neared the chair and had to be pushed forward by his guards. His face was concealed by a black mask; his trousers cut off at the knees so one of the electrodes could be attached to his right leg.

Smith stared through the glass as the initial jolt of 1,900 volts slammed into Schroeder's body one minute later, causing him to fairly leap against the restraining belt and clamps. The body relaxed as the current was momentarily shut off, then grew taut again with the second charge of 900 volts. Then it grew limp as the power was cut off at 12:07.

Father Ernest Kaufholdt, the jail chaplain, stepped forward and administered the last rights of the Catholic Church as Dr. Harold P. Sullivan pronounced Robert Schroeder dead at 12:09 a.m.*

Only then did Harold Smith take his eyes off the reddened, smoking corpse of the man who had taken his daughter's life. Rising slowly to his feet, and linking his arm with that of his brother, Phillip, who had accompanied him, he said, "Well, there's one man who will not harm any more children."

*Ironically, another man having the same name was electrocuted—by his own design—exactly ten years later. In 1950 Robert Schroeder, an unemployed electrician, stripped two electrical cords, attached them to a switch, and wound them around his wrists. Then he plugged the cord into a ceiling fixture, stretched out on his bed, and switched on the current.

30

HOLDUP SLAYERS OF TWO DIE IN ELECTRIC CHAIR

JUNE 20, 1941

By the summer of 1941 most of Europe had been overrun by the forces of the mad German dictator, Adolph Hitler, and his Axis partner, Benito Mussolini. Nazi troops occupied Poland, Austria, Czechoslovakia, the Netherlands, Belgium and Luxemburg. France had capitulated, and the German Juggernaut rolled across the Balkans, taking first Yugoslavia, then Greece, before turning its guns on Russia—all the while pounding England relentlessly with aerial bombs.

In Washington, President Franklin D. Roosevelt maintained a neutral attitude and assured American parents, "Your sons shall never fight on foreign soil."

In Chicago, two men who couldn't care less were about to die.

Two years earlier, on May 2, 1939, Orville Watson and Edward Riley, also known as Paddy Ryan, had attempted to hold up a tavern at 4623 North Western Avenue, not realizing that two police officers were inside.

In the gun battle that followed, Policeman Edward McIntyre was wounded, and policeman Philip Kelly was killed, along with Alex Ferguson, an undertaker. Watson was also wounded, but got away with his partner.

They fled to Detroit, where they were captured the next day and returned to Chicago.

Both men pleaded guilty to murder when they appeared a month later before Judge Robert J. Dunne in Criminal Court. If they expected mercy, however, they were mistaken.

Judge Dunne promptly sentenced both men to death. In imposing the extreme penalty the jurist declared:

"You men have pleaded guilty. I have found you guilty. I have read the record in every possible way and I can find no mitigating circumstances. Have you anything to say?"

Watson, 29, answered, "I wish your honor had read the testimony of the reenactment. Then you would know who fired the first shot."

Without commenting the judge turned to Riley, 37, who said, "I feel that my attorney has represented me better than I could have myself."

"Is that all?" the judge asked.

Watson nodded.

Omitting the customary, "May God have mercy on your soul," Judge Dunne pronounced sentence:

"Life, liberty and property must be protected in this city. I fix your punishment at death in the electric chair for both of you. I am sorry. Mr. Bailiff, take them away. Call the next case!"

The entire proceeding lasted less than four minutes.

Since 1919 seven judges in Cook County had imposed death penalties on ten defendants who pleaded guilty to the charge of murder, rather than place their fates in the hands of juries. Nine of them were put to death. Watson and Riley would be ten and eleven.

They managed to stay alive for more than two years, however, while their lawyers filed motions and appeals. By June 20, 1941, every legal remedy had been exhausted.

As the two prisoners sat in adjoining death cells,

counting the hours before the sheriff's men would come for them, they presented a contrast in character.

Watson, nervously pacing back and forth like a caged tiger, could talk of nothing but his faith in his lawyers to win a reprieve from Governor Dwight H. Green or the U.S. Supreme Court.

Riley, on the other hand, appeared almost indifferent. "It doesn't matter much whether I die because I never knew my father or mother. I was an orphan kicked around from one orphan home to another," he said. "Watson, he has a mother, father, sisters and brothers. He has someone who cares. Why don't they let me die in the chair and let him live?"

After Watson received a farewell visit from his mother, Bertha, who had come from Detroit, the two men asked for pencils and paper. Watson wrote a long letter to his parents, while Riley dashed off ten notes, seven of them to various women friends.

Then the doomed men said good-bye to Warden Frank L. Sain, and idly played dominoes and cards until the guards came for them.

Watson was summoned first, blindfolded, and led from the death cell. Then his legs buckled, and he had to be carried into the death chamber. He was placed in the electric chair at 12:06 a.m. The red button was pushed, his back arched, and his fingers snapped into fists. He was pronounced dead at 12:11. His limp body was removed and placed on a gurney as the chair was wiped off for the next man.

Riley walked unassisted to his doom six minutes later. He was pronounced dead at 12:25 a.m.

As the bodies were being prepared for delivery to the morgue, a jailer went back to the death cells and collected the letters the two men had written. In one of them Riley had included a joker and four aces from a deck of cards. The ace of spades was underlined, with the words, "You never know when."

In the note he had written:

> *Life is like a deck of cards and we are all the jokers. First it's hearts, then it's diamonds. Next it's clubs, and now it's spades.*

31

EXECUTE PARKS, SAWICKI NEXT

JANUARY 15, 1942

On December 7, 1941, Japanese bombers attacked the United States naval base on Oahu in the Hawaiian Islands, and America suddenly found itself mobilizing for a full scale war. Each day's newspapers brought screaming headlines about Japanese advances in the Pacific, and Allied casualties in Europe, where Germany and Italy had also declared war on the U.S.A.

The papers were so loaded with battle news from all fronts that the electrocution of Earl Parks just five weeks after Pearl Harbor barely rated four inches of type.

Parks, a black, 26-year-old ex-convict, shot and killed Lawrence Murphy, 27, of Gary, Indiana, during a robbery attempt in Jackson Park. After his arrest he also confessed to the murder of Gustaf R. Lindbloom, a 65-year-old carpenter, and to raping a white woman in Washington Park.

His arrest came in a most round-about way. Five blacks were detained in Georgetown, Kentucky, in a stolen car from Chicago. When Detectives John Foley and Fred Hinkens went down to bring the prisoners back to Illinois, they were told that one of them, 17-year-old Ernest Gaither, had been packing a pistol.

Routine ballistics tests showed that the weapon had fired the bullets that killed both Murphy and Lindbloom. Gaither, frightened at the prospect of facing a double homicide rap, told police he had gotten the gun from George Calhoun. Calhoun, in turn, said he purchased it from Parks.

Parks was picked up for questioning, and confessed to both murders as well as a series of other crimes.

From the moment of his arrest Parks seemed resigned to his fate. He was stoic as Judge John A. Sbarbaro sentenced him to die in the electric chair. And when his lawyers failed in an eleventh-hour attempt to have his life spared, he shrugged, "Well, I guess that's that."

He was led to the death chamber and placed in the electric chair at 12:01 a.m. on January 15, 1942. At 12:08 he was a dead man.

Parks left no one to mourn for him except 19-year-old Bernard Sawicki—and he had a special interest in the case. Young Sawicki, who occupied the death cell next to Parks, had his own appointment with the lethal chair in just twenty-four hours.

32

KILLER OF FOUR PUT TO DEATH IN ELECTRIC CHAIR

JANUARY 17, 1942

Towheaded Bernard Sawicki, who looked for all the world like an urban Huckleberry Finn, was not the kind of kid anybody would care to go rafting down the Mississippi with—and where he came from nobody knows.

Anna Sawicki, a babushkaed housewife from Chicago's Polish North Side, took him in when she found him abandoned as a baby on her doorstep in 1923 and gave him her name.

He grew up to be a mean little guttersnipe, and by the time he was nineteen he had killed four people, including a policeman. When a judge sentenced him to die in the electric chair he snarled, "The hell with you!"

Sawicki had earned the nickname "Knifey" while still in grammar school, when he showed up with a switch-blade knife to intimidate his classmates. He dropped out of school at the age of thirteen to become a full time bully and thief.

When he was sentenced to the St. Charles School for Boys for purse-snatching two years later, he was found to be "a boy of superior intelligence. However he seems to be without emotion. He has no love, no fear, no loyalties..."

The killing spree that would cost Knifey his life lasted

just seventy-two hours.

It began on June 27, 1941, when he used his long-barrel, .22 caliber target pistol to rob a man of $200. That gave him more than enough money for a round-trip bus ride to Momence, where he called on Henry Allain, a 72-year-old farmer whom he blamed for being sent to St. Charles. Allain was working in his barn when Sawicki strolled in, shot him through the head, and took $20 out of his overall pockets.

Back in Chicago, Sawicki went to the home of 17-year-old Charles Kwasinski, whom he had known at St. Charles. When Kwasinski refused to join him in a holdup, he shot him, too, and left him for dead.

An hour later, while ambling aimlessly through Sherman Park near 55th Street and Racine Avenue, Sawicki came upon 19-year-old John J. Miller, who was walking with his girlfriend. Sawicki robbed Miller of $2 and shot him three times. Leaving Miller dead on the ground, the young killer took a streetcar to an all-night restaurant, where he stuffed himself with five hamburgers.

By 7 a.m. he found himself at 59th Street and the Outer Drive, where he hijacked a car containing a man and a woman, which had stopped for a traffic signal. Pointing the gun at the couple, Sawicki took $8 and ordered, "Drive me to St. Louis."

The frightened motorist had just started to roll when he spotted Park Policeman Charles J. Speaker, 58, crossing the road in front of him. He slammed on his brakes and screamed, "Help! I'm being robbed." Speaker never had time to draw his service revolver. Sawicki shot him in the left eye, killing him instantly.

Sawicki fled on foot, and then hopped a streetcar back home—where police were waiting for him. Before young Kwasinski had died, he named Sawicki as his killer.

When he went on trial in Criminal Court for the policeman's murder, Sawicki mentioned to the bailiff, Joseph Lelivelt, "I bet I'll get the roaster."

"Naw, you won't get the chair. You're just a kid," Lelivelt scoffed.

"Oh, yeah? I'll bet a pack of cigarettes on it."

When the jury brought in an electric chair verdict, and Judge John A. Sbarbaro sentenced him to death, he retorted, "To hell with you! I can take it!" Then, turning triumphantly to Lelivelt he grinned, "You lose. You said I wouldn't get it. You owe me. Gimme a pack of cigarettes."

The bailiff sheepishly fished a pack of cigarettes out of his jacket pocket, and Sawicki snatched it out of his hand before being led back to the lockup. As they passed Assistant State's Attorney Richard Devine, who had prosecuted him, Sawicki quipped to the bailiff, "There's a guy I'd like to get a pot shot at."

While awaiting the death call the teenaged ruffian maintained his tough-guy facade almost to the end. On the afternoon of January 16, only hours before his appointment with the chair, he broke down and cried when Warden Frank Sain told him Governor Dwight H. Green had refused to grant him clemency.

Sawicki then asked for a pencil and paper, so he could write a letter of apology to the widow of the policeman he had slain.

"Dear Mother Speaker," he wrote. "I know that Mr. Speaker is up there praying for me; I will probably meet him there tonight if God wills it. Please say a prayer for me. I need it. May I always be your friend."

Sawicki's last visitors were his weeping foster mother, Anna Sawicki, who was accompanied by her son, Henry, her daughter, Jean, and the Reverend Leon V. Czyle of the Catholic Youth Organization.

At 10:15 p.m. Sawicki was served his last meal. He took four bites, and shoved the rest away.

At one minute after midnight on January 17 Sawicki regained his composure and walked, white faced but unassisted, to the electric chair. Three Roman Catholic priests stood alongside, intoning prayers, as the electricity coursed through his body. Eight minutes later he was pronounced dead.

Sawicki was buried the following day in Holy Sepulchre Cemetery. Six boys from the Catholic Youth Organization acted as pall bearers.

33

'3 HAT' KILLER EXECUTED; BODY CLAIMED BY FAMILY

SEPTEMBER 18, 1942

By the fall of 1942 nearly every able-bodied man in the 20-year age group was either in military service or waiting to be called. Those with leadership ability were especially in demand. John Pantano might have made a good officer candidate—except he was already in a position of leadership. Police knew him as head of the "Three Hat Gang."

As such he was the central figure in one of the most intriguing murder mysteries ever laid out before authorities up to that time—the fatal shooting of a policeman in Chicago and a tavern keeper in St. Louis, and an armed robbery.

By a strange coincidence, the slayers each lost a hat at the scene of the crime, while a third member of the gang left his hat at the scene of the holdup.

The bizarre skein of events began when the handsome Pantano, who had only a minor police record, persuaded Gene Landeck, also 20, and Herbert Dietz, 21, to join him in a series of cross-country holdups. After an armed robbery in New Orleans they drove to Dallas, and then headed back north. By the time they had reached St. Louis they were again out of "trump," as Pantano called it. They were flat broke.

Landeck and Dietz decided to hold up a St. Louis tavern. The saloonkeeper, Milton Scheuerman, drew his own gun, and Landeck and Dietz each pumped two bullets into him. As they fled from the scene of the slaying, Landeck's hat, with the initials G.L. in the band, flew off and was left behind.

Not long after that Pantano fatally shot Policeman Charles Williams during a tavern robbery on North Western Avenue in Chicago. Just outside the tavern a hat with the initials J.P. was found.

Then a friend of Pantano's, Joseph Burgo, tried to hold up a saloon on Belmont Avenue. The bartender, Stanley Migdal, hurled a bottle at Burgo, and when he ducked his hat flew off. Inside the hat police found a letter from the probation department bearing Burgo's name and address.

The letter took police directly to Burgo's door, and a subsequent investigation disclosed that he had friends with the initials J.P. and G.L. The three hatless holdup men were soon in custody.

Pantano was convicted for the murder of the Chicago police officer, and sentenced to die on September 18, 1942.

Shortly before he was scheduled to go to the chair, he handed Warden Frank Sain a letter addressed to his girlfriend, Joyce Christian, in which he had written:

"I'll never forget the swell times we had together. Now don't go blaming this thing on yourself, 'cause I was the dummy. If I should die tonight, don't worry about me 'cause I'll be in good hands, the Lord's hands."

As Pantano was being taken from the death cell he turned to Sain and said, "I'm sorry for what I have done. Tell the young fellows outside to keep on the right side of the law." He stumbled and had to be supported by four guards as he was led to the electric chair, in which he was seated promptly at 12 midnight.

The current was turned on and he was given four minutes of electricity at 12:01 a.m. At 12:07 three jail physicians examined the limp form in the chair and pronounced Pantano dead.

34

WISHON DIES, FALTERS
AT LAST MILE

NOVEMBER 26, 1943

Ernest Wishon never really had a great life, to hear him tell it. Born in the Missouri Ozarks, he began drinking moonshine whiskey when he was nine years old. He served forty-three months in prison at Jefferson City, Missouri, for robbery, and thirty-five months in Carson City, Nevada, on the same charge. In addition to that he was an alcoholic and a drug addict who used marijuana, morphine and cocaine, plus he suffered from both syphilis and gonorrhea.

When he was 38 years old he shot and killed a 79-year-old Chicago jeweler, Joseph Schulte, during a holdup. He was captured by a streetcar motorman who trailed him for five miles. Twenty-six days after the shooting a jury, that included ten women, sentenced him to death.

In an unusual move, when asked whether he had anything to say before the judge ratified the sentence, Wishon turned and addressed the jurors:

"Ladies and gentlemen, regardless of your verdict there is no ill feeling on my part. You were told that your conscience would bother you if you returned the death penalty. I hope not."

As he was being escorted from the courtroom he told

bailiffs, "I had it coming."

Wishon was sentenced to die on November 26, 1943, the day after Thanksgiving. For his last meal he enjoyed the same fare that was served to the 621 other prisoners in the Cook County Jail: turkey, cranberry sauce and pumpkin pie.

"This is a little different from last year," he joked. "A year ago today I was having Thanksgiving dinner at my mother's home in Rolla, Missouri."

Then he added, "Tell my mother I'm sorry, especially as far as she is concerned. Nothing in my past bothers me as much as the thought of how she will take this. It will be harder on her than it is on me."

After dinner the condemned man wrote two notes, one to Warden Frank Sain, and the other to the Reverend Albert E. Selcer, the jail's Episcopal chaplain.

His note to Father Selcer, written on the back of a holy picture, said, "The Lord is my shepherd. I thank God that He is my shepherd and that I am going back into the fold."

The note to the warden contained a passage from the scriptures, and concluded, "By my death, the state will gain nothing, while I will gain eternal life."

Wishon had been a loser all his life, and nothing changed at the end. He rose calmly from his bunk when jailers came for him, but after taking several steps his knees grew wobbly and he had to be almost dragged to the waiting chair.

The first charge of 1,900 volts shot into his body at 1:02 a.m., and a minute later the current was reduced to 900 volts. After the electricity was turned off four physicians examined him and pronounced him dead at 1:08 a.m.

Wishon's body was turned over to two sisters, who had traveled from Rolla to have one last visit with him on Thanksgiving Day, before he went to the chair.

35

KILLER GOES TO HIS DEATH PRAYING

MARCH 15, 1944

Paul Le Roy Williams, a gangling 25-year-old gunman from Chicago's Southeast Side, was not one bit happy when Criminal Court Judge John Sbarbaro sentenced him to die in the electric chair for the fatal shooting of Thomas Papayanis during a grocery store holdup.

"I was double crossed!" Williams stormed.

His lawyer had promised him that by pleading guilty he would escape the chair. Judge Sbarbaro wasn't in on the deal, however.

Sheriff Michael Mulcahy wasn't too happy either. This would be his first execution since taking office, and he was not looking forward to it. "Executions are distinctly the least pleasant part of the sheriff's post," he said.

Williams tried to cheat the executioner by hanging himself by a bed sheet in his cell, but a jailer foiled the attempt and he was placed under an around-the-clock guard.

Williams was scheduled to die January 16, 1944, but a highly unusual legal tangle resulted in a stay of execution until March 15. The stay was granted on January 12 by the Illinois Supreme Court to permit his lawyers to perfect an appeal to the United States Supreme Court on a writ of certiorari. At the same time, the U.S. Supreme Court notified the lawyers that the writ had been denied, and it would not hear the case.

Plans then went ahead for the March 15 execution.

Williams spent his last two afternoons with his 24-year-old wife, Genevieve, his mother, Evelyn Williams, of Jacksonville, Florida, and his sister, Gerry Meyers. They sat separated by two panes of glass, and talked through a telephone. Their final meeting lasted six hours, until jailers took Williams to the death cell at 7 p.m. As he was being led away Williams' wife threw him a kiss, and he threw one back to her.

At 9 o'clock he was brought his last meal, consisting of steak, salad, potatoes, peas and coffee. After that he had his head shaved, stripped naked, and put on his execution clothes, a white undershirt and black knee-length trousers.

"I didn't get a fair trial. They didn't believe me," he told Warden Frank Sain as he was being readied for the death march.

Just three minutes before the black mask was put over his head he accepted religion, and repeated the Lord's Prayer after the Reverend Albert E. Selcer, the jail's Episcopal chaplain.

Williams was then led into the death chamber supported by two deputies, who positioned him into the chair and affixed the restraints. More than 45 witnesses, including Sheriff Mulcahy, Warden Sain, and newspapermen watched as he drummed nervously on the black painted arm of the chair with his left hand until the 1,900 volt jolt stiffened him against the straps at 1:04 a.m. Eleven minutes later Doctors Frank L. Fartelka, Meyer Levy and V.C. Flowers pressed their stethoscopes to his chest and declared him dead.

36

SLAYER KRAUSE DIES IN CHAIR AT COUNTY JAIL

SEPTEMBER 15, 1944

The allies invaded Normandy in June of 1944, Paris was liberated in August, and by mid September American bombers were raining more than 3,000 tons of explosives—averaging more than three tons a minute—on key targets in Germany day and night.

Back on the home front Alvin Krause, who had been one bad guy, was preparing to face death in a different way. He was about to atone for his crimes in the Cook County electric chair.

A year earlier Krause, a well-groomed man of 29 who looked more like an accountant than a stick-up man, had shot and killed realtor Walter Bush during a currency exchange robbery at 5151 South Kedzie Boulevard. Two weeks after that he and a partner, Edward Damiani, a chemist, hit a currency exchange at 311 North Pulaski Road, where they sprayed the cashier, Agnes Olson, with sulphur dioxide gas. She died three days later.

Krause and Damiani were tracked down after a complex investigation by Captain Frank Pape and other detectives, who had just two clues—a photograph of Damiani's baby daughter and the key to a gas cylinder.

An all-woman jury, the first ever qualified to impose the death penalty, convicted both men for the poison gas murder of Agnes Olson. The twelve women spared the two killers, however, and sentenced them to life imprisonment.

Krause then refused an opportunity to plead guilty to the Walter Bush murder and accept another life term, to run concurrently. Instead he gambled on another jury trial. What his logic was is hard to understand, unless he wanted to die.

Assistant State's Attorney Richard Austin, in arguing the case before the jury, said, "The defendant is charged with murder, and murder is not new to him. How many killings is a man entitled to in a space of two weeks?"

The jury decided Krause had enjoyed his quota, found him guilty, and sentenced him to death in the electric chair. His execution would automatically cancel the life sentence imposed in the earlier homicide.

The six-foot two-inch, lantern-jawed prisoner turned to religion as he awaited his date with destiny, scheduled for September 15, 1944. He had his Bible out and was reading the Twenty-third Psalm when Warden Frank Sain broke the news to him that his last appeal had been turned down by the Illinois Supreme Court, and he would have to die.

"This book is preparing me to go," he told Sain. "I am not afraid now. I still hope something may be done to save me—but if not, okay, I'm ready."

On the day before he was to die, Krause was quartered in the jail hospital with a skin infection, induced by nervousness, according to jail physicians. While in the hospital he was visited by his mother, Mary, his stepfather, Walter, and a sister.

At 10 p.m. he was taken to the death cell, where he was served his last meal of steak and French fries, string beans, a fruit dessert and coffee. Then his long, dark hair was shaved off and he received the last sacraments of the Roman Catholic Church.

Shortly after 1 a.m., as Krause walked steadily to his

doom, the sixty-one newspapermen, law enforcement officials and other selected witnesses noticed that his hands were bandaged—the result of the skin infection. The Reverend Ernest Kaufholdt, Franciscan chaplain at the jail, walked behind the blindfolded prisoner as he was guided into the death chamber and clamped into the electric chair.

At a signal from the sheriff, the current was applied at 1:06 a.m. Nine minutes and four jolts later, Krause was pronounced dead.

The story of Alvin Krause had a heart-breaking ending. His parents could not read English, and Krause had never told them why he was in jail. "I just kid them along," he told his jailers.

On the afternoon of September 15, twelve hours after Krause was executed, his mother and father were escorted to Warden Sain's office by a jail guard who wore a look of consternation on his face.

"I would like to see my boy," Mrs. Krause told the warden.

It was then that Sain realized that the parents still did not know their son's fate. As gently as he knew how, the warden told the elderly couple that Alvin had "returned to God."

The woman screamed hysterically, broke away from her husband and ran out of the building in tears. He caught up with her in the corridor of the nearby Criminal Courts building and comforted her. When last seen, they were standing arm in arm on the corner across the street from the courthouse, waiting for a streetcar that would take them home with their grief.

37

TRIPLE MURDERER WALKS CALMLY TO DEATH IN CHAIR

OCTOBER 19, 1945

The world was suddenly at peace. The war in Europe had ended on May 1, and the Pacific war came to a stunning conclusion on August 14 after the United States unleashed the atomic bomb on Japan.

Two months later returning soldiers, catching up on the news back home, learned that a man named Kermit Breedlove was about to be electrocuted for killing his wife and two police officers.

That Breedlove, 35, ever lived to die in the chair is a miracle in itself.

Breedlove, a black stockyard worker, put six bullets into his wife, Goldine, because another man had flirted with her. As she lay dead on the floor of their Prairie Avenue apartment, he telephoned police and told them what he had done. Then he reloaded his pistol and awaited their arrival.

When Policeman Sam Black, 53, arrived at the apartment Breedlove shot him twice through the head. With Black's gun in one hand and his own in the other, he then ran downstairs, where he encountered Black's partner, Policeman Ezra Caldwell, 32. In an exchange of gunfire, Caldwell was fatally wounded and Breedlove took three bullets. A second police squad arrived, and Officer James McKenna shot Breedlove three more times.

Breedlove and Caldwell were placed in a squad car, which collided with a bus and overturned, injuring three more officers.

Breedlove somehow survived and went to trial. He was sentenced to 199 years in prison for Officer Black's murder. Then, in a second trial, a jury took just twenty minutes to find him guilty of killing Officer Caldwell and sentenced him to death.

As the clock ticked away on his life on the night of October 18, 1945, Breedlove sat quietly in the death cell, reading his Bible.

Daylight Saving Time gave the prisoner an extra hour of life, since jailers did not want to be accused of executing him on the wrong day because of a technicality.

After receiving the last rites of the Episcopal Church from the Reverend Albert E. Selcer, Breedlove offered no resistance when jailers came for him shortly after 1 a.m. and led him blindfolded to the electric chair. He was strapped into the lethal device at 1:12 a.m., and the red button was depressed one minute later. After the customary series of jolts, Breedlove was pronounced dead at 1:19.

He became the fifty-third man to die in the electric chair since it replaced the gallows in 1927. It was the twenty-ninth execution at which Warden Frank Sain officiated.

38

KILLER EATS STEAK,
DIES IN CHAIR

JUNE 20, 1947

The Great Depression ended with World War II, when every able bodied man and many women were in service, while just about everyone else who wanted to work held down a vital job of one kind or another. When the soldiers, sailors, marines, airmen and coast guardsmen, WACs, WAFs, WAVEs, and SPARs returned home, many went off to college on the G.I. Bill. Industry, meanwhile, gearing up for peacetime production for the first time in five years, welcomed the remainder back with open arms.

Violent crime appeared to be down, and the electric chair gathered dust in the basement of the Cook County jail for nearly two years. Then Charles Crosby, a black, 37-year-old ex-convict entered the picture.

Police Lieutenant Herman Ziebell and Sergeant Joseph Cortino surprised two burglars looting a gasoline station in the suburb of Forest Park, and Ziebell was shot to death as the pair tried to get away.

Cortino subsequently identified Crosby, alias Arthur Peterson, as the gunman. Crosby's partner, Henry Hitson, got 199 years in prison and Crosby got the chair.

"I'm willing and ready to die," Crosby told the

Reverend Theodore Harper, jail chaplain, who comforted him during his last hours. Shortly before midnight on June 19, 1947, Crosby ordered "a thick steak with all the trimmings."

Six comrades of the slain Forest Park policeman were among the forty-nine witnesses as Crosby was led blindfolded into the death chamber and clamped into the chair.

Sheriff Elmer M. Walsh, officiating at his first execution since taking office six months earlier, nodded when all was ready, and the switch was thrown at 1:06 a.m. Four minutes later the man in the chair was pronounced dead.

39

'TOUGH GUY' DIES
WITH HYMN ON LIPS

OCTOBER 24, 1947

Ernest Gaither was one of the more unusual men who ever abided on death row. A powerfully-built black man, who stood six feet tall and weighed 260 pounds, he looked more like a young choir boy than a hardened killer of 24.

In fact, by the time he was fifteen, he had already attained the nickname of "Little Gaither," and led his own gang by virtue of being the toughest kid in the bunch.

He earned a seat in the electric chair by fatally shooting Max Baran, 49, in a $300 tavern robbery on Chicago's West Side. He was arrested a week later in Atlanta, where he had gone on a spending spree with the proceeds.

As Gaither sat on death row he suddenly got religion, was baptized by the Reverend Theodore Harper, a Baptist minister, and spent his final hours reading the Bible and writing letters.

To Warden Frank Sain he wrote:

> *I am write you this letter to let you know how much I appreciate what you have did for me tell all the Boys in here and on the outside that Crimes don't pay no one but the lawyers.*

His last note to his mother, Mrs. Australia Gaither, said:

I am OK, Mother, so don't worry about me please because we all got to leave this world someday. I want you to meet me in heaven I will be waiting for you there.

And to his aunt, Lucille Brown, he penned:

I was very happy to see you today but sorry to see you crying. Well, darling, I only have five hours to live but still I am not worrying although I can't help from worrying our sister she is so sweet. Well, I hope you can read this letter. I am in a hurry. I got to get ready to leave this worried world. When you answer send it to King Jesus.

For his last meal Gaither made a most unusual request—"cornflakes with real cream."

At 10:23 p.m. he asked Chief Guard Rudolph Lee, "Can't we move up the clock, Lee? I'm ready to go now." When told that he must wait until a minute past midnight, he sat and sang "When the Roll is Called up Yonder," "Just a Little Talk with Jesus," and "I Know the Lord Has Laid His Hand on Me," until jailers came to shave his head. As he was taken from the death cell he said, "I'm going to sit in the chair and go to sleep."

Gaither walked bravely to the chair as seventy-five witnesses looked on. He took the seat just after midnight, and waited calmly as the clamps were tightened about his arms and legs, the death cap lowered, and the strap buckled across his chest.

Among the witnesses were Baran's two sons, Bernard and Leo, and a nephew, Maurice Baran.

The first jolt of nearly 2,000 volts flashed through Gaither's body at 12:03 a.m. After two more jolts of lesser voltage he was pronounced dead by Dr. Harold Levy, jail physician, at 12:06 as the jail chaplain uttered a prayer over his limp body.

Had any man ever gone to the chair before on a bowl of cornflakes?

40

KILLER DIES AS
EYE 'DEAL' FAILS

NOVEMBER 26, 1949

On November 26, 1949, the *Chicago Herald-American* printed one of the most remarkable newspaper pictures ever published. It was a photograph of 22-year-old James "Mad Dog" Morelli dying in the electric chair.

How the *American* got the amazing photo is a story in itself.

Morelli earned his nickname as the result of an insane murder spree in which three men were killed and two others were shot and left for dead.

He and two of his friends, Lowell Fentress and Thomas Daley, suspected that 36-year-old John Kuesis had informed on them in a grocery holdup. Kuesis was shot to death by Daley in a garage at 3600 Emerald Avenue. Four other men, who were in the garage at the time and witnessed the slaying, were "taken for a ride" in an effort to seal their lips permanently.

Two of them, Emil Schmeichel, 22, and Theodore Callis, 29, were shot to death. The other two, Nick Kuesis, John's younger brother, and Frank Baker, 17, were also shot and left for dead.

They lived to tell the story, however, and Morelli was

sentenced to death for slaying Schmeichel. Fentress got two 199-year prison terms, and Daley was shot to death by police.

Proclaiming his innocence to the bitter end, Morelli offered to donate his eyes to anyone who would provide financial assistance to his wife and baby after his death. The plan fell through on a technicality, however.

Morelli's last meal was the traditional turkey dinner, served to all jail inmates on Thanksgiving Day, the last day of his life.

He then spent his last hours with members of his immediate family—his 20-year-old wife, Genevieve, their infant daughter, Dorothy, and his parents, Fred and Dorothy Morelli. "Look after the baby. Take care of her," he told his wife, as she left sobbing hysterically.

After the family had gone, while Morelli was being consoled by a Catholic priest, the Reverend Ernest Kaufholdt, two of his friends tried to smuggle a pair of hacksaw blades to the prisoner. They were caught, and in searching the basement of one of the men's homes, police found an arsenal including a tommy gun, two rifles, a pistol and a sawed-off shotgun.

Morelli, meanwhile, broke into tears while kneeling in the death cell as Father Kaufholdt prayed, "Have compassion, oh Lord, on his tears and admit him who hath no hope but in Thee to the sacrament of Thy reconciliation."

The condemned man regained his composure when Chief Guard Rudolph Lee and his bailiffs came to get him at midnight for the short walk to the chair. "I can walk without help," Morelli said. "I'll do what I have to do."

Morelli, his face masked, and the top of his head shaved, entered the death chamber at 12:02 a.m., walking between Lee and deputy Warden Walter Makowski. He wore a white undershirt, and black knee-length shorts. Father Kaufholdt followed, chanting words of the final sacrament.

Guards, who had been rehearsing throughout the day,

quickly snapped the arm and leg clamps into place. A leather and metal mask was put over his head, and the electrode pressed against the bare spot on the top of his skull.

The guards stepped back while Lee made a quick inspection of their work. He then nodded to Warden Chester Fordney that all was in readiness. The warden gave the signal and four men—two jail officials and two electricians—pressed the switches in front of them. None of the four knew which one was depressing the "live" button.

Morelli jerked and strained at the clamps as the first jolt of 1,900 volts hit him, and coursed through his body for ten seconds while 154 witnesses watched through the plate-glass window in the adjoining room. He was then given three more charges—one of low voltage, one high, and another low. At 12:10 a.m. Lee stepped up to the chair and pulled the undershirt aside. Seven physicians approached the chair and, one by one, they pronounced him dead.

Morelli's body was kept in the jail for six hours, a customary procedure, before being turned over to the family's undertaker to be prepared for burial.

The next morning the *Herald-American* shocked the city with a graphic photograph of Morelli dying in the electric chair.

The newspaper had assigned two men to cover the execution, reporter Basil "Gus" Talbott, a former boxer, and photographer Joe Migon. Earlier in the day Vern Whaley, the *American's* picture editor, and Tony Berardi Sr., the chief photographer, had hollowed out the heel of Migon's right shoe and slipped a tiny Minox camera, three inches long, an inch wide, and three-quarters of an inch thick, into the opening.

Twice that evening Migon passed through an X-ray machine in the jail, along with other witnesses, but it failed to pick up the camera so close to the floor.

As the witnesses filed into the small basement room

and found places on the thirteen rows of wooden benches facing the chair, Talbott and Migon muscled their way into the front row.

While all eyes were on Morelli being fastened into the death chair, Migon casually slipped the camera out of his shoe and cupped it in his hands between his legs. He then gave Talbott a nudge with his elbow, and Talbott feigned a coughing spell to cover the clicking of the shutter.

When the extraordinary picture ran the next day the other newspapers screamed foul. Jail officials were furious, and Sheriff Elmer Walsh held a news conference to denounce the explicit photo as "impossible" and "a phony."

So Talbott and Migon went out to the jail the following day and demonstrated just how they did it. The newspaper then ran the photo a second time, along with the "inside story" of how the paper had achieved what it called "the picture scoop of the decade."

The *American* justified the stunt by telling its readers:

> *By this picture, the* Herald-American *has PROVED that the detection system is NOT fool-proof! And it points out a REAL DANGER to authorities that guns and saws COULD BE SMUGGLED INTO THE COUNTY JAIL AND EVEN PERMIT A WHOLE-SALE BREAK BY PRISONERS!*

The paper further rubbed it in by getting the respected Dr. Preston Bradley, pastor of the Peoples Church, to declare, "It is unfortunate to see such a young boy being killed by a society he has offended, but apparently talk and counsel aren't enough. Here is a living, visible, tragic picture showing conclusively that crime does not pay."

Then the paper massaged salt in the competition's wounds by quoting Police Commissioner John C. Prendergast:

"This is one of the greatest newspaper pictures I ever

saw. It is shocking, but it should serve as a stern warning to rapacious youths that tough guys come to a deadly, unglamorous end."

After the hullabaloo had died down, Whaley had Migon's shoe gold-plated and presented it to him at the National Press Photographers Convention in Hollywood, Florida.

41

YOUNG SLAYERS DIE IN CHAIR
FOR $18 KILLING

APRIL 21, 1950

A Mexican feast was prepared on the afternoon of April 20, 1950, in a most unlikely kitchen on Chicago's Southwest Side. Large helpings of tortillas, enchiladas, frijoles, chili con carne and other delicacies were lovingly cooked up in the kitchen of the Cook County Jail by Refugio Martinez, owner of the Acapulco Restaurant in the city's Mexican community. He was assisted by George Hernandez, a cook, who was a federal prisoner awaiting deportation.

The south-of-the-border menu was being prepared for Alfonso Najera and Fred Varela, who had requested it for their last meal.

Varela, 26, and Najera, 27, had been sentenced to death in the electric chair for the murder of Albert Brody, a 31-year-old cab driver, in an $18 robbery.

Their final appeal had been turned down by Governor Adlai E. Stevenson, and there was nothing to do now but count the minutes.

As the evening wore on, Varela sobbed in the arms of his parents, Stephen and Amada, choking out his last protests of innocence. In an adjoining cell Najera talked quietly with his wife, Josephine, while holding their two children, 6-year-old Mary and 3-year-old Alfonso Jr., on his lap. Najera's last request was that the children be let into his cell so he could hold them. The youngsters, laughing happily at the visit, did not know they would never see their father again.

The families were allowed to remain until 7 p.m., when the last meal was brought in. Afterward the two prisoners were given the last rites by the jail chaplain, the Reverend Ernest Kaufholdt and the Reverend James Tort of St. Jude's Seminary in Momence, Illinois.

At the same time Warden Chester L. Fordney, a former Army colonel, was deploying extra guards around the jail grounds and in tiers adjoining the death cells, after picking up rumors that the prisoners might try to escape.

Najera had already broken out once, by overpowering a guard and taking his keys, in September 1948 while still awaiting trial. He was recaptured by FBI agents in Texas while trying to get back into Mexico.

As the clock wound down on their lives, Warden Fordney brought his own television set down and set it outside the death cells for the condemned men to watch while they waited. When Fordney prepared to leave, Varela grabbed his hand through the bars and said, "How're things going, Colonel?"

At 11:30 p.m. a guard with an electric razor came down and shaved each man's head. That done, each stripped naked and put on the traditional white undershirt and black shorts that would make them look like blindfolded children as they walked to their deaths.

Eighty-four witnesses were crowded into the small room facing the chair as Varela was brought in first, since he had been the first of the two sentenced by Judge Charles E. Byrne. He was strapped into the chair at 12:01 a.m. Four minutes later—after receiving 1,900 volts for one minute, 900 volts for ten seconds, 1,900 again for thirty seconds, and then ten seconds more of 900 volts—he was pronounced dead.

Father Kaufholdt administered Extreme Unction over Varela's reddened body as it was removed from the chair at 12:12 and wheeled out on a gurney. Najera was brought in next. He was seated into the chair at 12:17, and five minutes later he, too, was history.

It was the first double execution in the jail since June of 1941 when Orville Watson and Edward Riley went to the chair.

Among the witnesses to the electrocutions was cab driver Brody's brother, Sidney, an appliance store owner. "We feel that justice has now been done," he said as he left the execution chamber.

Najera's wife, Josephine, his step-mother, Mercedes Rodrigues, and other relatives sat weeping in the jail lobby while the executions were carried out. As soon as guards informed them, "It's all over, folks," they left quietly.

42

KNIFE KILLER
DIES IN CHAIR

NOVEMBER 17, 1950

Willard Truelove was a lowly purse-snatcher, but his occupation earned him the highest penalty on the books.

The snag came when Truelove, 31, grabbed the purse of Mary Lo Chirco, the 26-year-old mother of two small boys, as she walked near her home on South Damen Avenue on October 26, 1949. When she refused to let go, he whipped out a six-inch knife and slashed her throat.

As the woman lay dying on the street, Truelove ran off with the purse, which contained $1 in cash and Mrs. Lo Chirco's $20.06 paycheck from the neighborhood toy shop. He then abducted a small girl, took her to his room, and raped her.

The child who, like Truelove, was black, had the presence of mind to remember the surroundings, and gave police information that led to her attacker's arrest.

Truelove confessed that he stabbed Mrs. Lo Chirco to death, but later claimed that police beat the confession out of him. He said the murdered woman's purse had been given to him by a stranger.

When lawyers made an eleventh-hour plea to save Truelove from the electric chair, on grounds that he had become insane since his conviction, Chief Justice Frank M. Padden of Criminal Court told the condemned man's attorney, "You might as well have given me a blank piece of paper."

Truelove, a Methodist, read the Bible as he sat in the death cell, just a few paces from the lethal chair. He refused offers of an elaborate last meal of steak, chicken or anything he wanted. "Just a pack of cigarettes, that's all," he said.

His last visitors were the Reverend Theodore Harper, pastor of a church on South Michigan Avenue, and his girlfriend, Charley Shorts, age 30.

At the stroke of midnight Truelove was carried, still protesting his innocence, to the electric chair. After three applications of high-voltage current he was pronounced dead at 12:06 a.m.

Among the witnesses to the execution were Mrs. Lo Chirco's husband, Joseph; her three brothers, Sam, Peter and Nick Salerno; her step-father, Frank Greco, and Greco's son, Frank Jr.

As he was leaving the jail afterward the elder Greco turned to his son and remarked, "I'm glad to see him get it."

43

JENKO DIES IN CHAIR; KILLED GIRL FOR CARFARE

JANUARY 25, 1952

Color television had only recently been introduced in the United States, Harry S. Truman was in the White House, and the second purse-snatcher in a row was about to go to the electric chair in Cook County.

Raymond Jenko, just 20 years old, had slashed 17-year-old Patricia Schwartz to death with a butcher knife when the Englewood High School student refused to relinquish her purse to him after he accosted her on the doorstep of her home.

Jenko, a drug addict, almost didn't survive to keep his appointment with the executioner. When he was brought under guard to the inquest into the teen-ager's death, the girl's parents, William and Florence Schwartz, pounced on him and wrestled him and the policeman he was handcuffed to to the floor.

"Why didn't I bring a knife and let him have it like he gave it to Patricia?" Mrs. Schwartz screamed. "I'm sorry we didn't get him. I'd like to slit his throat from cheek to cheek."

Later Mrs. Schwartz, 39, embraced Jenko's crippled mother, Ruby, 53, and the two women sobbed in each other's arms.

"I'm so sorry for you," Mrs. Schwartz cried.

"I'm sorry for him," Mrs. Jenko wept, motioning toward her manacled son. "But why did he have to do that to your little girl? I hope you can forgive him."

After being sentenced to death for the girl's murder, Jenko escaped briefly from the jail, but never got off the property. He fooled guards making their rounds by rigging up a dummy wearing blue jeans and a shirt stuffed with newspapers in his bed. He then removed a wall panel, possibly with a coin, and crawled up a ventilating shaft to the jail roof, five stories above the ground.

Harry Williams, a fellow death row inmate, lowered himself to the ground with a rope woven from sixteen bed sheets and got away. Jenko lost his nerve and was captured. From then on he was confined to the death cell, under 24-hour guard, until all appeals ran out and he was scheduled to die on January 25, 1952.

His last day on earth was an uneasy one all the way around at the jail, because neither the newly-elected sheriff, John Babb, nor the new warden, Phillip Scanlan, had ever executed a man before.

Patricia Schwartz' parents both requested permission to witness the electrocution. "He killed my little girl. I want to see him die," Florence Schwartz begged. Babb denied the mother's request, but issued a ticket to Mr. Schwartz.

Jenko was visited on his last day by his arthritic mother, whose legs gave her so much pain she was unable to kneel and pray with him. When it was time for her to leave at 6 p.m., both wept as he kissed her and she said, "Oh, Raymond. My son, my son. It isn't fair that I should lose both my husband and my son in two short years. I don't know what I'm going to do."

"Now, Mom, promise me that you're not going to do anything to yourself."

"I promise," she sobbed.

After his mother hobbled from the death cell on crutches, the prisoner was served a last meal of two hamburgers and two cups of coffee.

As the midnight hour approached, his head was shaved and he was dressed in the white undershirt and black short pants. He walked to the chair unaided between two jailers.

It took sixteen minutes to kill Jenko. Four physicians watched as the first electrical charge of 1,900 volts stiffened his body and turned his skin a sunburn red. It was followed in quick succession by charges of 900 and 1,900 volts.

When the current was turned off, the four doctors stepped forward and pressed their instruments to Jenko's chest. His heart was still beating! The physicians stepped away as a fourth charge was administered, after which Jenko was pronounced dead at 12:17 a.m.

As the murdered girl's father left the chamber after the execution, he told reporters, "It was a pleasure."

Five years later Jenko's crippled mother, Ruby, was found dead in her room at 5636 Princeton Avenue, where she had been living under an assumed name. A piece of clothesline was around her neck.

44

SLAYER OF TWO IS EXECUTED IN ELECTRIC CHAIR

MARCH 14, 1952

Ray Jenko's partner in the daring escape from death row, Harry Williams, bludgeoned a guard to death and took his shotgun as he went over the twenty-six-foot wall.

The murder of the guard, George Turley, so enraged Sheriff John Babb that he put up $1,000 of his own money as a reward for the escaped prisoner—dead or alive.

The fugitive was described as a 20-year-old Negro, 6 feet 2 inches tall, 180 pounds, wearing a polka dot cap, white shirt, tan suit and crepe soled shoes, and carrying the guard's shotgun.

Williams was captured two days later in a city-wide dragnet.

He had originally been sentenced to death for the fatal shooting of Mary Scott, 45, in a purse snatching. After his arrest he was identified as the rapist of a South Side housewife. Williams also shot and wounded two police officers who had earlier tried to arrest him.

Once back behind bars and under heavy guard, Williams' execution was set for 12:01 a.m. Friday, March 14.

As he awaited his fate he was visited in the death cell by Father Philemon Canavan, the jail chaplain. For his last meal the prisoner requested barbecued ribs.

Then he had his head shaved, changed into the short-pants death uniform, and went to the chair quietly at midnight. The initial jolt of 1,900 volts was administered at 12:05 a.m., followed by a second of 700 volts at 12:07, and a third shock of 300 volts at 12:09.

He was pronounced dead by a panel of three physicians three minutes later.

Williams never lived long enough to be tried for the death of the guard he killed during his escape from jail.

45

2 COP SLAYERS ARE EXECUTED; 3D GIVEN STAY

OCTOBER 17, 1952

A quadruple execution had been scheduled for four convicted cop-killers. It would have been the first since Frank Jordan, Charles Rocco, John Popescue and Richard Sullivan went to the chair in rapid succession in 1931.

The condemned men were:

• Bernice "Bernie" Davis, 31, who fatally shot Detectives Donald McCormick and Edward T. Crowley, a brother of Superior Court Judge Wilbert F. Crowley, when they went to his home to question him about a West Virginia robbery.

• Earlie Burton, 30, sentenced to death for the murder of Policeman William B. Murphy who interrupted the holdup of a liquor store at 455 W. 59th St.

• LeRoi Lindsey, 30, one of Burton's partners in the holdup.

• Emanuel Scott, 25, another member of the holdup gang.

Scott and a fourth member of the gang that killed Officer Murphy were also wounded during the shootout. Murphy shot and wounded Emil Washington 25, before he fell dead with eight bullets in him, and Scott, who had acted as lookout, was shot in the hand by Lindsey "because he let the copper walk into the store."

Washington died while in custody after ripping the stitches from his wounds. The coroner called his death "suicide."

On June 12, 1952, Burton's name was dropped from the roster when he died of tuberculosis in his cell.

That left Davis, Lindsey and Scott. They were scheduled to be executed on October 17.

All three had embraced religion since their arrest, and as they sat in the three death cells counting the hours of their last day, they talked to one another through the bars, or read their Bibles.

Lindsey was confirmed by Bishop Bernard J. Sheil of the Roman Catholic Church, who visited him in his cell.

"Trouble only hit me twice, but twice is enough," he told Sheil. "I served five years for a robbery committed when I was nineteen, and now—this."

Scott, still maintaining his innocence, even though he was shot at the scene by one of his fellow gang members, said, "I'm not bitter. I have nothing in my heart but Christ."

And Davis declared, "The world is in bad shape because man will not turn to God. I don't think I had a fair trial, but I have found peace in Christ."

Faced with a multiple execution, Warden Phillip Scanlan ordered the jail's 1,676 prisoners served their evening meal at 3 p.m., so the "boulevard" would be cleared for the midnight walk. The boulevard was the long corridor leading to the death cells, in the room next to the electric chair.

Lindsey, a barber by profession, was visited by his wife, Dolores, and their two children. He seemed resigned to his fate as he sighed, "I always had a Bible in the house, but never opened it. I never knew the beauty of religion until now."

An hour before the three were to have gone to their

deaths, Scott was given a reprieve by acting Governor Sherwood Dixon, to permit his attorneys to appeal to the U.S. Supreme Court.

Scott sat stunned for several minutes when Warden Scanlan gave him the news. "It's God's will," he said, as Scanlan led him from the death cell back to his old cell block.

Sheriff John Babb, as the county's official executioner, strode into the execution room at 11:35 p.m. to let the standing room only crowd of nearly 200 witnesses know that the show was about to begin.

Lindsey was brought in first, followed by the Reverend Philemon Canavan, the jail's Catholic chaplain. He was strapped into the chair at 12:05 a.m. and was pronounced dead at 12:14 as Father Canavan administered the last rights.

First Assistant Warden Rudolph Lee then went with several jailers to the death cell where Davis was waiting.

"All right, Bernie, time to go," he said.

Davis did not want to go. He was carried, kicking, screaming and praying into the death chamber and pushed forcibly into the chair. The restraints were fastened into place and the current was turned on at 12:26 a.m.

His body stiffened and strained against the clamps and the leather strap. A wisp of smoke curled up from the top of his head, and another from his right thigh. Urine dribbled from the chair as his bladder gave way. There was a slight commotion among the spectators as one of them fainted and tumbled to the floor.

Seven minutes later, at 12:33, Davis was pronounced dead as Father Canavan administered the last rights.

Policeman Frank McCormick of the Albany Park station, a brother of the slain detective, got up from the witness bench and wiped the palms of his hands on his trousers.

"Justice has been done," he said.

46

DRAG COP'S SLAYER
'LAST MILE' TO DIE
MARCH 19, 1953

Emanuel Scott's luck ran out at 12:01 a.m. on March 19, 1953. The 25-year-old Negro's appeal for clemency was vigorously opposed by State's Attorney John Gutknecht. Citing the fact that Scott had shot Policeman William Murphy to death during a holdup, he argued, "Extending lenience to Emanuel Scott would be damaging to police morale and law enforcement generally."

After hearing the arguments, Governor William G. Stratton denied executive clemency.

Scott's last visitor was his wife, Ruth, who came from Dayton, Ohio to spend several hours with the prisoner. Talking to her through a glass panel, he continued to deny his guilt, but told her, "I am ready to go. I have made my peace with God."

Scott refused a last meal, and made no last-minute requests. When jailers came for him shortly after midnight, however, he had changed his mind about being "ready to go." He refused to leave his cell, and had to be dragged into the execution chamber by the guards.

Two deputies held him down while others affixed the clamps and leather strap and lowered the leather mask over his face. The electricity was turned on at 12:01 a.m., and seven minutes later Doctors Thomas Carter and Irwin Hoffman agreed that he was dead.

Only thirty-five spectators, mostly police officers, witnessed the execution.

Scott had been the last survivor of the four-man gang involved in Policeman Murphy's death. One of his partners, LeRoi Lindsey, had preceded him in the electric chair five months earlier. Another, Emil Washington, had died in the Bridewell Hospital after ripping the stitches from wounds inflicted in a shootout with the lawman. And Earlie Burton had died of tuberculosis while awaiting the death penalty.

47

KILLER DIES
STILL DEFIANT

DECEMBER 19, 1958

After a hiatus of five and a half years, the worn black electric chair was returned to service on December 19, 1958—less than a week before Christmas—to dispatch convicted cop killer Richard Carpenter and strong-arm robber Charles Townsend.

Townsend, 23, had fatally beaten another man, Jack Boone, to death with a brick wrapped in a paper bag during a robbery on December 20, 1953.

Carpenter, 28, had been sentenced to die for the fatal shooting of Detective William J. Murphy in the Roosevelt Road subway on August 15, 1955. Coincidentally, the last man to die in the electric chair, Emanuel Scott, had also been executed for the death of a police officer named William Murphy.

Carpenter also shot and wounded another policeman, Clarence Kerr, 27, in a theater at 2046 Division Street when Kerr tried to take him into custody. Wounded himself, Carpenter forced his way into a home at 2040 Potomac Ave., where he held a family captive for twenty-three hours before being captured in a spectacular gun battle with police.

After his arrest Carpenter was beaten so unmercifully that he was never the same since.

Once in the county jail under sentence of death Carpenter went on a silence strike, and did not utter a word to anyone for months, pretending to have withdrawn from the world completely.

At a sanity hearing before Chief Justice Wilbert F. Crowley in Criminal Court, the Reverend James Jones, Episcopal chaplain at the jail, testified that Carpenter always appeared to be in a stupor. "In my opinion Richard Carpenter does not have sufficient mental power to know of his impending fate," the priest stated.

Assistant State's Attorney Edward Egan had just one question for Jones:

"Father, you are very strongly opposed to the death penalty, correct?"

"Yes," Jones responded.

Carpenter's lawyers then called the jail's current warden, Jack Johnson, who testified that he had tried on many occasions to talk to Carpenter, but said the prisoner would never speak in return.

However a jail guard, Frank Toberman, related that he had overheard the prisoner tell his mother and sister, "Don't worry. I'll never get the chair."

Judge Crowley, confused by the conflicting testimony, assigned Dr. William B. Haines, Criminal Court psychiatrist, to examine the prisoner and report back to him.

Haines went to the jail, where Carpenter was brought to a well-guarded room for the interview.

"Richard Carpenter, my name is Dr. Haines and I have come here to…" the psychiatrist began.

"Fuck you, Doc!" Carpenter interrupted.

"You're sane," Haines retorted.

After that Carpenter broke his twenty-two months of silence. Chatting idly with Johnson he said, "I know I'm going to make the chair, warden. I wonder if you can fix it so I can have commissary privileges, so I can buy cigarettes and newspapers to pass the time."

"That's no problem, Richard," the warden told him. "Glad you've decided to rejoin us."

A long-time loner in the sprawling jail, Carpenter became friends with Townsend, who occupied the adjoining cell on death row.

On what was to have been the last day of their lives, the two of them stood in their cells and chatted through the bars.

Meanwhile, twenty-two steps down the hall from Carpenter's cell, and only fifteen steps from Townsend's, where the electric chair was located, a macabre practice session was in progress. Seven guards were conducting a dry run, going through the procedures that had been assigned to each man for the double execution scheduled for midnight.

Since there had not been an electrocution in the jail since early in 1953, none of the guards assigned to carry out the death sentences had ever performed the task before.

Using members of their own group, one a white man the same height and weight as Carpenter, and the other a black jailer whose physique matched Townsend's, they took turns leading the blindfolded "prisoners" into the freshly painted 8-by-20-foot room where the black chair faced a 6-by-9-foot picture window.

"Let's try it again. That last time was a little clumsy," Chief Guard Walter Makowski suggested.

Once more a guard, his trouser legs rolled up to indicate he was the "prisoner," was guided into the room by two jailers who turned him facing the window, and pressed him into the chair in a sitting position.

A third guard quickly snapped a black leather belt tightly across the prisoner's chest, then lowered a black visor-like hood—with a triangular hole for the nose—over the man's face.

On either side of the chair guards depressed foot-pedals bringing heavy metal clamps over the man's forearms, holding them tightly to the arm of the chair. Another guard adjusted the leg clamps, and fastened an electrode to the man's right leg, while yet another adjusted the "contact" to the top of the prisoner's head.

The guards stepped back and Makowski, a beefy, blond-haired man, examined the man sitting in the chair and offered his critique.

"From the time you got him to the front of the chair it took six seconds," he said. "That's fine. Remember, don't get the straps too tight. We don't want to hurt the man."

Johnson, who himself had never officiated at an execution, had insisted on the rehearsals so everything would run like clockwork, enabling the "State of Illinois" to dispatch the prisoners as quickly and humanely as possible.

"In a few hours this will be for real," he said. "If you feel yourselves getting sick or nauseous, gulp air, or excuse yourself in time for another guard to take your place."

While the grim rehearsal continued, Carpenter received a last visit from his 19-year-old sister, Irene, and his aunt, Paulene Abene. "Yes, I killed Murphy, and I'm glad," Carpenter told them. "After I'm dead I'm coming back and kill more coppers."

"Oh, don't say that, Richard," his kid sister pleaded.

Carpenter chain-smoked and began to sing Irish songs he used to croon for his sister when she was a child. "Remember all those records I used to have? I've been thinking about them," he said. "I had quite a collection, didn't I?"

After his aunt and sister left, Carpenter tore the black leather loafers he would wear to the chair, and ripped the heel off one of them. "I don't want anyone else wearing my shoes," he said as he demolished them.

In the neighboring cell Townsend sang hymns while Carpenter carried on.

As the zero hour approached, the two condemned men were given the opportunity to order anything within reason for their last meals.

Townsend asked for chicken, sweet potato pie, a dozen biscuits with butter, a raw onion, a pound of rice with chicken gravy, a bottle of soda-pop, and a pint of walnut ice cream.

For his last meal Carpenter requested sirloin steak, a baked potato, vegetables, a biscuit, and coffee with cream.

As the dinners were being prepared, word was received that Justice Tom C. Clark of the U.S. Supreme Court had stayed Townsend's execution. It was the fourteenth reprieve his lawyers had won for him in three years.

Warden Johnson went down to the death cells to deliver the news himself.

Told that his life was being spared, at least for the time being, Townsend looked beseeching at Johnson and said, "Warden, does that mean I don't get to have my last meal?"

"No, you can have it, Charles," Johnson smiled. "Then we'll take you back to your old tier."

"Warden, if you don't mind, I'd like to stay here with Richard," Townsend said. "I'd want to pray with Richard. I want to stay nearby where I can do him the most good."

Johnson reluctantly agreed to let Townsend remain in the adjoining death cell to keep Carpenter company for the few remaining hours of his life. Carpenter had refused to talk to a Catholic priest or the jail chaplain. Townsend was allowed to stay with him until 11:30 p.m. Johnson did not want him looking on as his cellmate was being prepped for death.

Former Warden Frank Sain, who had since been elected Cook County sheriff, was Carpenter's last visitor. He was accompanied by Undersheriff Thomas Harrison.

"Is there anything you would like to tell us, Richard?' Sain asked him. "Did you kill Detective Murphy? Now is the time to get it off your chest and make your peace with God."

"I don't believe in God," Carpenter asserted. "I'm going to the electric chair, and there's nothing I can do about it." As he spoke a large tear ran down the side of his face.

At 11:45 p.m. five guards entered Carpenter's cell and waited while his head was shaved. Shorn of his long, black locks, he stripped naked and put on his death uniform—a sleeveless undershirt and blue shorts reaching only halfway down to his knees. One of the guards slipped a black, mask-like blindfold over the convicted killer's eyes.

In the next room, facing the chair, sixty witnesses—mostly jail guards, newspapermen and police officers—sat on wooden benches waiting for the death march to begin.

An hour earlier reporters assigned to cover the execution had to surrender everything in their pockets, including their handkerchiefs, which were placed in sealed manila envelopes bearing their names. Then every man was thoroughly searched, including their armpits and crotch areas. Their shoes were taken from them and twisted, bent, slammed on table tops, and minutely examined to make sure there were no hidden cameras.

Reporters even had to relinquish their pencils, pens and note pads. In return, each was given a pencil and yellow legal pad provided by the sheriff's office.

Authorities were taking no chances on a repeat of the 1949 execution in which James "Mad Dog" Morelli was photographed with a smuggled camera as he died in the chair.

Shortly after midnight Carpenter was marched under his own power into the death chamber. He looked pathetically comical in the undershirt and blue short pants, as he settled back into the lethal chair and the black visor was lowered over his face.

"Get it over with quick" his muffled voice was heard to say as guards backed away from the fatal apparatus.

Sheriff Sain, who was in charge of the operation, stood ten feet to the right of the chair, as Franciscan Father Cronan

Murphy, in his brown cassock, stood to the left and prayed. Warden Johnson, who did not believe in the death penalty and refused to assign any other man to the unsavory task of dispatching a fellow human being, stood alone before the panel of three levers and four red buttons in the control room.

The soft movement of newsmen's pencils over notepads was the only sound in the deathly silent witness room. Carpenter's adam's apple moved up and down three times as he swallowed his last gulps of air at 12:06 a.m.

Suddenly his extended fingers snapped into fists and his body jerked rigid at the impact of 1,900 volts of electricity. Smoke rose from the top of his head and his right leg, where the electrodes touched the skin.

Sixty-five seconds of high voltage later Carpenter's body went limp as the juice was turned off. Water from the brine-soaked sponge on Carpenter's head trickled down his left temple, and dripped from his ear onto his reddened shoulder and chest.

A uniformed guard entered the death chamber and unbuttoned the undershirt to expose the left side of Carpenter's chest. Doctors Achille Chreptowski, Victor Levine and Myron Charkewycz stepped forward, found no heart beat, and pronounced Carpenter dead at 12:10 a.m.

Chreptowski, chief of the county jail medical staff, filled out the death certificate:

Age of deceased: 28. Cause of death: Electrocution. Place of death: Cook County jail, 2626 S. California.

After the execution Johnson, who needed desperately to unwind, invited reporters to the warden's dining room above the jail for a post-midnight lunch before they returned to their papers.

Ironically, the menu—left over from a dinner served to jurors in an ongoing trial earlier in the day—consisted of smoked butt!

48

HOW CIUCCI FINALLY
KEPT DATE WITH DEATH

MARCH 23, 1962

The execution of Vincent Ciucci was detailed in an earlier chapter. The 35-year-old West Side grocer had been condemned to death for the murder of his wife and three children for the love of another woman who had borne him a child.

Talking to reporters as his head was being shaved, only minutes before he died in the electric chair, Ciucci admitted for the first time that he had indeed killed his 28-year-old wife, Anna, but claimed he had shot her with a rifle only after she had murdered their children, Vincent, 9, Virginia, 8, and 4-year-old Angeline.

For more than seven years after receiving the death sentence Ciucci avoided the electric chair through twelve stays of execution while his lawyers maneuvered the case back and forth through the courts.

Ciucci awakened at 8:15 a.m. on March 22, the last day of his life, and asked for a breakfast of bacon and eggs. He would have gotten his wish regardless, since bacon and eggs happened to have been the regular jail breakfast that day.

He skipped lunch, and told Warden Jack Johnson that he intended to forgo a condemned man's last privilege—to order anything within reason for his last meal. He also took a pass at the jail's regular dinner that evening, pot roast, brown gravy, potatoes, mixed vegetables and a hard roll.

Ciucci's only visitors during the day were the Reverend Aidan Potter, Catholic chaplain at the jail, his divorced parents, Frank and Virginia Ciucci, and his lawyer, George Leighton.

Warden Johnson had received a telephone call from a woman who identified herself as Carol Amora, Ciucci's former mistress. "I'm confused. I want to do what I can to help Vince," she told him. "But before I talk I would like legal advice."

Johnson told the woman to contact Leighton, but Ciucci's lawyer said he never heard from her.

Later another woman, who identified herself as Miss Amora's sister, telephoned the warden and told him, "Don't expect anything from Carol."

During the more than seven years Ciucci had been on death row, Carol had visited him twice. Four other times since 1955 she had called at the jail with their daughter, Rose, but at Ciucci's request only the child was permitted to see him. The last time Ciucci saw his daughter, who was then nine, was in November of 1961.

On the night of his death Ciucci waited vainly for a phone call from Governor Otto Kerner that could call off the execution. Kerner's press aide, Richard Thorne, notified Warden Johnson a few minutes before midnight that the governor did not intend to intervene.

When Johnson told Ciucci that the U.S. Supreme Court had turned down his lawyer's final plea, and the governor did not intend to act, Ciucci remarked, "Well, it's a rat race out there."

After meeting with reporters, Ciucci made his final confession to Father Potter, who gave him Holy Communion and said a final mass outside the cell door. He then gave the priest an envelope marked "personal," and asked that it be passed on to the warden after his death.

The letter, written in a flowing hand with a fountain pen, follows:

Death Cell County Jail
March 22nd. 1962

Warden Jack J. Johnson.

Sir, I have just made my peace with God, attened (sic) Holy Mass and received Holy Communion. Warden, I want you to know that what I revealed to you around three (3) or four (4) years ago with regards to what truly transpired on the night of Dec. 3 or 4, was the honest-to-Gods truth.

Like I informed you, I was in our bathroom for a period of fifteen (15) or twenty (20) minutes. I then heard strange sounds, similar to one that is made when a child or individual, fires a cap pistol in a closed area. I then rushed out and made my way into our bedroom. Now as I entered my bedroom I noticed my wife leaving the children's room with a rifle in her hand. Immediately I snatched the rifle from her. In the struggle I am sure that a shot was fired in the direction of the ceiling or wall. In the process of snatching the rifle from her, I spun her around and knocked her across our bed. Then I went into my children's room. I picked up my son Vincent's head and noticed that his face was completely covered with blood. I called his name several times and received no reply. I then also turned to my two daughters and was confronted with the same conditions. I then picked up the rifle and rushed to where my wife was lying. She was mumbling something. Anyway, I then emptied the gun into her.

Vincent Ciucci, Sr.

PS I forgive all who have injured me. And I beg pardon of all whom I have injured. Further more I thank you deeply for all you did for me. Vince

A notation on the side of the letter said: Signed in my presence 22 Mar 62 3:15 p.m. Aidan R. Potter, OFM, Catholic Chaplain, Cook County Jail.

After the execution, Ciucci's body was taken to the Cook County Morgue, where it would remain until 6:30 a.m., after which members of his family were told they could claim it.

Ciucci was buried in Mount Carmel Cemetery, thirty feet from a headstone marking the Turco family plot, where his murdered wife, the former Anna Turco, and their three children were buried.

His death brought renewed efforts to abolish the death penalty by foes of capital punishment. Among them was Warden Ross V. Randolph of the Illinois State Penitentiary in Menard, who had witnessed Ciucci's execution.

"If there were any doubts in my feeling against capital punishment, this put an end to it," he said. "I'm opposed to it. It serves no purpose. It has been proved that the number of murders is just as high in states with the death penalty as it is in states without it.

"Murderers should never be permitted to walk the streets, but execution is not the answer. It is one wrong compounding another, a futile attempt to rectify the situation. If persons in favor of the death penalty were made to watch it happen, they might change their minds."

49

SLAYER DUKES GOES
TO DEATH SILENTLY

AUGUST 24, 1962

Richard Carpenter's loyal cellmate, Charles Townsend, never did walk that "last mile." His death sentence was eventually commuted and he was shipped off to the state penitentiary. The last man to be legally executed in Cook County was James Dukes, alias Jesse Welch, a 37-year-old convicted cop killer, and a bad guy from the word go.

In 1947 Dukes, who had been kicked out of the Army with a dishonorable discharge, was indicted for the murder of a Chicago shop owner's wife. He disappeared, changed his name, and was never tried.

He didn't have the good sense to stay out of town, however. On June 16, 1956, two men who were painting the vestibule of the New Mount Baptist Church at 223 W. 47th Street heard a woman screaming and went to investigate. Seeing Dukes beating the woman, they called to him to stop.

"I'll kill you all," Dukes responded, as he fired three shots, hitting 49-year-old Charles Legget, a deacon, twice in the leg, and Thomas J. Sylvester, 23, the head usher, in the left shoulder.

Dukes stuffed the gun into the front of his shirt and ran toward Wells Street, where he encountered Detective Daniel

Rolewicz, who had heard the shots and was on his way to investigate. "What have you got there?" Rolewicz called out.

Dukes pulled the weapon from his shirt and got off two shots at the detective, missing both times. He continued running across the street, where Rolewicz's partner, Detective John J. Blyth, Jr., was waiting to cut him off. Dukes shot Blyth in the chest, mortally wounding him. Blyth returned the fire as he fell, while Rolewicz also fired several rounds at the fleeing felon.

Dukes was hit three times, but kept on running, leaving a trail of blood in the street. Police followed the crimson trail, and found Dukes lying under a station wagon in a lot at 48th and Wentworth, with a jammed .32 caliber pistol in his hand.

Detective Blyth lay dead in the street. A third generation policeman, he died wearing the same badge that his father and grandfather had worn before him.

When Dukes went on trial in Criminal Court for the policeman's murder, Prosecutor Robert Cooney told the jury, "If this man doesn't get the death penalty, no man who ever did deserved it." Dukes got the chair.

Some of the best criminal lawyers in the city then set about trying to save him, for any number of reasons. In one appeal his lawyers claimed he'd been intoxicated, and thus not responsible for his action. The state argued that if drunkenness become a legal excuse for murder, anybody who took a few drinks before committing a crime could claim that as a defense.

The lawyers then demanded a new trial because there were no blacks on the jury that convicted Dukes for killing a white police officer. Prosecutors pointed out, however, that the other shooting victims were fellow blacks, as were the witnesses who testified against him.

By the time six years had passed the appeals well finally ran dry, and Dukes was scheduled to be executed on August 24, 1962.

On his last afternoon he was permitted to visit briefly with his father, Jack Welch, in the warden's office. At nightfall his mother, Olivia Welch, accompanied by three daughters and a family friend, held a final 35-minute reunion with the prisoner in the same office. As they left in tears, and Dukes was being led back to his basement cell, he encountered a newspaper reporter in the hallway. Dukes paused, patted the reporter on the shoulder, and said, "Take it easy, now."

As the midnight hour approached, a crowd of nearly 700 people, including 200 pickets carrying signs protesting the death penalty, had gathered in front of the Criminal Courts Building.

Dukes spent his final hours in the death cell writing notes, praying, and nervously talking with his guards about his failure to win a reprieve. In a letter to his mother he enclosed a religious medal Warden Jack Johnson had given him when he was baptized in the jail three years earlier.

Dukes rejected the traditional "last meal." A breakfast of oatmeal, a sweet roll, and coffee sustained him through his last day on earth.

Resigned to the fate a jury had imposed upon him, he was conducted blindfolded to the black lacquered chair by two jail guards at seven minutes after midnight. The prisoner took his last twenty steps like a man who knew where he was headed, and was in no hurry to get there. He placed his feet far out in front of him and leaned back into the arms of his escorts.

When Dukes exhibited an understandable hesitance to sit down he was shoved firmly into the chair and held in place while other guards tightened the clamps around his arms and legs, and pressed the electrode with its dripping wet sponge down against the top of his shaved head.

The last thing Dukes did in this world, as the pale blue brine from the sponge dripped down over his face and onto his broad, brown shoulders, was to inhale deeply several times as though gulping down the last sweet breath of the stale, humid air that hung so heavily in the jail basement.

As the eyes of the thirty witnesses were transfixed with anticipation at the pathetic figure seated on the other side of the plate glass window, Chief Guard Walter Makowski lowered his arm as a signal that all was ready. Johnson, watching through a one-way mirror in the control room, pressed the red button with his thumb and Dukes was jolted into eternity.

Three minutes and forty seconds later three physicians, including Coroner Andrew Toman, approached the chair with their stethoscopes and officially pronounced him dead. The Reverend Aidan Potter, O.F.M., administered the last rites of the Catholic Church.

Among the spectators at Cook County's last execution was Detective Blyth's partner, Daniel Rolewicz. "I've been waiting a long time for this night," he said.

Left behind in Dukes' cell was a book, "Five Great Dialogues by Plato," in which he had marked a number of passages pertaining to being condemned to death. In Plato's "Apology" he had underlined the sentence:

> *The difficulty, my friends, is not to avoid death, but to avoid unrighteousness; for that runs faster than death.*

And moments before he went to his death he had circled the final paragraph:

> *The hour of departure has arrived and we go our ways, I to die and you to live. Which is better, God only knows.*

BOOK V

HOW ONE MAN BEAT THE CHAIR

1

DOLLY WEISBERG
DIES OF FRIGHT

MAY 20, 1947

One of the strangest stories ever attributed to the execution process is that of Julius "Dolly" Weisberg, a flamboyant prohibition era figure, whose demise was one of the most unusual ever recorded by the Cook County coroner.

We have seen how several other condemned murderers cheated the executioner. Haymarket anarchist Louis Lingg blew his head off by chewing on a blasting cap while awaiting the gallows; millionaire Russell Scott hanged himself in his cell with his belt; "Terrible Tommy" O'Connor went over the wall and hasn't been seen since; and Earlie Burton died of tuberculosis before they could put him in the electric chair.

How did Dolly Weisberg escape his fate? He was literally scared to death, just thinking about it.

But in escaping the hot seat he left behind one humdinger of a mystery: Who poisoned Dolly *after he died*, and why?

A familiar figure on the Rush Street honky-tonk scene for thirty years, Weisberg ran The French Cuisine, also known as the 885 Club, at 885 Rush Street.

He killed his first man on a Sunday night in March,

1925, when he put a bullet into the stomach of Morris Barnstein, alias "Mush" Goldman, a beer runner for the Alterie mob, in a crowd outside the Palace Theater in the Loop.

Although a mounted police officer witnessed the fatal shooting, the grand jury refused to indict Weisberg and he walked away free as a bird. Someone, it appeared, had filed what was known in Chicago as a "motion to fix."

Dolly then restored an old North Side mansion into the famed Colony Club, where he cut quite a figure with his constant companion, a German shepherd dog named Danger, who wore a $3,000 14-karat gold collar, a leopard skin coat, and had his own bank account.

On the night of October 23, 1945, just after the end of World War II, Dolly was soaking up some of the city's euphoria in the crowded Regent Room, a glitzy bar at the corner of LaSalle and Madison Streets, with Joseph McKnight, a 46-year-old automobile salesman from Evanston.

Weisberg was trying to cut a fast deal for a new Pontiac, once the auto industry returned to peacetime production. Suddenly the buzz of the crowd was interrupted by a series of gunshots, and McKnight dropped to the floor and tried to scramble behind the bar on his hands and knees.

As McKnight rolled over on his back, bleeding from bullet wounds to his left shoulder and abdomen, Weisberg calmly slipped a revolver into his pocket and sauntered out the door.

Everybody knew Weisberg was the shooter, but when police tried to round up witnesses, in true Chicago fashion, "nobody saw nothin'."

Inspector Edwin Daly and Detective Sergeant William C. Walsh picked up Weisberg at his home and took him out to the Bridewell Hospital where McKnight, with his dying breath, identified Weisberg as the man who had shot him.

Weisberg was charged with McKnight's murder, and

languished in his cell for eight months while Assistant State's Attorney Edmund Grant dragged his feet on the prosecution. The fact of the matter was, Grant did not have a case without an eyewitness, and he knew it.

Then Grant learned that there had been some uniformed sailors in the bar on the night of the shooting, apparently on their way home from the war. With the help of Naval officials and U.S. Senator Scott Lucas of Illinois, the prosecutor found three sailors who had stopped off at the bar between trains on the night the auto salesman was shot.

The sailors returned to Chicago from New Jersey, Connecticut and Georgia to testify against Weisberg, who was convicted of murder and sentenced to die in the electric chair at one minute after midnight on May 23, 1947. "I have a story and it'll break before I sit in that chair," Weisberg boasted to the press.

A bitter rivalry existed between Republican Sheriff Elmer Walsh, whose office provided guards for the jail, and Democrat Frank Sain, who at the time was still the warden. Sain, fearing that Weisberg might try to escape and embarrass him, ordered him placed in the death cell seventy-two hours before the scheduled execution.

After Weisberg was brought to the cell two of Sain's most trusted aides, Rudolph Lee and Michael Sabatello, ordered the prisoner to strip naked, and thoroughly body-searched him. He was not permitted to put his clothes back on until every garment had been examined, inch by inch.

Sain then assigned jailer Peter Lanz to keep Weisberg under observation day and night.

Weisberg's last words, just sixty hours before he was scheduled to be strapped into the chair, were to Lanz. "How does it feel to look at a man who's going to die in the electric chair?" he asked nervously. Lanz did not answer. Forty minutes later Lanz noticed the prisoner sprawled face-down on his bunk, "writhing strangely."

Lanz summoned Sabatello, who alerted Sain that something was wrong. Sain, along with Dr. Richard Buckingham of the county hospital staff, who was in the building on business, raced to the cell — but Weisberg was dead.

"How?" Sain demanded.

Dr. Meyer Levy, the jail physician, and two of his aides made a searching examination of the still warm body. "There isn't any odor of poison, and no sign of it around the mouth," Levy told Sain. "I'd say he died of a heart attack. If you wish, I'll sign a death certificate to that effect right now."

By all appearances Weisberg, a healthy man of fifty, had died of fright.

"Let's be sure," Sain insisted. "This thing can be political as hell. Turn the body over to the coroner for an autopsy."

Coroner A.L. Brodie ordered his chief pathologist, the eminent Dr. Jerry Kearns, to perform the post mortem examination, while he stood by to await the results along with a mob of newspaper reporters.

"It's heart disease," Kearns confirmed. "There's a spot near the heart. The stomach is clean, but the vital organs have been removed for a chemical test. Just a routine measure." He signed the death certificate, as Weisberg's organs were turned over to Dr. William D. McNally, the coroner's toxicologist, for a chemical analysis.

Nine days later, after the prisoner had been quietly buried, the coroner dropped a bombshell. Chemical tests showed that Dolly Weisberg's organs contained a fatal amount of strychnine sulfate. Traces of strychnine were found in the stomach, liver, brain and kidneys. Dr. McNally estimated the poison had been swallowed fifteen minutes before death.

Here were the makings of a monumental scandal, and Sheriff Walsh jumped in with both feet. He launched a full investigation, and ordered lie detector tests to determine whether Sain's men were in collusion to smuggle the poison to the prisoner. Other inquiries were begun by the coroner and the chief of highway police.

The mystery: Where did Weisberg get the poison, and how could he have taken it while under the watchful eye of the jailer?

Dr. Kearns, who originally declared Weisberg had died of a heart attack, was adamant. "If Weisberg actually died of strychnine, my pathological examination would have shown it," he insisted. "I'm making further microscopic examinations before I agree on another cause of death."

Two weeks later Kearns turned his report over to Coroner Brodie, who defused the bomb. "The finding of poison in the body was erroneous. Dolly Weisberg died of a heart attack," he declared. Contrary to his earlier report, Dr. McNally also agreed that no strychnine had been found in Weisberg's body.

Why the turn-about? McNally said John Polli, a coroner's chemist, had discovered the poison originally and turned the specimen over to W.L. Bergman, a fellow chemist to determine the quantity. But after the scandal broke, McNally, suspicious on the large dosage of poison that had been discovered, ordered new tests, which showed *not a trace.*

Meanwhile Dr. Kearns, his reputation on the line, asked Dr. Walter Camp, a University of Illinois toxicologist, to make tests for poison on fresh sections of Weisberg's internal organs, taken from the same jars as the tissue which Polli had reported to be loaded with strychnine.

Dr. Camp could find none!

Clearly, he reported, someone had introduced the poison to Weisberg's organs in the laboratory where they had been taken for examination in an apparent effort to discredit Warden Sain.

Polli, the chemist who "discovered" the poison, took a

lie test and flunked. An investigation by State's Attorney William J. Touhy indicated that the strychnine had, indeed, been introduced into parts of Weisberg's vital organs after the chemical tests had been initiated.

Who poisoned Dolly after his death, and why, was never determined. But an angry Coroner Walsh then asked for, and got, the resignations of Polli, Bergman and Dr. McNally.

A coroner's jury subsequently returned a verdict of death due to a heart attack. Dr. Kearns, who was exonerated, declared, "It's true, in effect, that Dolly Weisberg had been frightened to death."

BOOK VI

CAPITAL PUNISHMENT— YES OR NO?

1

THE CASE AGAINST CAPITAL PUNISHMENT

MARIO M. CUOMO
Governor of New York

It is difficult to imagine a more important subject for consideration than the one that brings us together this morning. Together the legislature and the governor every year make thousands of judgments that are important.

But occasionally we are confronted with a question that has transcendent significance: one that describes in fundamental ways what we are as a people; one that projects to ourselves, and to the whole world, our most fundamental values—one, even, that helps configure our souls.

I have spoken my own opposition to the death penalty for more than thirty years. For all that time I have studied it, I have watched it, I have debated it, hundreds of times.

The above remarks, used with Governor Cuomo's permission, were delivered at the College of St. Rose in Albany, N.Y., on March 20, 1989, when he declared that he would veto a death penalty bill sent to him by the New York State legislature.

Copyright 1989 by Mario M. Cuomo.

I have heard all the arguments, analyzed all the evidence I could find, measured public opinion when it was opposed, when it was indifferent, when it was passionately in favor. And always before, I have concluded that the death penalty is wrong, that it lowers us all, that it is a surrender to the worst that is in us, that it uses a power, the official power to kill by execution, which has never elevated a society, never brought back a life, never inspired anything but hate.

In recent years I have had the privilege of casting my vote on bills passed by the legislature to bring back the death penalty. And I have voted against it each time. On each occasion that I did, the legislature might have passed the bill despite my disapproval by obtaining a two-thirds vote. So far they have chosen not to.

Now the death penalty bill is before me again, and there can be another chance for the legislators of New York to speak on this subject in the name of the people they represent.

Because of the awesome significance of the matter, and the imminence of the decision, I sought a chance to speak directly to the public so that I could add my voice to and underscore the cogency of the arguments made by the bishop, the Assembly people, and so many of you—and made already so cogently, so forcefully, so eloquently.

Clearly there is a new public willingness to return to the official brutality of the past, by restoring the death penalty. And it is just as clear what has provoked this new willingness. Life in parts of this state, and nation, has become more ugly and violent than at any time I can recall.

Many, like myself, who have spent more than fifty years in this state are appalled at the new madness created by drugs and frustrated by what appears to be the ineffectuality of the federal, state, and local governments to deal with this new problem. Savage murders of young, bright, and committed law-enforcement people and other citizens enrage us all. Our passions are inflamed by each new terrible headline, each new report of atrocity. We know the people have a right to demand a civilized level of law and peace. They have a right to expect it.

When it appears to them that crime is rampant, and the criminal seems immune from apprehension and adequate punishment, and that nothing else is working, then no one should be surprised if the people demand the ultimate penalty. It has happened before, it will probably happen again. To a great extent it is a cry, a terrible cry of anger and anguish born of frustration and fear in the people. I know that, and I understand it.

I have been with the victim, too. I have felt the anger myself, more than once. Like many other citizens I know what it is to be violated, and even to have one's closest family violated, in the most despicable ways. I tremble at the thought of how I might react to someone who took the life of my son: anger, surely, terrible anger. I would not be good enough to suppress it. Would I demand revenge? Perhaps even that. I know that despite all my beliefs, I might be driven by my impulses.

So how could I not understand a society of people like me, at times like this, wanting to let out a great cry for retribution, for vindication, even for revenge, like the cry we hear from them now? I understand it. But I know something else. I know this society should strive for something better than what we are in our worst moments. When police officers are killed, violence escalates and lawlessness seems to flourish with impunity. It isn't easy for people to hold back their anger, to stop and think, to allow reason to operate. But that, it seems to me, is the only rational course for a people constantly seeking to achieve greater measures of humanity and dignity for our civilization.

We need to respond more effectively to the new violence; we know that. But there is absolutely no good reason to believe that returning to the death penalty will be any better an answer now, than it was at all the times in the past when we had it, used it, regretted it, and discarded it. There are dozens of studies that demonstrate there is simply no persuasive evidence that official state killing can do anything to make any police officer, or other citizen, safer. There is, in fact, considerable evidence on the contrary. Consider this: For the decade before 1977, we had the death penalty in New York State. In that period eighty police officers were slain. For the decade after, without the death penalty, fifty-four were killed. The argument for deterrence is further weakened by realization of how rarely and unpredictably it is applied.

For hundreds of years we have known that the effectiveness of the law is determined not by its harshness, but by its sureness. The death penalty has always been terribly unsure. The experts of the New York State Bar Association's Criminal Justice Section, and the Association of the Bar of the City of New York, have come out strongly against the death penalty after hundreds of years of cumulative lawyers' experience and study.

One of the points the state section made is that the death penalty must be regarded as ineffective as a deterrent, if for no other reason than because its use is so uncertain. Execution has occurred in only about five hundredths of one percent of all the homicides committed in America over the past decade.

Then, despite Ted Bundy, it seems to threaten white drug dealers, white rapists, white killers, white barbarians a lot less than others. Think of this: Of the last eighteen people executed in this state, thirteen were black and one Hispanic. That seems an extraordinary improbability for a system that was operating with any kind of objective sureness. And there's more. Some of the most notorious recent killings, like the gunning down of the DEA Agent Everett Hatcher and the killing by Lemuel Smith, occurred in the face of existing death-penalty statutes.

Psychiatrists will tell you that there is reason to believe that some madmen, like Ted Bundy, may even be tempted to murder because of a perverse desire to challenge the electric chair.

For years and years, the arguments have raged over whether the death penalty is a deterrent. That used to be, frankly, the only argument when I first began debating it. But the truth now is that because the proponents have never been able to make the case for deterrence convincingly, they have moved to a different argument. It is phrased in many ways, but in the end, it all comes down to the same impulse.

The argument was heard in the debates in recent weeks on the floor of the Senate and Assembly, which I listened to and read with great care. Such things as this were said: "Whatever the studies show, the people of my area believe that the taking of life justifies the forfeiting of life." Or: "Our people have the right to insist on a penalty that matches the horror of the crime." And even this: "An eye for an eye, a tooth for a tooth." Where would it end? You kill my son, I kill yours. You rape my daughter, I rape yours. You mutilate my body, I mutilate yours. You treat someone brutally, and I, the established government of one of the most advanced states in the most advanced nation on earth, will respond by officially and deliberately treating you brutally, by strapping you to a chair and burning away your flesh, for all to see, so the barbarians will know that we are capable of official barbarism. We will pursue this course, despite the lack of reason to believe it will protect us, even if it is clear, almost with certainty, that occasionally the victim of our official barbarism will be innocent.

Think of it: at least twenty-three people are believed to have been wrongfully executed in the United States since the turn of this century. Twenty-three innocent people officially killed. But it is not called murder. And tragically, New York State, our great state, the Empire State, holds the record for the greatest number of innocents put to death over the years. We lead all the states in the nation with eight wrongful executions since 1905.

The proponents of the death penalty in this state assume that the criminal justice system will not make a mistake. They seem to be unconcerned about the overly ambitious prosecutor, the sloppy detective, the incompetent defense counsel, the witness with an ax to grind, or the judge who keeps courthouse conviction box scores. But that, ladies and gentlemen, is the human factor, and it's the deepest, most profound flaw in their argument.

In this country, a defendant is convicted on proof beyond a reasonable doubt, not proof to an absolute certainty. There's no such thing as absolute certainty in our law. The proponents of the death penalty, despite this, say we should pretend it cannot happen.

They do not discuss the infamous case of Isadore Zimmerman, who got so far as to have his head shaved and his trouser leg slit on the day of his scheduled execution in 1939, before Governor Herbert Lehman commuted his sentence to life imprisonment. And then twenty-four years later, Zimmerman was released from prison, after it was determined that the prosecutor knew all the time he was innocent and had suppressed evidence. Zimmerman died a free man just a few years ago.

They do not discuss William Red Gergel, age 62, released in Queens just this year after spending 535 days in jail for a triple murder he did not commit. It was a case of mistaken identity.

They do not discuss a young man named Bobby McLaughlin of Marine Park, Brooklyn. Bobby McLaughlin was convicted of the robbery and murder of another young man in 1980. This was a one-witness identification case, the most frightening kind. In July of 1986, Bobby McLaughlin was released after serving six years for a murder he did not commit. Wrongly convicted by intention or mistake, take your pick of the fact, right here in the state of New York.

It all started when a detective picked up one wrong photograph: one wrong photograph, one mistake, one date with the electric chair. It could have been one more tragically lost life. It didn't happen, but it took an almost superhuman effort by his foster father and some aggressive members of the media to keep the case from falling between the cracks of the justice system. Bobby McLaughlin had this to say after he was released, "If there was a death penalty in this state, I would now be ashes in an urn on my mother's mantle."

Yes, it can happen. And it will happen if we allow it to. And what would we tell the wife or the husband, or the children or the parents, of the innocent victim that we had burned to death in our official rage? What would you say to them? "We had to do it"?

Then we would be asked, "But why did you have to do it, if you were not sure it would deter anyone else? Why did you have to do it?" And what would we answer? "Because we were angry"? "Because the people demanded an eye for an eye, even if it were to prove an innocent eye"?

What would we tell them? Should we tell them that we had to kill, because we had as a society come to believe that the only way to reach the most despicable among us was to lie down in the muck and mire that spawned them?

I hear all around me that the situation has so deteriorated that we need to send a message to the criminals and to the people alike, that we as a government know how bad things are and will do something about it. I agree. Of course we must make clear that we intend to fight the terrible epidemic of drugs and violence.

But the death penalty is no more effective a way to fight them than the angry cries that inspire it. We need to continue to do the things that will control crime by making the apprehension and punishment of criminals more likely. We've made a good beginning. Since 1983 we have increased funding for local law enforcement alone by 65 percent.

The legislature should finally vote for a real, tough, effective punishment for deliberate murder. And there is one: better, much better, than the death penalty; one that juries will not be reluctant to give; one that is so menacing to a potential killer, it could actually deter; one that does not require us to be infallible in order to avoid taking innocent life; one that does not require us to stoop to the level of the killers; one that is even, for those who insist on measuring this question in dollars, millions of dollars less expensive than the death penalty, millions—true life imprisonment, with no possibility of parole, none under any circumstances.

If you committed a murder at 20, and you live to be 81, you'll live 61 years behind bars. You'll go in alive, and come out only when you die. Now that's a tough penalty. Ask the people who know how tough this penalty would be, the people who know Attica or Auburn. Ask the people who know how hard such places are. They will tell you that to most inmates, the thought of living a whole lifetime behind bars, only to die in your cell, is worse than the quick, final termination of the electric chair.

Just recently in an article in *The New York Times Magazine,* a young man on death row named Heath Wilkins was asked whether people underestimated the deterrent power of life without parole.

"Absolutely," Wilkins responded. "Death isn't a scary thing to someone who's hurting inside so bad that they're hurting other people. People like that are looking for death as a way out."

For the six years I have offered it to the legislature, I have heard no substantial arguments in opposition to the proposal for life imprisonment without parole. I've heard none.

Finally, while we are fighting the criminals in the street with the relentless enforcement of firm laws and with swift, sure punishment, we must at the same time continue to provide all the things we know dull the instinct for crime— education, housing, health care, good jobs, and the opportunity to achieve them. The old fashioned effort to deal with root causes has never lost its relevance, even when it lost its popularity.

That, in the end, I think personally, may be the best antidote of all against the kind of terrible crime we are now experiencing. Certainly it offers us more hope than does the politics of death.

There will be few questions more difficult for us than the one we now face, and few opportunities as good as this to prove our commitment as a people to resisting the triumph of darkness, and to moving our society constantly toward the light.

For a politician, like the people from the Assembly who have joined us today, and myself, rejecting what appears to be a politically popular view can be troublesome. But I...make the same decision I have before. In my case, I make the same decision now that I have for more than thirty years, this time I believe on the basis of even more evidence and with a firmer conviction than before.

And I do it with a profound respect for the people who have raised their voices—and occasionally even their fists— asking for the death penalty. I have not as governor ignored those voices. I have listened intently to them. But after the sincerest effort, I have not been able to bring myself to agree with them. I continue to believe, with all my mind and heart, that the death penalty would not help us...it would debase us; it would not protect us...it would make us weaker.

I continue to believe, more passionately now than ever, that this society desperately needs this great state's leadership. We, the people of New York, ought now, in this hour of fright, to show the way. We should refuse to allow this time to be marked forever in the pages of our history, as the time that we were driven back to one of the vestiges of our primitive condition, because we were not strong enough, because we were not intelligent enough, because we were not civilized enough, to find a better answer to violence...than violence.

Today I will veto the death penalty bill sent to me by the legislature and return it with my proposal for life imprisonment without parole with the hope and the prayer that this time the legislature will once again choose the light over darkness.

2

A VOTE IN FAVOR OF THE DEATH PENALTY

GEORGE MURRAY
Author and Philosopher

Sooner or later the American people are going to wake up to one of the greatest swindles of our time: the idea that law-abiding citizens who have been victimized by habitual criminals should be expected to support criminals in luxury for years or for life.

This con job has been put over on the people by politicians and penologists, those who profit by the scheme. The ordinary American has been too busy earning a living and paying taxes to pay much attention to crime and punishment.

But now that his standard of living is falling, with no bottom in sight, he is compelled to face up to the fact that it is all he can do to support his own family, much less support the criminals.

The ordinary American is going to wake up to the fact that his leaders in politics cannot and will not do anything much about crime and criminals. The problem rests squarely in the laps of the law-abiding, as it has since pioneering days along the American frontier.

The ordinary citizen is going to realize that if crime is

to be stopped, it is the citizen who must stop it. The way to stop crime is to stop criminals. And the way to stop habitual criminals is to put them to death, quickly and painlessly if possible.

This is not a plea for lynch law. Few Americans want to take the law into their own hands so long as they believe our system of laws and courts is working in the interests of justice.

But the compassion of Americans can and must be aroused for the victims of habitual criminals. Statutes must be changed so that the victims of crime can get at least as much consideration as those who set out consciously to victimize them.

Capital punishment should be visited by our courts not alone upon those who commit capital crimes. Capital punishment should be mandatory for those who set out to make a career of victimizing decent, hard-working American citizens.

Habitual criminals, those convicted of three or more felonies, should be put to death after they have exhausted all the appeals possible under our court system.

Habitual criminals, sentenced to death by our courts, should not be freed on bail while pursuing endless appeals. Rather, they should be held in the public stocks, in view of passersby, in fair weather or foul, until their final appeals have been decided.

The punishment for the first and second felony, before a criminal has been found to be habitual, should not lie in confinement but in the whipping post, the public pillory, the humiliation which comes with exposure to the scorn of one's fellow citizens. Although there will always be drunk tanks for Saturday night revellers, and jails in which to hold suspects awaiting trial, the prison system as America has come to know it should gradually be phased out.

Philip Jenkins, professor in the Administration of Justice Department at Pennsylvania State University, has told us:

"Taking federal and state prisons together there were 210,000 inmates in 1974, 454,000 by 1984, and more than 800,000 in 1991."

The prison population is constantly growing and if the experts are to be believed it will reach four million by the turn of the century, by the year 2,000.

There are not now enough prisons in the fifty states to house such a body of criminals. Even today, many states are "furloughing" criminals—freeing them because of lack of space—far before the time they are eligible for parole or probation.

New prisons are being built at a cost of nearly $50,000 per cell. Prisoners are being maintained in these facilities at a cost of nearly $36,000 a year apiece. For that kind of public outlay, the prisoners could be maintained in our finest motels, fed gourmet meals, have their every want attended by butlers, maids and chauffeurs. Why build more prisons?

Our criminal justice system seldom sentences a first offender to prison. The prison population in every state is made up of men and women who have consciously set out to prey upon society, criminals determined to lie, cheat, kill if necessary rather than work for a living. These are the people who laugh at law-abiding citizens.

It is ridiculous for the law-abiding to be compelled by their political leaders to pay taxes to keep such criminals in virtual luxury.

Every dollar spent to provide prison inmates with food, clothing, medical and dental care, surgery and hospital facilities—and, yes, with color television sets—is a dollar's worth of food which never will be provided to the children of taxpayers supporting the prisons.

Society, which has been victimized by the prison inmates, is further victimized by the politicians and penologists who constantly ask more money to provide further luxuries for those same inmates.

The men and women who make up the prison populations, and who now demand uxorious visits by spouses or girl friends as the price of a comparatively riot-free prison atmosphere, have not been committed to prison for playing tiddlywinks.

They are there for such crimes as rape, murder, incest, getting children hooked on drugs, looting banks of the savings of the hard-working and law-abiding.

Probably worse than the criminals under confinement are the politicians and penologists who get rich by arranging to change the laws so that decent people must take bread out of the mouths of their own children to support habitual criminals in comparative luxury.

For luxury is the only word to describe the modern prison with its recreational facilities, its television sets and movies, its libraries to prevent boredom, its guaranteed health care which goes far beyond any such guarantee for the taxpayers who have to foot the bill.

The penologist speaks of vocational training for criminals, of re-educating the criminal for eventual life on the outside, of "rehabilitation." Every drunk in the gutter knows that rehabilitation never comes from the outside, but only from the inner will to reform.

The ordinary citizen who pays the bill for all this is less interested in the rehabilitation of criminals than he is in simply getting the criminal off his back. He wants to feel safe in his own home, safe in his own streets, safe to go anywhere in this country without fear of being mugged, bullied, made the victim of extortion or worse. He wants to know that his wife and children are safe.

The ordinary citizen knows that the only way to get rid of crime is to get rid of the criminals. He knows that the only sure way to get rid of criminals is to put them to death. He might prefer that this be done quickly and painlessly, without the fanfare and ceremony—and expense—of the electric chair.

But the important thing, to the ordinary citizen, is to be assured that the habitual criminal once caught be permanently prevented from ever again being a burden to society.

The entire system of prisons which we have been given by our greedy politicians is of comparatively recent origin. It is an experiment which began about the time of the American Revolution. It has grown like Topsy, proving a bonanza for the politicians who will fight to keep it. It is time to acknowledge that the experiment has failed.

Modern prisons grew out of the 16th century work houses in which were confined paupers, vagrants, and debtors rather than criminals.

Only in 1773 did jails and work houses begin confining indicted prisoners awaiting trial. They were confined only until executed, banished, or freed. Jailers fed only those able to pay.

The death penalty was decreed for virtually every offense until the mid-18th century. There was no argument as to whether it was or was not a deterrent. The important thing was to get rid of the offender so that other people could get on with their lives.

After the death penalty came banishment, the galleys, and corporal punishment. Everyone remembers "The Man Without a Country," "The Scarlet Letter," flogging either before the mast or on land at the whipping post. Everyone knows the use of the stocks, the public pillory. Corporal punishment was not considered "cruel or unusual" by the men who drew up the Constitution of the United States.

In 1773, only two years before the Battle of Bunker Hill, an experiment was tried in Belgium. The Belgians built a prison to which offenders could be sent for a certain term of years for certain offenses against society. Even then, taxes paid by the general public were not expected to support those so confined.

The thieves and rapists and killers and scofflaws were expected to work. Their work was even to show a profit for the society which paid the guards. Contractors used prison labor, paying the state for the privilege.

In 1773, Connecticut used an old mine in which to chain prisoners. In 1796, New York State erected a prison. New Jersey built a prison in 1798, Virginia in 1800, Massachusetts in 1803, Vermont in 1808, Maryland in 1812, Ohio in 1816.

The Quakers were the first to interest themselves in improving the lot of felons who preyed upon society. In 1787, Quakers organized the Philadelphia Society for Alleviating the Miseries of Public Prisons.

This was called "the Pennsylvania Plan." Under this plan, felons were incarcerated apart from each other. They could not leave their cells. Work was prohibited. Only chaplains and other officials could visit prisons. Only the Bible could be read.

Out of these modest beginnings was our prison experiment born.

Today the prison industry with its appendages is estimated to be the ninth or tenth largest industry in the United States—and growing. It employs more men and women than the auto industry. It costs taxpayers more than Social Security, health care, and welfare for the able-bodied.

Yet no politician running for office ever suggests its reform.

The multi-billion dollar prison industry in the United States today is a result of quiet lobbying on the part of the "science" of penology, as distinct from the "science" of criminology. The criminologist studies crime and criminals. The penologist calls his field the study of punishment for wrongdoing or crime, from the aspect of deterrence and reform.

The greatly-inflated prison industry begins with architecture. There is wide differentiation in prison architecture, prison location, prison equipment, prison administration, prison discipline.

Needless to say, prison architects work hand in glove with the politicians who grant the contracts. The politician who knows in advance the site of a proposed prison can arrange for his brother-in-law or a favored campaign contributor to option the land. The optioned site can later be sold to the state or federal goverment at a nice profit to all. At an additional cost to the taxpayer.

Every newspaperman knows of such things and seldom mentions them.

The architect who wants the work of designing a proposed new prison—such as that now abandoned at Alcatraz in San Francisco Bay—knows he must kick back part of his fee to the politician. Such kickbacks are often covered by calling them campaign contributions.

Up till now the taxpayer has seldom stopped to think that the campaign for United States senator is likely to cost 20 million dollars every six years. That works out to a sum of $10,000 a day for six years which must be raised to pay the campaign costs of re-election. The politician cannot get that kind of money—$10,000 a day—from his neighbors. The prison industry is expected to pay its share of the cost of any senator's re-election.

The prison architect, as part of the penology industry, knows he is expected to deal with the criminal "intelligently." This means taking into account the prisoner's physical and mental status, his or her physical and mental age, character and conduct, the nature and cause of the delinquency. If this sort of thing continues, the next step will be to take into consideration the prisoner's sexual orientation.

Last, but by no means least, the architect must figure on the psychotheraphy and training deemed by the penologist required to fit the habitual criminal for return to society as a "useful" citizen.

All of this mumbo-jumbo, when all the ordinary citizen wants is to get the habitual criminal permanently off his back. Instead, the ordinary citizen is expected by his political leaders to stand still for a constant increase in his taxes to pay the criminal's keep for years.

The penologists, getting rich in the process, have even given names to the kinds of institutional government or discipline they would like to see in their $50,000-a-cell prisons.

They speak of the types of discipline as autocratic, benevolent despotic, mixed autocratic and despotic, mixed benevolent and Hamiltonian republican, Jeffersonian democratic, and so on.

With autocratic discipline (in their words, a repressive system) they pretend to shrink with horror at the idea of a confined criminal being totally subordinate to the will of prison authorities.

Under benevolent discipline (acceptable, if not endorsed by the modern penologist) they anticipate that prison authorities will be "benevolent of purpose and expedient in action" while dealing with these dregs of society.

Under the half-and-half, autocratic and despotic, any discipline required is expected to be "administered with kindness." Cheerfulness is supposed to permeate this type of discipline. Work assignments and other activities are expected to be "developmental and reformative."

In the mixed benevolent and Hamiltonian republican system, the penologists want classification and promotion among the prison's inmates to be based on individual effort. Self-government is to be granted, so far as possible, to those groups deemed deserving and capable of exercising such control.

The Jefferson democratic ideal among penologists is total self-government. This is supposed to be limited to those institutions from which the incorrigible, the low-grade, the feeble minded, the degenerate, and seriously abnormal, the insane, the old rounders and the feeble inebriates have been removed.

In all cases, say the penologists, the systems are to be so administered "as not to offend the better impulses and instincts" of the felons.

The modern penologist is always more concerned with the criminal than with the crime. He would make the punishment fit the criminal, rather than seeking the Gilbert and Sullivan ideal of making the punishment fit the crime.

One wonders that the modern penologist can bury his head so deep in the sand as not to know that the modern prison is simply an over-crowded graduate school in felony. Most prisons degrade the inmates without deterring the commission of future crimes. They are simply breeding places for crime and homosexuality. Any new "fish" under the age of forty starts his sentence by being subjected to gang rape by all the veteran criminals confined in his cell block.

The prison system as we know it is hard to defend in a modern state.

The Liberals complain that the system is brutal and inhumane. And they are right. The Conservatives insist that Liberal reforms such as furloughs and work-release programs simply turn vicious criminals loose once again to prey upon society. And they are right.

Everyone knows this modern prison experiment has failed. Far from being deterrents to crime, our prisons—both federal and state—seem to be breeding places for ever-more-sophisticated crime and its practitioners. They are more expensive to the taxpayers than any finishing school or university in the land.

The annual cost of the correctional apparatus in the United States by the year 2,000 is expected to exceed forty billion dollars.

This is only the taxpayers' cash outlay for such

personnel as wardens, guards, psychologists, physicians, nutritionists and chauffeurs. It does not count the peripheral outlays for food purveyors, weapons and ammunition, automobiles and trucks, all the other expenses incurred in maintaining hundreds of prisons and prison farms.

This expense on the taxpayer might have been justified in the days of prosperity when every household had two or three colored television sets, two or three cars in garages and driveways, two or three credit cards in every wallet and purse. But the United States, supporting two-thirds of the world with foreign aid, has entered upon a period of belt-tightening for its citizens. No longer do taxpayers have the money to support an experiment in luxury for habitual criminals.

There is an alternative to our modern prison, the alternative of corporal punishment and public humiliation such as that known to the founding fathers of this Republic.

There will always be crime, as there will always be war, so long as one man envies another his woman or his wealth. There will always be the lazy and the indigent, the slick and the smooth, the natural-born criminal who is determined to live by the sweat of somebody else's brow.

No system ever devised will deter all of those with a criminal bent. After everything has been done that can be done to instruct people as to what the public good requires, there will always be found two classes: those who abide by demands of the public will—and those who do not.

The common will develops a powerful tribal conscience which demands universal obedience to certain general rules called laws. Those who consciously choose to flout such laws are, by common consent, to be punished. The primary object of such punishment is to maintain or restore the common will or social order.

And to do so without penalizing the law-abiding in the process.

When we seek an alternative to the modern prison experiment the first rule to bear in mind is that it must not penalize the decent citizens of the community. The law-abiding must not be expected to take food out of their children's mouths to maintain the criminal classes.

The question is:

How does society deal in the least expensive manner with those who are mentally capable of understanding society's demands, physically able to conform to them, but who still act in a manner contrary to society's requirements?

That question has been asked since men first formed themelves into organized "society." The answer has always been punishment.

Capital punishment, originally a retaliation, has become society's only sure protection against recidivism. In all history, no criminal subjected to capital punishment has ever returned to repeat his crimes.

Our forefathers, the men who drew up the Constitution, felt they had dealt with the question of enemies of society when they wrote in Article VIII of the Bill of Rights:

"Excessive bail shall not be required, nor excessive fines imposed, nor cruel and unusual punishments inflicted."

Inasmuch as prisons were generally unknown at the time, the founding fathers clearly expected corporal punishment to be sufficient for lesser crimes, with capital punishment reserved for greater crimes.

No modern politician could be expected to approve the system of punishment approved by the founding fathers. This would remove from the politicians' purview the thousands upon thousands of patronage jobs ushered in with the prison experiment; and the millions upon millions of dollars in campaign contributions to be anticipated from those who profit by this failed prison experiment.

Here is a suggestion as to how to handle criminals of any age or sex, at a minimal cost to the law-abiding:

Upon first conviction for a felony, the criminal could be taken directly from court to a public whipping post and stripped to the waist. The judge, guided by statute, could determine the number of strokes with a lash, based upon the age and sex of the felon and the nature of the crime.

After this humiliation of a public whipping, the felon would be released with a warning. The taxpayer would not be stuck with his upkeep.

Upon second conviction for a felony, the criminal can be taken from court to the public pillories. The judge, once again guided by statute, can determine the number of days or weeks the felon is to stand in the public stocks. Once again, the criminal will be exposed to public humiliation, on public view in fair weather or foul, until his or her sentence has been served.

After the sentence has been served, the two-time loser will be released with a stronger warning. The judge will ask that the criminal refrain from committing and being found guilty of a third felony, which would result in his being labeled habitual and subjected to a mandatory death penalty.

The criminal so warned will, upon conviction of a third felony, face the death penalty. The judge who presided over the conviction will decree death by hanging or shooting.

The electric chair, poison gas in an airtight chamber, the lethal injection are all expensive ceremonies. The hangman's rope is cheap. The firing squad, only half of whose guns would be loaded, is cheap and expeditious. The idea is to save the taxpayers' money.

No habitual criminal would be prevented from appealing his third and final conviction. But he or she would not be eligible for bail in the course of what might be lengthy appeals processes. He or she would remain outdoors in the public stocks until the appeal was decided.

Far from being considered cruel and unusual, such punishment would have been considered normal by the authors of the Constitution.

Prisons now standing might be protected by a grandfather's clause. Those now sentenced to prison could serve out their terms.

But after such a program went into effect, no criminal could ever again be sentenced to prison. In time this prison experiment would be looked back upon as a period of man's greatest inhumanity to his fellow man.

As Thomas Fleming said in "Chronicles," many men would give up a hand or even an arm in preference to spending years in a state prison as the "wife" of Mike Tyson.

The public whipping post and the public pillory, outdoors in winter or summer, would require a minimum of supervision by guards. The taxpayer might provide bologna sandwiches and nothing else to sustain those held in the stocks for a period of days or weeks. In every community there are likely to be those whose compassion runs more to the criminal than to the criminals' victims. Such people could, if they wanted, bring to the convicted felons a few delicacies such as hot coffee or cold lemonade—and could change the criminals' clothing when the odor became too offensive.

The law need make no distinction as to crimes of violence, white collar crimes or the so-called "victimless" crimes such as possession and sale to school children of narcotics. (No dope handler, selling the stuff to feed his own habit, ever knows where the product might end up.) As far as the law is concerned, a felony is a felony.

Humiliation before one's peer group might discourage a first- or second-offender going on to become a habitual criminal. The teenager who brings a lethal weapon to school or physically attacks a teacher could be expected to lose prestige among his fellows by confinement for a day or so in the public pillory in a school yard.

Capital punishment on a wide scale might be expected to cut down abruptly on the population of habitual criminals. The habitual criminal's body, by statute, could be declared property of the state so that suitable organs might be removed for use by hospitals needing transplants.

The politician accustomed to routinely dipping in the public till, or selling favors to campaign contributors such as the thieves of the savings and loan debacle, might be brought up short by the realization that conviction—even for a United States senator—would result in a mandatory public flogging.

Such a program as is here suggested would require a change in public thinking. But the public has been too long brainwashed by politicians. For too long, the politicians have sold their votes so that the law-abiding are compelled to support the criminals.

It is high time for a sweeping change in public thinking.

George Murray, a former newspaperman, is the author of The Madhouse on Madison Street, The Legacy of Al Capone, New Horizons, *and numerous plays. He currently resides in Eureka Springs, Arkansas.*

3

STRICTLY PERSONAL
EDWARD BAUMANN

The publisher of Bonus Books suggested, "After you finish this book, tell us how you feel, personally, about the death penalty. You have seen men die, both as a newspaper reporter and as an official witness for the State of Illinois. In researching this book, you have examined the causes and effects of capital punishment in this state more thoroughly than any other person in history. Based on your research and your own experience, how do you feel about it today?"

The answer to that question is: I don't know.

As the Criminal Courts reporter for the *Chicago Daily News* in the 1950s and '60s, the electric chair was part of my beat. I felt absolutely no emotion in watching a man with whom I had chatted less than a half hour earlier sizzle to death in the chair.

Reporters, like policemen, learn to leave their emotions and personal prejudices on the shelf when they go to work. Those who cannot do so should find another line of employment, or they will end up on a psychiatrist's couch.

I listened to Vincent Ciucci ramble as he was having his head shaved before going to the chair. I was the reporter who lagged behind after the execution, pulled the sheet off the still form on the hospital cart, felt his warmly-cooked body, and examined the crimson circle the electrode had burned into the top of his skull.

I did not know that I would write a book about it some day. I just had to see for myself what electrocution did to a human body. An insatiable curiosity is one of the qualities that separates career newspaper reporters from the transients who eventually go into public relations.

I can tell you this. The electric chair is a horrible way to die. Dr. Harold Hillman, a British expert on executions, says, "Execution by electrocution is extremely painful, not only because of burning, but because body fluids must have heated up to a temperature close to the boiling point of water in order to generate the steam" that witnesses see rising from the body. "There is no scientific evidence whatsoever to support the notion that a person being electrocuted loses consciousness."

Supreme Court Justices William J. Brennan and Thurgood Marshall likened the electric chair to such ancient forms of punishment as disemboweling and drawing and quartering. "Death by electrical current is extremely violent and inflicts pain and indignities far beyond the mere extinguishment of life," Brennan declared.

Just thinking about the electric chair literally scared condemned killer Julius "Dolly" Weisberg to death.

And remember, the electric chair was introduced because it was considered more humane than the gallows. If a hanging was not done right, as we have seen, it could (a) fail to break the subject's neck and cause him to slowly strangle at the end of the rope, or (b) it could snap the victim's head clean off, spraying the spectators with warm blood.

Sometimes the agony of waiting for the penalty to be carried out can be as torturous as the final moment itself. Take the case of William Andrews, sentenced to die for his role in the murders of three people who were forced to drink liquid Drano before being shot.

Andrews sat on Utah's death row for *eighteen years* before he was finally dispatched by lethal injection on July 30, 1992. Another condemned murderer, Carl Eugene Kelly, after eleven years of awaiting death by injection in Huntsville, Texas, told a reporter, "This is more torture than taking a person out and tying him up and peeling his skin or setting him on fire."

I once heard a defense lawyer, pleading his client's case before a Criminal Court jury, argue, "Turn him loose or give him the juice!" Not a bad idea.

If we are going to keep capital punishment on the books, and juries are going to condemn men and women to death for crimes they committed, let's get on with it. Let's not keep pampering them for another decade or more, at yours and my expense, as George Murray argues in a preceding chapter.

On the other hand, before we act in haste, let's make damn sure they're guilty. Michael Radelet, the University of Florida sociologist, has documented twenty-five innocent people executed in the United States between 1900 and 1985. These were twenty-five wrongly convicted people who cannot be brought back—ever.

The biggest problem with capital punishment, as Governor Cuomo points out, is its irrevocability.

I cannot agree with Governor Cuomo, however, that capital punishment penalizes blacks and minorities more than whites.

Of the 171 men executed in Cook County over a 122-year period, only forty-nine were black.

Does that tell us that capital punishment penalizes whites more than blacks? Of course not. We know that, for the greater part of that period, there were more whites than blacks living in the area, and consequently more whites than blacks were committing crimes. In later years, as the black population increased, so did the black census on death row.

Governor Cuomo points out that, of the last eighteen people executed in New York, thirteen were black and one was Hispanic. But he does *not* tell us the ratio of crimes committed by blacks and Hispanics compared to the homocides committed by whites.

If the whites still dominate white-collar crime in America, anyone who reads the daily police blotter can tell you that more and more violent crimes in urban areas are committed by blacks. Regardless of why this might be—disadvantaged childhoods, lack of education, poverty, racial discrimination—it stands to reason that if more blacks are committing violent crimes today than a hundred years ago, then more blacks are going to be joining, and outnumbering, the whites on death row.

And, of course, there is just as great a likelihood of an innocent black landing on death row as an innocent white. Which brings us back to the permanence of the death penalty. Once it's carried out, it can't be undone.

Among the stories in this book are those of men who should not have been executed; and of those who had it coming.

Based solely on what I know about hangings in America, and the men I have personally seen dispatched in the electric chair, I would have to say that I am dead set against capital punishment. I do not believe in it, nor do I believe it serves as a deterrent to crime.

But there are exceptions to any situation, such as the vile and inherently evil Henry "Junior" Brisbon, the so-called "I-57 killer."

He took his first life at the age of sixteen, when he blew a grocer's head off with a shotgun because he didn't like something he said.

Then came the I-57 killings, so called because they occurred along Interstate Highway 57 south of Chicago. The first victim was a truck driver, David Spur.

Next were Dorothy Cerny, a school teacher, and her

fiance, James Schmidt, both 25. Their killer forced them to lie face down by the side of the road. Then he said, "Make this your last kiss," and shot each in the back with a shotgun blast so forceful that it blew them right out of their shoes.

But the worst—the worst—was Betty Lou Harmon, a 29-year-old hospital worker. Her killer stripped off her clothes and forced her to lie naked on the grass alongside the highway. Then he rammed a shotgun up her vagina—literally raping her with the long, steel barrel—and pulled the trigger! The blast tore out her abdomen, but not her lungs and her heart. As she lay writhing in agony, the man put the bloody shotgun against the side of her head and pulled the trigger again.

Brisbon, a convicted rapist, was charged with the crimes after he boasted to a fellow jail inmate, "I know who killed those white folks on I-57."

Described by prosecutors as "an incredibly evil person," he was convicted for the crimes. Because he was only seventeen, however, he could not be sentenced to death.

Judge James M. Bailey, declaring, "You are by far the most evil coward I have ever seen; I'm sorry I can't execute you," sentenced him to 2,000 to 3,000 years in prison.

Despite the longest prison term ever handed down in the state, under Illinois law he could become eligible for parole after eleven years and three months!

Yet while in prison for the I-57 murders Henry Brisbon kept on killing. Using a home-made knife, he stabbed a fellow inmate, Richard Morgan, to death and boasted that he would keep on killing just as long as he lives.

For the 1978 prison murder Brisbon was ultimately sentenced to death. That was fifteen years ago, and still counting.

Did I say I was opposed to capital punishment?

Henry Brisbon is a walking testimonial for the death

penalty. Only he shouldn't get that "humane" needle they use at the state prison these days. What Henry needs is 1,900 volts.

And if they asked me to, I would pull the lever myself, and enjoy a good night's sleep afterward.

BOOK VII

WE ARE THE DEAD

1

COOK COUNTY HANGINGS

1840-1927

1	John Stone	July 10, 1840	Public
2	William Jackson	June 19, 1857	Public
3	Albert Staub	April 20, 1858	Public
4	Michael McNamee	May 6, 1859	Courthouse
5	Walter Fleming	Dec. 15, 1865	Courthouse
6	Jerry Corbett	Dec. 15, 1865	Courthouse
7	George Driver	March 14, 1873	New County Jail
8	Andrew Perteet	Dec. 12, 1873	Joliet Prison
9	Chris Rafferty	Feb. 27, 1874	Waukegan Courthouse
10	George Sherry	June 21, 1878	County Jail
11	Jeremiah Connelly	June 21, 1878	County Jail
12	James Tracy	Sept. 15, 1882	County Jail
13	Isaac Jacobson	Sept. 19, 1884	County Jail
14	Ignazio Sylvestri	Nov. 14, 1885	County Jail
15	Agostino Gilardo	Nov. 14, 1885	County Jail
16	Giovanni Azzaro	Nov. 14, 1885	County Jail
17	Francis "Frank" Mulkowski	March 26, 1886	County Jail
18	James Dacey	July 16, 1886	Woodstock Jail
19	Albert Parsons	Nov. 11, 1887	County Jail
20	August Spies	Nov. 11, 1887	County Jail
21	George Engel	Nov. 11, 1887	County Jail
22	Adolph Fischer	Nov. 11, 1887	County Jail
23	Zephyr Davis	May 12, 1888	County Jail
24	George H. Painter	Jan. 26, 1894	County Jail
25	Thomas "Buff" Higgins	March 23, 1894	County Jail

26	Patrick Prendergast	July 13, 1894	County Jail
27	Harry Lyons	Oct. 11, 1895	County Jail
28	Henry Foster	Jan. 24, 1896	County Jail
29	Alfred Fields	May 15, 1896	County Jail
30	Joseph Windrath	June 5, 1896	County Jail
31	Julius Manow	Oct. 30, 1896	County Jail
32	Daniel McCarthy	Feb. 19, 1897	County Jail
33	John Lattimore	⎧ May 28, 1897	County Jail
34	William T. Powers	⎩ May 28, 1897	County Jail
35	Christopher Merry	April 22, 1898	County Jail
36	John Druggan	⎧ Oct. 14, 1898	County Jail
37	George H. Jacks	⎩ Oct. 14, 1898	County Jail
38	Robert Howard	Feb. 17, 1899	County Jail
39	August A. Becker	Nov. 10, 1899	County Jail
40	Michael E. Rollinger	Nov. 17, 1899	County Jail
41	George Dolinski	Oct. 11, 1901	County Jail
42	Louis G. Thombs (Toombs)	Aug. 8, 1902	County Jail
43	Louis Pesant	April 15, 1904	County Jail
44	Peter Neidermeier	⎧ April 22, 1904	County Jail
45	Gustav Marx	⎨ April 22, 1904	County Jail
46	Harvey Van Dine	⎩ April 22, 1904	County Jail
47	Frank Lewandoski	Sept. 30, 1904	County Jail
48	John Johnson	Jan. 20, 1905	County Jail
49	Robert F. Newcomb	⎧ Feb. 16, 1906	County Jail
50	John Mueller	⎩ Feb. 16, 1906	County Jail
51	Johann Hoch	Feb. 23, 1906	County Jail
52	Richard G. Ivens	June 22, 1906	County Jail
53	Daniel Francis	Oct. 12, 1906	County Jail
54	Richard Walton	Dec. 13, 1907	County Jail
55	Andrew Williams	Oct. 23, 1909	County Jail
56	Ewald Shiblawski	⎡ Feb. 16, 1912	County Jail
57	Frank Shiblawski	⎢ Feb. 16, 1912	County Jail
58	Philip Somerling	⎨ Feb. 16, 1912	County Jail
59	Thomas Schultz	⎢ Feb. 16, 1912	County Jail
60	Thomas Jennings	⎣ Feb. 16, 1912	County Jail
61	Roswell Smith	Feb. 13, 1915	County Jail
62	Edward Wheed	⎧ Feb. 15, 1918	County Jail
63	Harry Lindrum	⎩ Feb. 15, 1918	County Jail
64	Dennis Anderson	July 19, 1918	County Jail
65	Lloyd Bopp	Dec. 6, 1918	County Jail
66	Albert Johnson	Feb. 28, 1919	County Jail
67	Earl Dear	June 27, 1919	County Jail

68	Thomas Fitzgerald	Oct. 27, 1919	County Jail
69	Raffaelo Durazzio (Durrage)	Jan. 2, 1920	County Jail
70	John O'Brien	Feb. 20, 1920	County Jail
71	William Y. Mills	April 16, 1920	County Jail
72	Frank Campione	⌠Oct. 14, 1920	County Jail
73	John Reese	⌡Oct. 14, 1920	County Jail
74	Frank Zagar	Oct. 15, 1920	County Jail
75	Arthur Haensel	Nov. 19, 1920	County Jail
76	Nicholas Viana	Dec. 10, 1920	County Jail
77	Edward Brislane	Feb. 11, 1921	County Jail
78	Sam Cardinella	⌠April 15, 1921	County Jail
79	Sam Ferrara	⟨April 15, 1921	County Jail
80	Joseph Costanzo	⌡April 15, 1921	County Jail
81	Grover Redding	⌠June 24, 1921	County Jail
82	Oscar McGavick	⌡June 24, 1921	County Jail
83	Antonio Lopez	July 8, 1921	County Jail
84	Harry Ward	July 15, 1921	County Jail
85	Carl Wanderer	Sept. 30, 1921	County Jail
86	Frank Ligregni	Nov. 9, 1921	County Jail
87	Harvey W. Church	March 3, 1922	County Jail
88	Casper Pastoni	June 15, 1923	County Jail
89	Lucius Dalton	⌠April 17, 1924	County Jail
90	Henry Wilson	⌡April 17, 1924	County Jail
91	Lawrence Washington	May 15, 1925	County Jail
92	Willie Sams	June 19, 1925	County Jail
93	Frank Lanciano	Oct. 15, 1925	County Jail
94	Campbell McCarthy	Jan. 29, 1926	County Jail
95	Jack Wilson, alias Woods	⌠Feb. 13, 1926	County Jail
96	Joseph Holmes	⌡Feb. 13, 1926	County Jail
97	Ray Costello	⌠April 16, 1926	County Jail
98	Charles Hobbs	⌡April 16, 1926	County Jail
99	Richard Evans	Oct. 29, 1926	County Jail
100	James Gricius	⌠Dec. 31, 1926	County Jail
101	Thomas McWane	⌡Dec. 31, 1926	County Jail
102	Oscar Quarles	Feb. 17, 1927	County Jail
103	John W. Winn	April 15, 1927	County Jail
104	Elin Lyons	June 24, 1927	County Jail

End of hangings.

2

COOK COUNTY ELECTROCUTIONS

1929-1963

105	Anthony Grecco	⎰ Feb. 20, 1929	County Jail
106	Charles Walz	⎱ Feb. 20, 1929	County Jail
107	Napoleon Glover	⎰ June 20, 1929	New County Jail
108	Morgan Swan	⎱ June 20, 1929	New County Jail
109	Aaron Woodward	April 11, 1930	New County Jail
110	August Vogel	May 9, 1930	New County Jail
111	Leonard Shadlow	⎰ Oct. 3, 1930	New County Jail
112	Lafon Fisher	⎱ Oct. 3, 1930	New County Jail
113	Leon Brown	Nov. 28, 1930	New County Jail
114	William Lenhardt	Dec. 12, 1930	New County Jail
115	Frank Jordan	⎧ Oct. 16, 1931	New County Jail
116	Charles Rocco	⎪ Oct. 16, 1931	New County Jail
117	John Popescue	⎨ Oct. 16, 1931	New County Jail
118	Richard Sullivan	⎩ Oct. 16, 1931	New County Jail
119	Frank H. Bell	Jan. 8, 1932	New County Jail
120	Ben Norsingle	⎰ Jan. 15, 1932	New County Jail
121	John Reed	⎱ Jan. 15, 1932	New County Jail
122	Morris Cohen	Oct. 13, 1933	New County Jail
123	Ross King	Oct. 16, 1933	New County Jail
124	John Scheck	⎧ April 20, 1934	New County Jail
125	George Dale	⎨ April 20, 1934	New County Jail
126	Joseph Francis	⎩ April 20, 1934	New County Jail
127	George Walker	⎰ Oct. 12, 1934	New County Jail
128	Alonzo McNeil	⎱ Oct. 12, 1934	New County Jail

129	Armando Boulan	⎰ Dec. 15, 1934	New County Jail
130	Walter Dittman	⎱ Dec. 15, 1934	New County Jail
131	Chester Novak	March 21, 1935	New County Jail
132	Andrew Bogacki	⎰ Oct. 21, 1936	New County Jail
133	Frank Korczykowski	⎱ Oct. 21, 1936	New County Jail
134	Rufo Swain	Feb. 26, 1937	New County Jail
135	Joseph Rappaport	March 2, 1937	New County Jail
136	Francis "Doc" Whyte	⎰ April 16, 1937	New County Jail
137	Stanley Murawski	⎬ April 16, 1937	New County Jail
138	Joseph Schuster	⎱ April 16, 1937	New County Jail
139	Peter Chrisoulas	Oct. 15, 1937	New County Jail
140	J.C. Scott	April 19, 1938	New County Jail
141	John Henry Seadlund	July 14, 1938	New County Jail
142	Robert Nixon	July 16, 1939	New County Jail
143	Steve Cygan	Oct. 13, 1939	New County Jail
144	Charles Price	Oct. 27, 1939	New County Jail
145	Howard Poe	April 19, 1949	New County Jail
146	Victor Wnukowski	⎰ May 17, 1949	New County Jail
147	Frank Michalowski	⎱ May 17, 1949	New County Jail
148	Robert Schroeder	Dec. 13, 1949	New County Jail
149	Orville Watson	⎰ June 20, 1941	New County Jail
150	Edward Riley (Paddy Ryan)	⎱ June 20, 1941	New County Jail
151	Earl Parks	Jan. 15, 1942	New County Jail
152	Bernard Sawicki	Jan. 17, 1942	New County Jail
153	John Pantano	Sept. 18, 1942	New County Jail
154	Ernest Wishon	Nov. 26, 1943	New County Jail
155	Paul L. Williams	March 15, 1944	New County Jail
156	Alvin Krause	Sept. 15, 1944	New County Jail
157	Kermit Breedlove	Oct. 19, 1945	New County Jail
158	Charles Crosby	June 20, 1947	New County Jail
159	Ernest Gaither	Oct. 24, 1947	New County Jail
160	James Morelli	Nov. 26, 1949	New County Jail
161	Fred Varela	⎰ April 21, 1950	New County Jail
162	Alfonso Najera	⎱ April 21, 1950	New County Jail
163	Willard Truelove	Nov. 17, 1950	New County Jail
164	Raymond Jenko	Jan. 25, 1952	New County Jail
165	Harry Williams	March 14, 1952	New County Jail
166	LeRoi Lindsey	⎰ Oct. 17, 1952	New County Jail
167	Bernice Davis	⎱ Oct. 17, 1952	New County Jail
168	Emanuel Scott	March 19, 1953	New County Jail
169	Richard Carpenter	Dec. 19, 1958	New County Jail
170	Vincent Ciucci	March 23, 1962	New County Jail
171	James Dukes	Aug. 24, 1962	New County Jail

End of executions in Cook County.

3

A FEW LAST WORDS

Executions lost much of their public fascination with the introduction of the electric chair, when condemned men were no longer asked whether they had any last words, as was customary when they stood on the trapdoor with a noose around their neck.

The people in charge of electrocutions had only one thought in mind: get it over with fast. It was almost a contest to see how quickly a blindfolded man could be pushed into the chair, strapped down, and zapped.

A death row inmate at San Quentin, about to go to the chair, did leave some last words behind in his cell, in the form of verse:

> "If I could have my last wish,"
> Said the prisoner one day,
> As they led him from the death cell
> To the chair not far away,
>
> "Please grant me this request, sir,
> Ere you tighten up the strap.
> Just tell the Warden I would love
> To hold him on my lap."

In Chicago, Edward Riley also left a message before going to the chair:

"Life is like a deck of cards and we are all the jokers. First it's hearts, then it's diamonds. Next it's clubs, and now it's spades."

But the gallows, that was different. The condemned man stood on the high platform looking out over the crowd as the rope was tightened about his neck, and was often moved to oratory.

The words most often uttered, it would seem, were, "I am innocent."

The last words John Stone, the first man legally executed in Cook County, were, "I swear to you, sheriff, I'm an innocent man."

Henry Foster, then, was quite refreshing when he declared, just before the floor dropped out from under him, "Gentlemen, I did the deed."

Some men were philosophical. Train robber Jack Ketchum, before his head was ripped off by an inept hangman in New Mexico, announced, "I'll be in hell before you start breakfast. Let 'er go, boys."

Others relied on religion as they took their last breaths.

"Oh! Lord God, save and receive me," said William Jackson, before the trap was sprung in 1857.

"I am going to Heaven," declared Walter Fleming.

"Good-bye, all! God bless us," cried out Isaac Jacobson.

Thomas "Buff" Higgins just said, "Good-bye."

Some men expressed elation, such as James Dacey, who announced from the gallows, "This is the happiest day since I came into the hands of (Sheriff) Udell."

Or Haymarket anarchist Adolph Fischer, who said, "This is the happiest moment of my life."

And who could have appeared happier than Richard Ivens? He said, "I wouldn't change places with John D. Rockefeller."

Some condemned men simply made statements, such as Lloyd Bopp, who gushed, "Gee, the night went fast!"

Julius Manow opined, "I believe the word of a

confessed murderer is better than that of a murderer who has not yet confessed."

Other prisoners admonished the hangman or the spectators, such as Michael Rollinger who said, "Don't look upon me with a bad face when I am gone."

"Don't let me suffer. Do it quick," were Albert Johnson's last words.

And John O'Brien complained to the hangman, "Don't get that rope too tight."

A few men died with questions on their lips, like Antonio Lopez, who inquired, "Can't you shoot me instead of hanging me?"

And Frank Campione, who couldn't seem to grasp what was about to happen, asked, "Are they really going to hang me?"

Edward Brislane condemned his executioners, when he said, "Let the State of Illinois take shame upon itself."

Chris Rafferty had nothing to say, and he said it: "I have nothing to say, sir."

Grover Cleveland Redding had something to say, but he didn't say it: "I have something to say, but not at this time."

John Lattimore's last request was, "Take off my shoes."

A Jewish inmate awaiting execution in Sing Sing ordered a ham sandwich for his last request. "I never tasted ham before," he said. "It isn't bad."

And Joe Hill, bitter about being sentenced to die before the firing squad in the Utah State Prison in 1915, made this last request of a friend:

"Could you arrange to have my body hauled to the state line to be buried? I don't want to be found dead in Utah."

Joe's friends did better than that. They had him cremated, and scattered his ashes in forty-seven of the forty-eight states — every one but Utah.

BIBLIOGRAPHY

Asbury, Herbert. *Gem of the Prairie.* Alfred A. Knopf, 1940.

Bross, William. *History of Chicago.* Jansen, McClurg & Co., 1876.

Death Row. Glen Hare Publications, 1991.

Drimmer, Frederick, *Until You Are Dead.* Pinnacle Books, 1990.

Fara, Finis. *Chicago — A Personal History.* Arlington House, 1973.

Gilbert, Paul, and Charles Lee Bryson. *Chicago and Its Makers.* Felix Mendelsohn, 1929.

Hecht, Ben. *Charlie.* Harper Brothers, 1957.

Information Please Almanac. Houghton Mifflin Co., 1992.

Levy, Barbara. *Legacy of Death.* Prentice-Hall, Inc., 1973.

Lyle, Judge John H. *Dry and Lawless Years.* Prentice-Hall, Inc., 1961.

McWhirter, Norris and Ross. *Guinness Book of World Records.* Bantam Books, 1971.

Murray, George. *Madhouse on Madison Street.* Follett Publishing Co., 1965.

Weinberg, Arthur. *Attorney for the Damned.* Simon & Schuster, 1957.

Capital Punishment Hearings before the Committee on the Judiciary of the United States Senate, April 10, 27 and May 1, 1981.

Columbia Journalism Review.

Chicago American, Chicago's American, Chicago Chronicle, Chicago Daily News, Chicago Daily Journal, Chicago

Evening American, Chicago Evening Journal, Chicago Herald-American, Chicago Herald-Examiner, Chicago Inter Ocean, Chicago Evening Post, Chicago Press, Chicago Record-Herald, Chicago Sun, Chicago Sun-Times, Chicago Times, Chicago Tribune, Daily Chicago American.

INDEX

ABOUT THE AUTHOR

Edward Baumann, a lifelong resident of Kenosha, Wisconsin, served with the U.S. Army Air Corps in New Guinea, the Dutch East Indies and the Philippines during World War II. He subsequently spent 37 years as a reporter or editor for the *Waukegan News-Sun, Chicago Daily News, Chicago's American, Chicago Today* and *The Chicago Tribune* before turning to full-time freelancing. He is a past president of the Chicago Press Club and the Chicago Press Veterans Association, a director of the Chicago Newspaper Reporters Association, a member of the Milwaukee Press Club, and winner of two Chicago Newspaper Guild Stick-O Type awards for investigative reporting. In 1988 his peers honored him as Chicago Press Veteran of the Year.

OTHER BOOKS BY EDWARD BAUMANN

Step Into My Parlor — The Chilling Story of Serial Killer Jeffrey Dahmer

Chicago Originals, with Kenan Heise

Chicago Heist, with John O'Brien

Getting Away With Murder, with John O'Brien

Murder Next Door, with John O'Brien

Teresita — The Voice from the Grave, with John O'Brien

Polish Robbin' Hoods, with John O'Brien